MW00998998

ILL-FATED FRONTIER

PERIL AND POSSIBILITIES IN THE EARLY AMERICAN WEST

SAMUEL A. FORMAN

Guilford, Connecticut

To Clio

*The muse of history is a living person who propelled this book
from concept to completion.*

An imprint of Globe Pequot, the trade division of The Rowman & Littlefield Publishing Group, Inc.
4501 Forbes Blvd., Ste. 200
Lanham, MD 20706
www.LyonsPress.com

Distributed by NATIONAL BOOK NETWORK

Map by Jeffrey Ward
Front cover: *The Signing of the Treaty of Greeneville* by Howard Chandler Christie, 1945, © The
Ohio History Connection

British Library Cataloguing in Publication Information available

Library of Congress Cataloging-in-Publication Data

Names: Forman, Samuel, 1952– author.
Title: Ill-fated frontier : peril and possibilities in the early American West / Samuel A. Forman.
Description: Guilford, Connecticut : Lyons Press, [2021] | Includes bibliographical references and
    index. | Summary: "*Ill-Fated Frontier* is at once a pioneer adventure and a compelling narrative of
    the frictions that emerged among entrepreneurial pioneers and their sixty slaves, Indians fighting
    to preserve their land, and Spanish colonials with their own agenda. [. . .] Endorsed by *New York
    Times* best-selling author Nathaniel Philbrick, it is a startling and frank portrait of a young
    America that examines the dream of an inclusive American experience and its reality—a debate
    that continues today"— Provided by publisher.
Identifiers: LCCN 2021014817 | ISBN 9781493044610 (hardback) | ISBN 9781493044627 (epub)
Subjects: LCSH: United States—Territorial expansion—History—18th century. | Frontier and
    pioneer life—United States—History—18th century. | Foreman family. | Forman, Ezekiel,
    1736-1795. | Forman, Samuel S., 1765-1862 | Forman, David, 1745-1797. | Indians of North
    America—Government relations—1789-1869. | Plantation life—Mississippi—Natchez
    Region—History—18th century. | Natchez (Miss. : District)—History—18th century.
Classification: LCC E179.5 .F67 2021 | DDC 973.3—dc23
LC record available at https://lccn.loc.gov/2021014817

♾™ The paper used in this publication meets the minimum requirements of American National
Standard for Information Sciences—Permanence of Paper for Printed Library Materials, ANSI/
NISO Z39.48-1992.

Contents

THE FORMAN PIONEERS

· 1789–1797 ·

← Path of Forman pioneers, 1789-1790	✕ Battles and conflicts
·······▸ Return of Gereral David Forman, 1797	▨ Spanish Influence asserted

L. Superior

BRITISH NORTH AMERICA

(MASS.)

VT.

N.H.

L. Huron

L. Ontario

Cazenovia

Boston

MASS.

Mississippi River

L. Michigan

NEW YORK

CONN.

R.I.

NORTHWEST TERRITORY

Detroit

L. Erie

PENNSYLVANIA

New York

Fallen Timbers

Fort Pitt/Pittsburgh

Washington's Crossing

Monmouth

FORBE'S ROAD

Philadelphia

Kekiongo/Ft. Wayne

Gnaddenhütten

Lancaster

NEW JERSEY

St. Clair's Defeat

Marietta

DELAWARE

Fort Washington/Cincinnati

Gallipolis

MARYLAND

St. Louis

Ohio River

VIRGINIA

Falls of the Ohio/
Louisville

SPANISH LUISIANA

FORT MASSAC

New Madrid

NORTH CAROLINA

SOUTHWEST
TERRITORY

SOUTH
CAROLINA

SPANISH TERRITORY

Mississippi River

Chickasaw Bluffs/Memphis

Charleston

Atlantic Ocean

Ball Game at
the Noxubee River
Beaver Pond

GEORGIA

Savannah

Nogales/
Walnut Hills/
Vicksburg

SPANISH WEST FLORIDA

Natchez

31st Parallel

St. Augustine

New Orleans

Pensacola

EAST
FLORIDA

Taken by
Privateers

Gulf of Mexico

Bahama Islands

0 Miles   200   400

New Providence

0 Kilometers   400

© 2021 Jeffrey L. Ward

Preface

"SURELY YOU MUST BE A NAMESAKE OF THE REVOLUTIONARY ERA Formans of New Jersey and Philadelphia!" observed a solicitous reader of my biography of Dr. Joseph Warren, the early Revolutionary patriot hero. One of that old Forman clan, Samuel S. Forman, had written *Narrative of a Journey Down the Ohio and Mississippi in 1789–90*. Her observation piqued my curiosity, resulting in the quest that ultimately led to my writing *Ill-Fated Frontier*.

The answer to her genealogical question is, oddly enough, an unequivocal "no." Although my surname is identical to the autobiographical travel narrative's author, I am no more related to him and his clan than any early twentieth-century Eastern European Ellis Island immigrant could be kin to the seventeenth-century English immigrant Forman settlers.

Arriving by 1680, these English Formans went on to multiply and prosper in Monmouth County, New Jersey, and parts of Maryland by the late eighteenth century. Among them were a number of officers and enlistees in the Continental Army and the New Jersey militia.

As I found out more about them, I was captivated by the *Narrative* and drawn in by its richly related incidents concerning a pivotal period that bridges the American Revolution and first few years of the Early Republic. Written from the viewpoint of a young man accompanying a plantation enterprise in the role of business agent or supercargo, this rare first-person narrative chronicled the Forman pioneers' epic 2,400-mile overland and riverine migration across virtually the entirety of the then-western frontier.

The old *Narrative* further suggested three additional, distinct human dramas: that of enslaved people in the Forman party, Native Americans encountered en route, and Spanish colonials at the destination. The emigration from Monmouth, New Jersey, to Natchez was the final inland passage of sixty enslaved African Americans. The group then encountered natives of the Northwest Indian Federation at a time and place where the Indians had the upper hand in their resistance to American settlers. At the Natchez destination, the key people governing the pioneers' lives were engaging and effective Spanish colonials looking out for the interests of their European homeland. This multiethnic and racially diverse cast is not some latter-day add-on, but rather in every way integral to the saga.

As I retraced their epic trek, I sought corroborating primary sources for this, one of the largest single pioneering groups of its day. I caught up on recent scholarship of the past twenty-five years addressing Indian, African American, and Hispanic experiences in the era in order to place the Forman pioneer *Narrative* into its larger context. I invite those who wish to delve deeper to consult an extensive foundation in primary sources and scholarship that is freely available on my website Ill-FatedFrontier.com.

I seek to provide not only a rousing early frontier true adventure, but also a window into the complex issues that threatened to stifle the infant American Republic in its cradle. The title *Ill-Fated Frontier* recognizes the travails experienced by many of the book's protagonists.

Dramatic events, occurring "offstage" but contemporaneously with the Forman pioneers' immediate travels, shaped the immigrants' fates. I present chapters on them: French scientist and physician Dr. Antoine Saugrain sets the stage for the perils of immigrant flat-boating on the Ohio River; the American Army experiences setbacks during the Northwest Indian War; Chief Little Turtle and his allies seek self-determination in the Indians' Middle Ground; the Whiskey Rebels resist federal authority; Indian groups compete for hegemony in the Southeast backcountry; America confronts Spain over Mississippi River navigation, and ultimately establishes the United States' southern border.

I want to alert the reader to several textual conventions. I make frequent reference to the ethnicity and race of people in the tale, as group identities are integral to the history. Such naming can be an important and nuanced topic to modern readers. My choices balance terms that are recognizable to general readers, true to the source material, and acceptable to—if not universally endorsed by—the several groups among present-day Americans. I use the term *Indians*—as do most modern federally recognized nations and tribes—interchangeably with *Native Americans* and *Indigenous People*. Where the specific Indian nation or tribe is known and relevant to the history, I name it. I use *African Americans* most frequently, with *Blacks* as a synonym. Recognizing the coerced nature of their social position, I refer to bonded house servants and field hands as the *enslaved*. I use *Spanish* for Hispanic colonials, a usage following the source manuscripts precisely.

American, French, and Spanish personal names appear in their original form. For Indian leaders, I generally identify them by Anglicized name rather than with phonetic or conceptual translations, or alternative monikers according to Indian traditions. Few of the enslaved African Americans are named in the primary sources. In instances where key proto-abolitionists remain unnamed, I identify them as did the chronicler: "Two Disaffected Fellows" and the "Ladies of Lancaster." I employ modern place names where the tale permits one to do so.

I modernize spelling, punctuation, and capitalization in direct quotations, but scrupulously preserve the intent and meaning of the original. Where quotation marks appear, these are direct quotes spoken, written, or credibly attributed to the speaker concerning the specific interactions. All source material is identified in the endnotes found on Ill-FatedFrontier .com. Where thoughts, intimations, and comments are speculative or circumstantial, I identify them as such.

I cannot and do not provide direct quotations of any of the Formans' enslaved African Americans, for no words uttered by the Black Forman emigrants to Mississippi survive. Employing surrogate quotes from similarly situated bondsmen is not possible for this era.

I quote some Native American speeches and conversations as recorded by others. With allowances made for the prejudices of non-Indian scribes, an impressive tradition of influential and colorful oratory by Indian leaders in their own languages comes through the structural filters.

Surviving written accounts and letters by and about Spanish colonial leaders lend themselves to direct quotes. Women—Caucasian, Black, Native, and Hispanic firsthand voices—are absent due to the limitations of the source material.

Weather is an important element of a travel account that pits adventurers against the elements. I include moon phases as derived from standard astronomical references. Meteorological data and river freeze/thaw conditions are pieced together from other travel accounts and scientifically minded diarists.

Unlike popular conceptions of American history, which tend to jump from the Revolutionary War to the Civil War, with whistle stops on Broadway for a singing Alexander Hamilton and at the War of 1812, *Ill-Fated Frontier: Peril and Possibilities in the Early American West* sweeps us into the realities and challenges along the frontiers of the fledgling United States. North *becomes* South by the choice of some and the compulsion of others, in the face of fierce Indian resistance, and with the encouragement of Hispanic colonials. It is a uniquely American adventure and origin saga of a goodly portion of the United States.

Please join me in this compelling and consequential pioneering and early settlement adventure. This odyssey changed the lives of everyone involved, and manyfold more who followed. The pioneers could not have foreseen how their own experiences would turn out for themselves, their progeny, and for what would become a great nation.

Timelines

WORLD OF THE FORMAN FAMILY

- 1775–1782: Numerous Formans and their associates in New Jersey fight in the Revolutionary War. General Forman acquires the moniker "Black David" for his excessive zeal in suppressing Loyalists during the prolonged guerrilla conflict in his native Monmouth County.
- Fall 1789: David Forman obtains a land grant for Spanish West Florida.
- November 1789: Ezekiel Forman (David's brother), his family, Samuel S. Forman, overseer Benajah Osman, and sixty enslaved African Americans depart Monmouth, New Jersey, by wagon train.
- December 1789: They arrive at Pittsburgh three weeks later. The Ladies of Lancaster and "two disaffected fellows" incite resistance by the enslaved en route.
- January 1790: They depart on the Ohio River by flat and keelboat, visiting Marietta and Fort Washington at Cincinnati en route.
- February 1790: They arrive at Louisville, Falls of the Ohio.
- March 1790: Ezekiel Forman, his family, Benajah Osman, and the enslaved African Americans depart Louisville. Samuel S. remains to conduct business.
- April 22, 1790: Ezekiel and the pioneer party arrive at Natchez, Spanish West Florida, *Luisiana*. Wilderness and later Second Creek plantations are founded.
- June 22, 1790: Samuel S. arrives at Natchez.
- June 1790 to June 1795: Twenty-seven children are born into the enslaved African American immigrant families.
- May 1791: Samuel S. departs Natchez for Philadelphia.

- June 1793: Samuel S. cofounds Cazenovia along the northern New York frontier.
- June 1795: Ezekiel Forman dies.
- March 1797: General "Black David" Forman arrives in Natchez to contest Ezekiel's estate.
- August 1797: General Forman departs for the North.
- 1800: William Gordon Forman arrives at Natchez to inherit Wilderness Plantation.

NATIVE AMERICANS

- March 8, 1782: Massacre of Christian-convert Delaware Indians at Gnadenhütten, Ohio.
- 1785–1795: Northwest Indian War.
- October 22, 1790: Indians inflict Harmar's Defeat on the US Army and militias. Piomingo (Chickasaw) leads a faction sympathetic to Americans, and brings warriors north into Ohio to fight as American allies against the Northwest Indian Federation.
- 1790: Choctaws versus Creeks at the great Noxubee River ball game in the Spanish West Florida backcountry.
- 1790–1793: Chief McGillivray negotiates separately with the Americans and Spanish to maintain and extend Creek influence.
- November 4, 1791: Chiefs Little Turtle (Miami), Buckongahelas (Delaware), and Blue Jacket (Shawnee) of the Northwest Indian Federation devastate the US Army at St. Clair's Defeat.
- 1793: Fruitless peace negotiations between Americans and the Northwest Indian Federation at Sandusky, Ohio Territory.
- 1793: The Spanish sign treaties at Nogales (Vicksburg) reinforcing peace among Wolf's Friend's Chickasaw faction, Choctaw, Creeks, and Spanish.
- August 20, 1794: General "Mad Anthony" Wayne defeats the Northwest Indian Federation at the Battle of the Fallen Timbers.
- August 3, 1795: The Treaty of Greenville ends the Northwest Indian War.

- 1790s: Numerous Indian delegations, including ones led by Chief Little Turtle following the Treaty of Greenville, are invited to the American capital in Philadelphia. They are received by George Washington and other ranking officials.

WORLD AND NATIONAL EVENTS

- 1783: The Treaty of Paris ends the Revolutionary War.
- 1784: Spain closes the Lower Mississippi River to American commerce.
- 1787: US constitutional federal republic begins.
- 1787: General James Wilkinson obtains Spanish monopoly to trade American goods in Spanish New Orleans.
- 1789: The French Revolution begins.
- 1793: Citizen Genêt, Revolutionary France's envoy to the United States, foments American mercenaries to attack Spanish *Luisiana*.
- 1795: Treaty of San Lorenzo with Spain. The United States–Spanish border is set at the thirty-first parallel.
- 1795: Pinckney's Treaty between United States and Great Britain. British forts are withdrawn from the Northwest Territory.
- 1796–1798: Manuel Gayoso is slow to transfer territory to the Americans.
- February 1797: American border commissioner Ellicot and military escort arrive in Natchez.
- February 1797 to March 1798: Two flags fly over the Natchez district.
- April 1798: US Mississippi Territory is established. New Englander Winthrop Sargent is appointed the first governor.

Introduction:
Monsieur Piqué's Watch, 1788

THE OHIO AND MISSISSIPPI RIVERS, AS THEY HAD BEEN SINCE prehistoric times, were the vast riverine highways to and within the immense North American mid-continent. To Americans and immigrants from abroad the region came to be known as the trans-Allegheny West, the lands over the mountains, a contested borderland full of promise and peril. To Native American nations like the Delaware, Miami, and Shawnee, these domains were their homes and hunting grounds—their refuge from the displacement of previous generations from the eastern lands of the rising sun. The Ohio River, which early French explorers named *La Belle Rivière*, served as the gateway to this West.

By late 1783 newly independent America claimed ownership of the entire Northwest Territory by provisions of the Treaty of Paris, which ended the Revolutionary War and rewarded the country victory. America's late-arriving ally Spain also formally gained British West Florida, legitimizing its conquest by Bernardo de Gálvez, the last conquistador and governor general of sprawling Spanish *Luisiana*.

Land companies recruited investors and settlers. Scientists were excited about reports of fossilized bones of mammoth beasts that might still roam the earth, while cryptic pyramids and earthworks loomed at the confluence of as yet unnamed rivers. Land was plentiful and fertile. Only the hard labor of clearing its forest cover, then dealing with the Indians who had not yet settled with the Americans, stood in the way of realizing a seemingly limitless range of possibilities.

The Ohio country, with its leafy forests, flowing rivers, lakefront vistas, and abundant game now beckoned a postwar torrent of land speculators encroaching on the Indians' "Middle Ground," that swath of land from the Great Lakes to the Upper Mississippi Basin. These hordes included impoverished veterans claiming land bounties, squatters, recent European immigrants breaking free of manorial lords in Europe, Christian evangelists, and not a few desperadoes. Reeking of backwoods whiskey, sporting stained fringed buckskins, and brandishing flintlock Pennsylvania long rifles and muskets from the war, ragtag militiamen and pioneers tangled with the Indians in an endless cycle of raids and reprisals.

From this volatile brew came a seemingly unending stream of mutilated body parts, human scalps, and atrocities committed against and by Indians, settlers, the American Army, and militiamen in almost all possible combinations. A typical incident might be triggered by an Indian raiding party attacking an isolated pioneer settlement, only to be answered by an ad hoc settler posse delivering a "mad, brutal action against the first available target."

*

The late winter breezes of March 1788 whipped Dr. Antoine Saugrain's face as he surveyed the dark Ohio River waters urging him and his little flatboat crew westward from their embarkation at Pittsburgh. Damp and chill air charged over the river's surface, tingling and inducing shivers. All four sojourners had their stations, were on constant lookout for river hazards, and were taking turns handling the oars. So long as their small flatboat maintained the main current, all would be well. Or so they thought.

Born Antoine François Saugrain de Vigny in Paris on February 17, 1763, the doctor came from a long line of government-connected printers, people with aspirations to the minor nobility of the *ancien régime*. Apprenticed as a physician and apothecary, and educating himself further as a natural philosopher of chemistry and physics, Saugrain felt the pull of the new American land almost viscerally.

This was his second trip in North America. The first was in the employ of Governor Bernardo Gálvez prospecting for mineral wealth within Spanish *Luisiana*. With Gálvez's passing in 1785, Saugrain had lost his patron and returned to France.

Dr. Antoine François Saugrain de Vigny. Born in Paris and well connected to leading scientists, Saugrain became an American frontier pioneer and physician. 1904 engraving after an anonymous miniature oil painting in color, circa 1785, at the Missouri Historical Society.

Passing through Philadelphia on the way west, he heard and read about the wonders and opportunities on the far side of the Allegheny Mountains. Saugrain could anticipate that his medical, pharmaceutical, and chemical assaying skills would be in demand at every turn.

He found his opportunity soon enough. Thanks to a small group of Parisian investors who engaged him to travel in concert with a young botanist, M. Piqué, the pair was "destined to explore the natural products of this country." And they had the good fortune to meet the aged Benjamin Franklin in Philadelphia, who penned a letter of recommendation. Franklin judged both as "young men of uncommon knowledge and most amiable manners, so that I have scarce ever met with persons for whom I had in so short acquaintance so much esteem and affection." Saugrain held the letter close, hoping it would open doors to him on the frontier. So strong was this new connection that M. Piqué entrusted his gold and other valuables to Franklin for safekeeping while he ventured on the western American frontier.

Franklin encouraged the capable and adventurous pair to take their skills into the Ohio country, where the living legend had both land company investments and interest in advancing scientific understanding of the region. Saugrain likely knew, however, that he was following a proven avenue to scientific recognition. The ethnographer Antoine-Simone Le Page Du Pratz had sought out and documented the customs of the Natchez Indians during the French Mississippi Bubble of the 1720s. More recently the Philadelphians John and William Bartram described new species of plants to Europeans and cultivated the most promising ones for commercial agriculture in their suburban greenhouses and gardens. Hector St. John de Crèvecoeur, whose writings rhapsodized on the possibilities of the American West, included the then-exotic flora and fauna of East and West Florida in his best-selling essays. Saugrain could aspire to become, through careful observations and discoveries, one among this distinguished company.

Departing Philadelphia, the two scientists made their way west across Pennsylvania, itself a difficult journey. There were no regular overland conveyances or stagecoaches west of Lancaster, making for an arduous trip crossing the Alleghenies. Perhaps they traveled in concert with the ponderous Conestoga freight wagons that lumbered along the poorly maintained roads to and from Fort Pitt.

When they arrived in Pittsburgh, then a tiny town outside the decaying fort at the confluence of the Allegheny and Monongahela Rivers, it was too late in the autumn of 1787 for floating down the Ohio, since the river had frozen over early that year.

So the two commissioned the building of a small flatboat during the winter, and awaited the breaking of the ice and reopening of river traffic while assaying ore samples brought into town by speculators and settlers assessing their lands. They cooked their own food, "for the greater part venison and potatoes, for bread was scarce and dear," and made the rounds of town, engaging strangers for company and inquiring about conditions downriver. There they met and engaged a Frenchman, Monsieur Raguet, and an American surnamed Pierce, from Baltimore. Both sought passage toward Kentucky. They were probably welcomed by Saugrain and Piqué as stronger, experienced hands who could wield the oversized flatboat's oars and rudder. Surely they were more confident using firearms, should that be necessary, than were the two scientists from France. Franklin, though, had counseled that such concerns, amplified in the press, were overblown: "Travelling on the Ohio has for some years past been thought as safe as on any river in France, so that there was not the least suspicion of danger. Many thousands . . . having gone down that way to the new settlements at Kentucky."

The little band of four departed on March 19, 1788, under an incandescent moon that made for good visibility and long days of swift travel along with their horses, saddles, and bales of hay lashed onboard. The onset of astronomical springtime, the vernal equinox, of which the scientists were well aware, promised that nighttime frosts would end soon.

Hours on the river passed quickly as the Frenchmen grew accustomed to maneuvering their craft into the swift current and letting the river do the rest. They made good time those first days. Brief stops at the tiny settlements at Wheeling, Fort Harmar, and Limestone hardly registered in their memories. The sojourners probably lashed their boat to stout tree branches reaching over the shoreline, settling in for the night. Here they could let their horses stretch their legs and perhaps share a meal with the locals. "We continued our voyage without accident until the 24th," Saugrain wrote, "always admiring both banks of the Ohio, which in places are magnificent."

Their first encounter with Native Americans occurred opposite the mouth of the Big Miami River. They were five days departed and already 430 miles downriver from the headwaters of the Ohio River at Pittsburgh. The place struck pioneer observers as a prime area for settlement and perhaps a fort.

At half past four in the afternoon Saugrain noted that "as the wind had thrown us a little upon the shore of the Ohio on the Pennsylvania side, M. Piqué called my attention to a flatboat which was upon the same bank."

Just as the little crew maneuvered their boat away from the shore to regain the current opposite the Big Miami, Indian calls pierced the tense silence. Next followed a ragged volley of musket fire from unseen attackers.

> *The Indians all went aboard the flatboat we had seen near the shore and in front of which they had put some planking to prevent their being seen. And in this same planking they made holes to put their guns through so that they might fire upon us without danger of being killed themselves. . . . To get beyond the range of the [musket] balls we all four took to the oars.*

The first shot killed Saugrain's mare, who in her death agony jostled Monsieur Piqué's horse. The gunfire, shrieking attackers, and sudden deathly collapse of the equine's companion caused the surviving horse to involuntarily kick Saugrain in the abdomen, throwing him flat.

The still unseen attackers fired a fusillade of twenty gunshots, their staccato reports echoing over the river. The Indians then ceased firing, showed themselves, and hopped into their canoes to give the flatboat chase. If they were Shawnee, painted in garish colored bear grease and traditional designs whose meanings were unknown to the Europeans, they would have presented an otherworldly and terrifying sight.

Saugrain "left my oar to see if our guns were in order. Of the three we had, I found two loaded; one of these was mine, the other, M. Raguet's carbine. I hastened to load the third as well and to prime two pistols" belonging to Raguet. Yet in the confusion either Raguet or Pierce proposed to raise a white handkerchief and to surrender "judging it would be better to be a prisoner among Indians than to be killed."

The ten Indians gained on the unwieldy flatboat. Silencing their guns, and now in plain sight, the lead attackers gestured in a manner that could be interpreted as "some sign of friendship" or at least nonlethal intent. After long minutes of suspense that felt as if time itself had been taken prisoner, the lead Indian came alongside and prepared to board.

Saugrain saw a knife in his hand. "I judged with some reason, I believe, that he had no praiseworthy intention." Acting reflexively, he aimed the pistol and fired, sending "two balls into his stomach."

No sooner was the handgun fired and the attacker felled than the rest of the Indians prostrated themselves in their canoes and returned to firing their muskets, but now at much closer range than before.

Among the defenders, Monsieur Raguet commenced a spirited response. Yet, in order to present the musket and take proper aim, he was forced to expose himself. Raguet "put his arm outside the boat and it was once broken by a gunshot," leaving a gaping open fracture of shattered bone and bloodied flesh.

Instead of making a stand, Monsieur Piqué jumped overboard into the chill waters along with Pierce, the American, and swam for shore. The naturalist perhaps perceived further opposition useless, and thought his chances swimming to shore and then being pursued on land better than being shot at or cornered on the confines of their craft. Saugrain thought otherwise. "This did us much harm, for then the Indians . . . fired much more."

Somewhere in the confused melee, an Indian gunshot mangled Dr. Saugrain's left index finger, leaving Raguet and Saugrain little choice but to abandon their resistance in the face of the encroaching assailants. Both threw themselves into the water. But Raguet did not know how to swim. His injured arm was useless. Back in Pittsburgh, he had confided to Saugrain, perhaps in jest, that he preferred "to be drowned to being scalped by the Indians." His wish was fulfilled that day.

Once Saugrain gained the shore, he was immediately confronted by two Indians, who had already captured the passive Piqué. One Indian bound Saugrain's hands behind his back with the same hide strips the natives used to bind their blankets. The other unceremoniously threw

Piqué to the ground, pulled open his coat and ruffled shirt, and then inflicted multiple "stabs with a knife" between his ribs. Then he proceeded methodically to scalp the expiring Piqué with the same knife. He placed the trophy into Piqué's own pocketbook and secured it to his person.

Saugrain expected a like fate. But instead of murdering him outright, the two Indians indicated he should proceed with them toward the abandoned flatboat, now drifting slowly downstream. Saugrain surmised that they intended to take him into Indian territory as a captive once they had crossed the Ohio River to the north side in the captured boat. A "cruel fear seized" him, as he pictured being burned alive as the guest of honor at some incomprehensible Indian ritual. Or maybe he would be ransomed, enslaved, or even forcibly adopted into the tribe. Having earlier dispatched one of the Indians personally with a pistol, he anticipated the worst.

He made a violent and sudden effort that tore through the straps that bound him. "I swam away with such force that [the Indian guard] did not risk following. . . . And he did well, for my plan was, if they came after me, to seize one of them and drown with him."

Saugrain, who had swum to what he judged a safe distance, clung to a projecting tree branch. The remaining assailants dived from their boat, boarded and captured the still drifting flatboat, and began to cross the Ohio. The Indians now seized the weapons abandoned there, fired at Saugrain, and wounded him in the neck.

He waited until the Indians had gone halfway across the river. When they showed no signs of deviating from their course, Saugrain stumbled ashore. Returning to the scene of his capture, he found Piqué "quite dead." He also came upon Pierce, who all along "had concealed himself in the ravine."

Together they turned over their unfortunate companion's corpse to more closely examine the Indian's insults. They were surprised to find that the raiders had left the man's gold watch, a knife, and two dollars in cash. Saugrain retrieved those items, hoping they would be useful in the course of their escape into the wilderness. Pierce cut off a large swatch of M. Piqué's greatcoat. Saugrain recalled later that he "had not the same forethought, of which I much repented." The two survivors had neither strength nor tools to bury the botanist in a proper grave in this godforsaken place, so far from his native France. Nor did they want to tarry.

The two began to walk westward paralleling the river, hoping to encounter anyone other than Indian marauders. Saugrain "had nothing upon me but a shirt and a pair of large breeches," having lost his shoes while swimming. They maintained a course just inland and out of sight of the river and the Indians who rampaged freely on the other side.

Saugrain had lost blood from his neck wound. He was exhausted. Pierce had no such encumbrance. They made their way almost five miles. As the eastern sky darkened, the cold increased. A grass meadow beckoned. Pierce covered them both in the brittle high grass and saw to his companion's comfort as best he could.

They slept for several hours before resuming their walk, continuing most of the night and into the predawn hours. Pierce selected a large fallen tree. They sheltered beneath it, huddling together for warmth. As they slept insensibly, a wet snow commenced. Saugrain's feet protruded from under the tree while Pierce covered his with the rag cut from Piqué's greatcoat. "I found my feet frozen when I awoke."

Undaunted, the duo continued to follow the south bank of the Ohio River, on the Kentucky side "in the hope we might see some boat" bound for Louisville that would take them aboard. Although tens of thousands of settlers swarmed over the Appalachian Mountains from Virginia to Kentucky, most of the newcomers steered clear of the lands close to the Ohio River, where Indian war parties ranged with impunity. One could travel for days at a stretch without encountering a soul, be they white, red, or black, friend or foe.

The two survivors were obliged to ford several streams emptying into the big river. Some were large enough to require swimming, or detouring upstream and inland to find a more conducive crossing place.

Wildlife abounded. To Saugrain, the American West was a wonder. "The number of deer, of turkeys and of pheasants we saw is quite inconceivable. We saw also four or five troops of buffalos, which came so near us that with a pistol I could have killed some."

The next morning, Saugrain's feet hurt so terribly he "could hardly walk." Pierce grew impatient, ranging ahead but always returning. The pair continued to walk but made little progress. Hunger added to their afflictions.

Saugrain indicated to Pierce what he called a *bête puante* (stinking beast) ambling ahead. Without hesitation Pierce gave chase, and clubbed the chattering skunk to death with a heavy stick. Having skinned the carcass, Pierce could not bring himself to even try to taste the raw meat. But Saugrain's hunger induced him to overcome revulsion. "I cut off some little bits and I swallowed them like pills. This did me little good, I assure you."

They thought of improvising a fire for cooking the beast. Saugrain mused on how he would remove the crystals from two watches—his and Piqué's—to make a bi-convex lens, concentrate the emerging sun's rays, and start a fire. Pierce may have found the Frenchman's idea ingenious, but their fear of smoke betraying their location nixed the enterprise. The duo moved on.

Late in the afternoon they came upon an abandoned log cabin. They estimated it to be about fifteen miles downriver from where they had been attacked. Resting briefly, they devised a plan to escape by raft. This would entail stripping and binding together the cabin's doors and "some fence [posts] or *poteaux de barrier*." Pierce did the heavy work, while Saugrain cut cords from Pierce's buckskin breeches for binding the wooden parts together. He also fashioned crude buckskin socks for covering his feet, now turned oddly gray.

Their project proceeded apace. The duo was about to launch their makeshift raft when Indians spotted them from the other side of the river, startling them and triggering new fears.

"Then I took to my heels and never in my life do I think I made so good use of them." Although his own frostbitten feet no longer pained Saugrain, Pierce, being unimpaired but just as frightened, far outran him. "And in two minutes I lost sight of him."

Pierce fortunately retraced his steps to stay with Saugrain as the sun set. They judged that darkness would conceal them from pursuing Indians and spent the night where they were. "It was one of the worst nights I have passed in my life. I could not sleep, and at each moment I thought I saw Indians."

The march the next day increased Saugrain's anxiety to the point of hallucination. "I saw Indians behind all the trees; each bit of wood was a gun and I believe, to alarm us more, all the deer had conspired" with the Indians. Hunger, immersions in cold water, clothing inadequate for the weather, extreme exertion while wounded, and blood loss were all taking their toll.

Before sunrise they were trekking again, staying close to the Ohio River in order to search for friendly river traffic. As noon approached, the sun shone brightly and warmed them. Eventually Pierce caught sight of two boats floating downstream.

They shouted to get their attention. The boats kept their distance at first, their helmsmen apparently believing the distressed pair were Indians, "but seeing our white shirts and our breeches, they determined to come to us." But not without great care, as the fraternal rescuers could only approach the shore on a diagonal on account of the current and the ubiquitous overhanging tree branches. Saugrain and Pierce were obliged to hurry along the shoreline as the boats approached. "At last we swam out to join them."

Saugrain was surprised that their saviors all had their "carbines in hand." The boatmen were on their guard for a new and dreaded Indian tactic: white adoptees and Native American sympathizers, feigning distress and claiming that murderous Indians were about to overtake them on land, were known to decoy pioneer river traffic into ambush. Unwary boatmen coming to the rescue would then face a fusillade of bullets and arrows from armed Native Americans hidden among trees and bushes. War Chief Little Turtle's own son-in-law William Wells, taken captive as a redheaded preteen years before and adopted into the Miami, was said to decoy regularly on behalf of the Indians.

So at last, Saugrain had escaped the Indian pursuers. "Arrived on board, they undressed me, warmed some whiskey and rubbed all my body, which did me much good." He drank some of the whiskey, the universal spirit and medium of exchange on the frontier, and ate some bread. The boatmen dressed his neck wound, but deferred definitive care for his injured hand, hopeful that a competent physician or surgeon in Louisville would conserve his limbs, all now in very bad condition, from amputation.

The two flatboats and their providential crews negotiated the Falls of the Ohio without incident. There remained just a mile or two more to Louisville. The waters being high, they arrived there two days after the rescue, on March 29, 1788. Saugrain and Pierce reckoned on being 620 miles on the Ohio River west of Pittsburgh, and some 180 miles downriver from the ambush near the Great Miami. Once assured that his wounded traveling companion was in a situation to find aid, Pierce continued on alone with his business errand.

The next day an army surgeon at Fort Finney ministered to Saugrain's wounds. Happily, his foot's circulation and vitality gradually improved. His injured finger similarly rallied over time. And there in Louisville a most relieved Saugrain tarried for almost seven weeks until May 11.

*

Months after the incident Benjamin Franklin heard of the disaster and relayed the melancholy news to one of the French investors, Saugrain's brother-in-law Dr. Joseph-Ignace Guillotin in Paris. "Probably the Company may now be discourag'd and drops their project." Guillotin concurred that Saugrain's travails and Piqué's grizzly demise likely "reverses projects dear to our hearts." The enterprise had failed.

The river ambush of the Frenchman's party generated alarm throughout Kentucky and was covered widely in newspapers from Vermont to South Carolina. Print coverage muted Raguet's spirited and armed resistance, Piqué's passivity or cowardice, the American Pierce's cutting and running, and Saugrain's murky shooting of the Indian boarder who was possibly under a flag of truce. Instead, newspaper stories fed a nascent blanket hatred for the "savages" in the West, vilifying all Indians, regardless of tribal affiliation and whether or not they were allied or neutral to the United States. The Franklins and Guillotins, however, perhaps due to their own rosy ideals of *sauvages nobles* in a state of nature, combined with their continuing economic interest in Western land speculations, avoided libeling an entire race. Rather, they characterized the incident impersonally as "this melancholy event," an "unfortunate accident," and a "horrible misfortune."

For their part, the war parties of Chief Little Turtle of the Miami nation and his allies Buckongahelas of the Delaware and Blue Jacket of the Shawnee, comprising the core of the Northwest Indian Federation, had succeeded in disrupting the aspirations of Saugrain as well as many American would-be settlers. To the Frenchman, his assailants were all simply Indians. To his credit, Saugrain, though maimed for long months by his wounds, never became hobbled by hatred of the Indians. In contrast, many of his fellow pioneers magnified Indian-hating into a genocidal mantra.

On a map, the entirety of the Northwest Territory fell within the borders of the fledgling United States. It was another matter entirely on the ground. South of the Ohio River was the Kentucky district, now on the cusp of statehood. The Ohio River itself was the gateway to the Southwest Territory of Tennessee, Spanish West Florida, and the largely unexplored lands of *Luisiana*, as well as to the mighty Mississippi River, linking these borderlands to New Orleans, the Caribbean, and to the Atlantic maritime mercantile world.

Although Monsieur Piqué's dreams had expired with him—his scalp now adorning a nameless warrior's abode at Kekiongo, principal center of the Northwest Indian Federation—his gold pocket watch tellingly remained with Dr. Saugrain. Time, numbers, and technology seemed to be on the side of the increasing numbers of settlers and adventurers going west. Their program of more "productive" use of Indian lands for permanent settlement, commercial agriculture, and industry, rather than subsistence farming, deer hunting, and fur trapping, seemed likely to prevail. But the Indians were far from passive witnesses to the encroachment on their lands. And European imperial powers and the nascent United States continued to jockey for influence. The conflicting plans and interests of all these groups were fatefully intertwined. The outcome was far from certain.

Chapter 1

West of the Revolution

As a twenty-four-year-old young man from Monmouth, New Jersey, Samuel S. Forman came of age in the shadow of dozens of his extended family members, veterans all of the recent Revolutionary War. Everyone had shared tales of their dangerous and sometimes heroic exploits. Everyone except Samuel S. Forman. . . . He was just young enough to have missed the excitement of military service against Loyalist neighbors, British regulars, Native Americans, and German mercenaries. He nevertheless relished the tales and repeated them at every turn.

But Samuel S. also felt acutely the challenge of making a living in the postwar world. Rural farmers were plagued by debt, and regional businesses offered him scant opportunities, for the country was in the midst of a postwar economic recession.

East Coast events and politics, including the 1787 Constitutional Convention, dominated the press and informed discourse. Disputes smoldered and flashed, involving natives in the interior, erstwhile Spanish allies, and the English along the entire long arc of the western and southern frontiers. These were more immediate preoccupations to people like General David Forman and his diminutive younger cousin Samuel S. Forman, as both of their prospects were entwined with international and domestic trade.

Frontier opportunities and danger beckoned variously to many adventurous, enterprising, desperate, impoverished, religiously enlightened, runaway, and even criminal souls. These descriptors were far from mutually exclusive, and in this the Formans were far from alone.

*

Samuel S. Forman. Frontier businessman who accompanied a large group of pioneer settlers immigrating to Natchez in Spanish West Florida. Oil on ivory miniature by an unknown artist, circa 1800, courtesy of the New York Public Library

American leaders faced a chasm between their Rousseauist ideals of noble savages capable of Christian enlightenment and the lived reality of the Northwest Territory. While the Confederation Congress could congratulate itself on laying out expectations for the creation of up to five new states, and an orderly transition from territory to future statehood, this American blueprint hardly captured life in the verdant Ohio forests and along its river highways. The Founding Fathers' achievement in the Northwest Ordinance appears impressive in hindsight, but when enacted, it did not recognize the confederated Indian tribal inhabitants. Native Americans dominated throughout the expansive territory, save for a few scattered, feeble forts and vulnerable pioneer settlements.

The British had ostensibly ceded the lands to the Americans in the 1783 Treaty of Paris, but without first consulting their native allies. From forts and trading posts in the far reaches of the Northwest Territory—Niagara, Detroit, and Michilimackinac in far Northern Michigan—the wily British also quietly encouraged Indians inhabiting the vast expanse to establish an autonomous state, a buffer from their viewpoint that would limit expansionist Americans from encroaching on British Canada. Additionally, Britain would continue to enjoy the lucrative fur trade. Ever since Pontiac's Rebellion (1765) the British had become more accommodating to Indian interests. The "Middle Ground" of largely peaceable interactions among British colonials and Indian tribes characterized the Northwest in the decade before the Revolutionary War.

However the departing British may have viewed the natives as subordinate clients to be bought off with gifts and incited at their whim to action against American settlers, the Indians hardly needed British encouragement. Inspired Indian leaders skillfully organized among themselves, balancing their British sources of guns and trade goods, raiding or dealing with rival American and Spanish traders, and trading with more distant native tribes.

Indian nations and tribes conducted their own foreign policies, at times divided into factions among themselves. Yet Chiefs Little Turtle, Blue Jacket, and Buckongahelas formed a powerful confederation of tribes residing in the Northwest Territory while also appealing when they could to more distant groups to oppose American settler encroachments.

The Eastern Woodlands Indians from time immemorial lived a life of farming and hunting. They were less demanding of the land's natural resources than the settlers' envisioned farms, orchards, dairies, mills, mines, and nascent factories. From the standpoint of American settlers and land speculators, the Indians were simply an impediment to progress.

Following intermittent periods of accommodation and strife, Delaware Indian life in Samuel S. Forman's New Jersey was a faint memory, as that nation had been swept first into central Pennsylvania by the mid-eighteenth century and then further west into the Ohio country. There, the Delawares became new neighbors to the Miami, Shawnee, Ojibwa, Potawatomi, and others who had earlier borne their own displacements.

The current Delaware leader Buckongahelas, and his Confederation allies, would have agreed with a fellow chief, Cornplanter of the Seneca, in chafing at dislocation and imposition. He had a message for the Americans:

> *Your forefathers crossed the great waters and landed on this island [Continent]. Their numbers were small. They found friends and not enemies. They told us they had fled from their own country for fear of wicked men, and had come here to enjoy their religion. They asked for a small seat. We took pity on them, granted their request and they sat down amongst us. We gave them corn and meat. They gave us poison [i.e., whiskey and rum].*

He bristled with defiance.

> *[But later settlers] . . . wanted more land. They wanted our country. Our eyes were opened, and our minds became uneasy. Wars took place . . . and many of our people were destroyed.*

The Northwest Indian Federation sought to enforce its collective sovereignty to stop further American settlement. They chose to employ the Line of Demarcation, articulated in a 1768 British treaty with Indian signatories that aimed to defuse their grievances following the French and Indian War. That action and treaty in the name of King George III sought to confine settlers east of the Appalachian Mountains and south of the Ohio River. Not surprisingly, Americans wanted none of it. Daniel

Boone and his Virginia pioneers succeeded in advancing settlements into Kentucky and Tennessee during the Revolutionary War into traditional Indian hunting grounds.

Consequently, hunting and raiding parties ranged out from clusters of Indian villages with impunity across the region. Some Indian tribes continued to raid across the Ohio River into Kentucky well into the 1780s. Daniel Boone's daughter Jemima was famously abducted and rescued in 1782. Likewise the river decoyer William Wells, whose biological father had been killed by a Miami Indian war party just two years before. Wells would become an important figure, unseen but strongly influencing the Formans' pioneering venture.

By 1783 an astounding 7 percent of Kentucky settlers—men, women, and children, both free and enslaved—had been murdered outright in Indian raids. Countless others had been wounded or maimed, and still others adopted or ransomed. A few years later the main theater of frontier guerrilla warfare largely shifted north of the Ohio River or onto the river itself. And with the now independent Americans claiming ownership of the entire Northwest Territory by right of the Treaty of Paris, the stage was set for bloody conflict among Northwest Federated Indians, the feeble American Army, settlers, squatters, and freebooting criminals.

*

One notorious episode, even more brutal than most, involved a community of neutral Indians, mostly Delawares, who had converted to Christianity. Encouraged by well-meaning Moravian missionaries to adopt a settled agricultural life, they gathered in a location they thought secure, the village of Gnadenhütten in the eastern Ohio Territory.

In April 1781 American Colonel Daniel Broadhead, with Tennessee militia in tow, attacked and disrupted Coshocton, the principal Delaware town in Ohio Country. Defeated but not bowed, Delaware Chief Buckongahelas warned the Gnadenhütten settlers that their asserted neutrality would not protect them.

The fatal stroke came not from fellow Indians but from disgruntled and vengeful militiamen from Western Pennsylvania and Fort Pitt. In retaliation for a nameless Indian raid by unknown assailants, the incensed militiamen surrounded undefended Gnadenhütten on March 8, 1782. The militiamen systematically butchered all the men, women, and children, one victim after the other. The assailants "Fell on them while they were singing hymns. . . . Many children were killed in their wretched mother's arms." Only one escaped to tell of the massacre.

Within months Delawares near Sandusky perpetrated their own massacre on American militiamen, reserving an especially prolonged three-day ritual execution for Colonel William Crawford, who had not been at Gnadenhütten but was killed in reprisal. The reported excruciating details of his murder would fuel the flames of anti-Indian sentiment, even though the coverage glossed over, or altogether omitted, any reference to the Gnadenhütten atrocity committed on the Christianized Indians. A generation of unremitting violence on the frontier gradually incubated an anti-Indian racist sentiment that hardly distinguished among Indian nations, be they friend, foe, neutral, or former American allies during the Revolutionary War.

Christian Delaware survivors of the Gnadenhütten massacre fled from Eastern Ohio. Some determined to resist further American settlement and joined with Buckongahelas in the northwest Ohio tribal towns. Others moved on, north into British Canada, or further west into Spanish Upper *Luisiana* just across the Mississippi River to Cape Girardeau, near the confluence with the Ohio River.

For those Indians remaining and standing their ground, Gnadenhütten only served to feed the flames of violence, resulting in ever-growing cycles of barbarity and reprisals. Aggrieved Indian speakers at British Fort Niagara declared that they "would redouble their attacks on the Americans, treat them as they were treated, and show them no mercy." In July 1782 Seneca Chief Guyasuta, up until then neutral in the hostilities, attacked and destroyed Westmoreland County's seat, never to be rebuilt. Mobilized Shawnee then defeated Daniel Boone and Kentucky militiamen at Blue Licks in Kentucky and set upon Bryan's Station at present-day Lexington. In retaliation George Rogers Clark invaded Shawnee country on a village- and crop-destroying raid.

A January 1785 treaty signed with the Americans at Fort McIntosh under Northwest Territory Governor General Arthur St. Clair did little to quell the mayhem. While it ceded several tracts of land north of the Ohio River to Americans for surveying and subsequent settlement, most tribes of the Northwest Indian Confederation were not party to the negotiations and treaty. They did not recognize its terms and continued their terror campaign against settlers.

Most pioneers traveling on the Ohio River bound for Kentucky, Tennessee, or further to Spanish West Florida just wanted to survive crossing the bloody Northwest borderlands in order to get to friendlier and generally more peaceful territory. Though they posed no settlement threat to the Indians in the immediate area, Northwest Confederation raiding parties targeted immigrant river traffic.

The unwieldy pioneer river flatboats and keelboats were loaded to the gunwales with cattle, horses, food, clothing, tools, and guns. They offered tempting targets for valuables, captives, or scalps. Canny Indian leaders like Little Turtle judged that their terror campaign was justified against the existential threat to their homelands, and that news of the violence would dissuade the torrents of settlers tempted to follow earlier pioneers.

Spanish West Florida was far more peaceful and beckoning, if no less complex, with respect to the relations among European colonial powers, the Americans, and Indian nations. Here the fearsome Chickasaw and more numerous Choctaw dominated the interior east of the Mississippi River Upper Delta. Farther east were the areas claimed by Georgia, the Creek and Cherokee. French colonials and Natchez Indians had prosecuted a mutually genocidal war fifty years prior, leaving much of West Florida mostly depopulated of both natives and settlers.

Spanish Governor-General Bernardo de Gálvez held court at New Orleans, capital of *Luisiana*. Asserting sovereignty over a huge swath of territory, Gálvez had endeared himself to the Americans during the Revolution by supplying arms and munitions for use in the Americans' western campaigns, among other invaluable initiatives.

But, within two years of the Peace of Paris, Spanish interests chafed against those of the Americans. The northern and eastern borders of Spanish West Florida, roughly encompassing the modern states of Mississippi and Alabama, remained ill-defined, while Chickasaws, Choctaws,

Creeks, and Cherokees jostled one another, and paid deference to Spanish and American interests only as it suited them.

The State of Georgia, whose legislature was dominated by land speculators, cast acquisitive and jingoistic eyes all the way west to the Mississippi River. The relationship between the United States and Spain, with its thriving Natchez district astride the great river, quickly degenerated from that of gratitude for assistance at a critical juncture late in the war to that of rivalry for the mid-continent east of the Mississippi River down to the lucrative port of New Orleans. As intended by the Spanish, western American settler farmers and traders, already feeling second to American centers on the East Coast and frustrated by the government's feeble protection against Indian disturbances, began to develop an affinity for the Spanish. Extensive tracts of fertile land, offered free in return for cultivation, increased the allure of *Luisiana* to potential settlers.

Samuel S. Forman and his cousin "Black David" may have had some awareness of these trends, thanks to newspaper articles about the latest pronouncements on Mississippi trade barriers and the lurid accounts of Indian depredations in the West. They could talk to Middle-Atlantic businessmen involved in the western and New Orleans trade. Like many of their restive peers, they must have wondered about opportunities for themselves and their families along those frontiers.

Soon David Forman would initiate a bold plan that would forever link them, their employees, enslaved workers, and their progeny to far-off Natchez in Spanish West Florida.

CHAPTER 2

Art of the Deal

THE LATE AUTUMN AIR WAFTED AND STUNG, BLOWING OVER PUNGENT heaped manure, sweet ploughed dirt, and musky withered cornstalks. It was November 21, 1789, on the east central New Jersey plains, the year following ratification of the US Constitution by a super-majority of state conventions. The infant United States had just established a temporary capital in New York City, which was much closer to the Formans' home-town of Monmouth County than to Philadelphia.

Samuel S. Forman was considering an opportunity sure to take him far afield from his familiar haunts in New Jersey and nearby New York City. If he were to accept, he would of necessity depart from his brother-in-law John Burroughs's Freehold house and a wooden shack of a storefront, perhaps never to see them again. But his trade of selling local farmers' produce into the New York City market, carting north by wagon and then by boat across the saltwater Narrows, had diminished to a trickle now that the harvest was in. Summer vegetables—Indian corn, pumpkins, and beans—offered him a tidy little profit if acquired directly from farm-ers, then transported to the city promptly for resale. New Jersey soil, well suited to growing such temperate garden crops, was productive during the hot and humid summer months. But as the season turned cool and the fields went dormant, so would his business.

Samuel S. was impatient to make a place for himself in the world. He set his mind on some larger horizon than that afforded by the seasonal arbitrage of corn, pumpkin, and beans between country and city. Yet in addition to buying and selling farm produce, he had cobbled together

General David Forman. George Washington's eyes, ears, and often extralegal bullying kept British Loyalists in check during a protracted guerrilla war in Northern New Jersey during the Revolutionary War. Obtaining a Spanish land grant for the Natchez district of Spanish West Florida, he dispatched family members and 60 enslaved African Americans on a 2,400-mile pioneering and settlement odyssey. Though a commissioned likeness, the artist managed to capture Forman's imperious and querulous nature, as well as his pride in being a member of the prestigious Society of the Cincinnati. Photo of a 1795 pastel by James Sharples appearing in the Forman Genealogy by Dandridge, 1903. Whereabouts of the original piece is unknown and thought to be privately held.

"business in various ways for Gen. David Forman," the most significant of which were attempts to recover the general's losses from his having received counterfeit New York bonds. Should he pursue whatever further opportunities his older cousin General David Forman might proffer?

Walking along to his cousin's home where the two were to meet, he may have recalled incidents of his childhood and adolescence in "Forman Square" to aid in his decision-making. A sickly child not expected by his parents to live past his earliest years, Samuel S. had rallied and caught up with other youths in study and play. A compact stature and easy manner led many to believe he was younger than he actually was. Rather than correct people, he allowed them to believe what they would. But his age remained a touchy subject with him.

At Christmas when a youth, Samuel S.'s father's Black servant Daddy French would tote him about on his shoulders. Together they caroled holiday songs. The pair presented a mirthful contrast of tall and short, old and young, black and white, low and high musical registers. And what a view of the world for a boy from such a commanding perch! Daddy French's confident old shoulders remained steadfastly strong for the frolic even after many years of labor on the Forman farms. Glasses of punch and festive little cakes were part of the merriment, and whatever remained unconsumed Daddy French would take back to his family.

Samuel was but ten years old when the war began at Lexington and Concord. He and his friends play-acted at war. Armed with wooden guns and swords, "We formed ourselves into a grenadier company. [I] had the honor of being chosen captain."

As he aged, he conceivably could have enlisted in the Continental Army or New Jersey state militia before the peace of 1783, but he decided not to. Conflict was neither in his nature nor preference. Perhaps he was dissuaded by the ugly, prolonged guerrilla conflict between Patriot and Loyalist neighbors that had developed in Monmouth County. Perhaps he appeared too young or simply unfit to serve on the basis of his sickly early years. In any case, the decisive battle of Yorktown had already been fought by the time he was sixteen.

With so many Forman brothers, uncles, nephews, and cousins, many sharing the same Christian name, as he came to majority just after the

war, Samuel S. took as his middle name "Samuel," an informal convention adopted in his generation. In this way younger men could distinguish
themselves from identically named relatives by employing their fathers'
first names as their middle names. In addition, with every male family
member a war veteran, Samuel S. would have to strike out on his own and
achieve in his own way. Surely it must have been frustrating to find his
way in the footsteps of such titans.

Samuel S. soon walked within sight of Reverend Woodhull's church,
with its many-paned windows, severe white clapboard, and assertive spire
pointing heavenward. Right ahead was the Reverend's school, where
Samuel had studied grammar and the classics. He may have indeed
remembered a smattering from his studies of Fénelon's *Telemachus*: "I love
my family more than myself; more than my family my fatherland; more
than my fatherland humankind." He could have fancied himself as that
teenager depicted in the epic poem of yore, the son of Odysseus, compelled to seek his own distinctive place in a postwar world.

Many of his classmates would excel at classical studies and natural
philosophic sciences in preparation for Princeton College. But Samuel
S.'s proclivity toward his numbers, account books, and dreams of adven-
turing would take him far from Monmouth County and the heartland
of his extended clan. However much Samuel may have liked the tales
of ancient philosophers and mythological exploits, reading them in the
original Greek and Latin, as would be expected at college, neither resonated with his mastery nor his desires.

Now, as he fought to summon the power and confidence that would
be required of him in his upcoming interview with his imperious cousin,
Samuel S. tossed recollections of his childhood aside. He would have to
rein in a wandering mind and focus on the road ahead. Mud, puddles, and
detritus left by horses and livestock still mired country roads, and would
continue to do so until the first firm frost solidified the way.

After another half mile he reached General David Forman's house.
The two-story clapboard residence with dormered roof was set among
outbuildings fifty yards back from the road. A row of servants' one-room
shacks was set off to one side, their chimneys emitting dense plumes of
acrid wood smoke into the chill blue sky. The bondsmen's houses were

within easy calling distance of the big house and an easy walk for the field hands venturing to and from their assigned labors.

Samuel S. Forman alternately anticipated and dreaded his meeting with his cousin David, addressed as *General* David Forman by friends and most family. Samuel S. rarely ventured the honorific term *uncle*. That affectionate appellation was easier to utter with respect to the general's elder, rotund brother Ezekiel. Ezekiel and General David had been close since well before the war. Ezekiel and his first wife had hosted David's marriage ceremony at his house, then in Princeton, in 1765. Both were of an age to be Samuel's uncles, though they were in fact cousins to him. He was comfortable referring to the elder brother as uncle in that familiarly affectionate way, but not the general. Ezekiel had become a widower, the children of that marriage now responsible adults making their own way. Ezekiel moved to Philadelphia, met the considerably younger widow Margaret Neilson, and remarried in 1775. Imperious and self-important General Forman, late terror to the Tories, had been George Washington's eyes, ears, and ofttimes extralegal strong arm in the continued guerrilla skirmishing in Northern New Jersey post-Yorktown. "His person was commanding; his address gentlemanly." A dark and swarthy complexion, coupled with his reputation among regional Loyalists, was said to have been the inspiration for his nicknames: "Black David" and sometimes "Devil David."

Although Samuel was fairly certain that he had been summoned to be offered a job in the general's latest venture, he did not want to appear too eager, for that might convey desperation or incompetence. The general might incorrectly infer that Samuel's current circumstances were tenuous. He might in turn deride the young man's abilities in such a manner as to make a piddling compensation appear to be a big favor.

Once ushered into the general's paneled study, Samuel S. listened to the outlines of his opportunity. The general had made "an arrangement [a grant of land] with the Spanish Minister, Don Diego de Gardoqui, then residing in New York, to emigrate with his family and sixty Negroes into Louisiana, then belonging to the King of Spain." David Forman wanted Samuel S. to accompany his brother Ezekiel Forman and his family; Benajah Osman, overseer on the Monmouth plantation; and the general's sixty enslaved African Americans, to relocate to Natchez in Spanish West Florida. Once there, Ezekiel, who had studied law as a youth and had served as a minor Continental Congress bureaucrat, would execute the Spanish land grant and establish a plantation with the muscle of the enslaved. Samuel S.'s role would be business agent, or supercargo as the position was then known, of the enterprise, entrusted with important papers and trading goods along the way. As General David's agent, he would have considerable autonomy for making deals, and could also trade on his own account. Samuel S. need not concern himself with Black people, since Benajah Osman would do that, both during the trip and once the enterprise was established in Natchez.

Samuel S. may have regarded his cousin coolly as he weighed the general's offer and his options. His cousin was clearly not an "I'll get back to you" type. David Forman had retained his military bearing in spite of the peace, and expected deference to be paid to him by inferiors. That would have included younger family members, his wife Ann, former military subalterns, and practically everyone else, excepting George Washington himself, Governor William Livingston of New Jersey, and perhaps a handful of former Continental ranking veterans in the prestigious Society of the Cincinnati.

One person who did not observe the general's implicit expectations was his attractive eldest daughter Sarah. Sixteen and unmarried, she may have been at home at the time of this most consequential interview. Samuel S. may well have met and beheld his second cousin in the course of this visit. Perhaps he briefly entertained courting her. But Sarah Marsh Forman was out of his league, he was sure. The general trusted and held this daughter in high esteem, unlike everyone else in his orbit. Family gossip may have already linked Sarah romantically to her first cousin William G. Forman, a Princeton College graduate who had studied law.

The only small talk offered by the general would have been pertinent to the scheme at hand. Perhaps the general may have minimized the extent of services he expected, and therefore the amount of salary he was willing to pay—100 English pounds in Spanish milled dollars, per year—for the job of supercargo, selling the owner's wares on the best possible terms, on the pioneering and settlement expedition.

Perhaps in consequence Samuel S. was able to negotiate some terms that were important to him. Salary would be payable at Samuel S.'s discretion, either at the ultimate destination, Natchez, by Ezekiel, or back in New Jersey if Samuel S. chose not to remain. Return transportation and board would be payable separately. And the general would pay annual interest at seven shillings/sixpence if the endeavor dragged out for more than a year.

The broad outline, however, was not up for discussion. Samuel S. would "proceed with Capt. Benajah Osman & a number of the aforesaid David's tenants or slaves to Fort Pitt, that during their travel to Fort Pitt, he will aid & assist the said Benajah." Ezekiel Forman, with his wife Margaret and children in tow, would proceed separately from Philadelphia and rendezvous on the road to Fort Pitt. From there on, the trek and settlement would be under the direction of David's elder sibling.

Samuel S. would serve as business agent, receiving "such dry goods as the aforesaid David & Ezekiel shall have provided [and] . . . proceed to sell or barter such goods & in such place as the aforesaid Ezekiel shall direct." If the general had not inserted over a dozen legal sounding "aforesaids" into the half-sheet scrap of paper memorializing the arrangement, it could easily have been mistaken for a military order from the last war.

There was not much to negotiate with the general. Samuel S. accepted. Cousin Tunis Forman witnessed the agreement while the general, who could be solicitous at times of his associates, offered a gesture guaranteed to cement his cousin's resolve and to assure he would not change his mind. David called for his own carriage, drawn by a four-horse team and guided by his trusted Black coachman Philip, to take Samuel S. home. The general further directed that the impressive conveyance stop by his wealthy Conover neighbors, where Samuel S. would cut an impressive figure while calling on one of the Conover daughters, whom the general perceived the young man fancied. "I went in such style Miss C[onover] could not refuse."

Meanwhile, probably eavesdropping on the proceedings was bondwoman Ginnie, forty-five years old, David's chief house servant. As a result, her view of the young and untested Samuel S. as supercargo for the proposed trip may well have changed from polite deference to a member of the master's extended family. He would be the repository of owner-ship and passport documents, at least until the rendezvous with Ezekiel Forman at Pittsburgh. This meant that Samuel S. was destined to play a critical part in her life and and the lives of those dear to her.

CHAPTER 3

Embarkation, 1789

THE TRAIN OF WAGONS, SUPPLIES, AND ENSLAVED PEOPLE ASSEMBLED ON General David Forman's Monmouth County farm on November 29, 1789. It was not a mile distant from Rev. John Woodhull's Old Tennent Church, and the grammar school of Samuel S.'s youth. As it was almost two years since New Jersey ratified the US Constitution, the third state to do so, with President George Washington having declared Thursday, November 25, 1789, as a day of Thanksgiving, the general's neighbors had likely extended their particular celebrations, indulging in additional days of libations and games. Not so the pioneer party, preparing and perhaps anxious about embarking on their long and arduous trek.

The final leave-taking was distressing "for the General's family and Blacks were almost all in tears." We can only imagine what was going through the sojourners' minds. Whites and Blacks, masters and enslaved alike would have borne the weight of finality. In all likelihood they would never again see friends, neighbors, acquaintances, or their familiar habitations. They may have also contemplated whether they would ever reach their destination, or whether they would fall prey en route to disease, the elements, or frontier savagery.

Some of the African Americans might also have considered that remaining in place in New Jersey might offer the prospect of gradual emancipation, as laws passed in Pennsylvania and Massachusetts recently had. Departing the North and the United States altogether for Spanish territories annihilated that possibility. That alone would reduce some to tears.

Surely some knew that disruptions of the late war in Monmouth County had provided opportunities for slaves to run away to the British in New York City. The Formans certainly still remembered Colonel Tye, the most notorious of the Loyalist irregulars.

Apparently hearing of Virginia Royal Governor Lord Dunmore's offer of freedom in exchange for military service in 1775, Titus, as he was then known to his Monmouth County plantation owner, promptly ran away. Once in Virginia Titus trained and saw combat as a British soldier, remaining undeterred even when his unit was decimated by a smallpox outbreak.

Traveling back north to British-occupied New York City and now styling himself "Colonel Tye," he had become a competent and aggressive leader of Loyalist irregulars. He commanded soldiers of both races on daring raids targeting Patriots deep in Monmouth County. On one such raid to capture New Jersey militiaman Colonel Joshua Huddy, Tye was wounded in the hand and suffered an agonizing lock-jawed death by tetanus within days.

Hostilities between opposing American and British forces did not abate following the decisive victory at Yorktown in October 1781. The venom if not the scale of fighting reached a crescendo both in Monmouth County and on the faraway western frontier. It was ofttimes impossible to distinguish among official British military operations, desperate strikes of Loyalist refugees into their former neighborhoods, and criminal freebooters using the war as an excuse for their depredations.

The anti-Loyalist fervor of New Jersey plantation owners like David Forman assumed an added edge born of racism and class warfare. British Army policy, encouraging runaways to enlist as warriors on the side of Great Britain, posed a grave challenge to slave-labor-based plantation owners' livelihoods. Indeed, much of General David Forman's and his neighbors' fortunes were tied up in Black "human capital."

Fear of vengeful mayhem appeared to play out as Loyalists and runaway slaves streamed forth from refugee lairs on Sandy Hook and the Pine Barrens, attacking Patriot businesses and farms in central and northern New Jersey. Samuel S.'s father in Middleton Point fell prey to such raiders, who killed guards and destroyed the family mill. The irregulars "boasting that they had aided in building the mill . . . now assisted in kindling the fire in the bolting box to burn it down." Plundering could include the capture and freeing of Patriot-owned slaves.

One of David Forman's slaves had the temerity to run away in 1781 to join the Black Brigade of Loyalist irregulars, as had a female slave three years earlier. They were among thirty-one African Americans from Monmouth County who fought with the British during the war, second only to Hunterdon County's one hundred. Unlike Massachusetts and Pennsylvania, New Jersey never permitted slaves to enlist in their state's Patriot militias.

So while the general would not have discussed the plan with his "servants," the size of the pioneering enterprise and his deliberate amalgamation of enslaved families into one emigrant group, leaving none behind, would have indicated that their destination was to a place friendlier to the institution of slavery. The general's reputation was such that all his enterprises were ultimately of benefit to him. Enslaved people themselves were worth more to their owner if they were transplanted to a fertile agricultural destination where emancipation was not even a remote possibility.

*

As Ginnie reconciled herself to the journey ahead, she would have seen these same people as individuals and families. She most likely focused on her husband and the fellow house servants she knew so well. The enslaved Forman plantation servants included people they had known for years, often since birth. Enslaved servants had toiled together, shared intimate moments and meals in their shacks, visited one another, and performed tasks together. A few had married enslaved people on adjoining farms.

She would have counted twelve family units in all, including her own, and a dozen or so unattached youngsters and elderly. The largest families, and most valuable to the masters, included fifty-five-year-old Cato and Dinah, forty, and their four children, ranging from fourteen to four—Cato, Jim, Darky, and Dick. Their brood was second in size only to that of strapping Toddy, and his decade-older wife Nanny. Due to the age difference, he was likely her second husband. Nanny's eldest, Wiring

Jack, was twelve, followed closely in age by Ben, Kate, Alley, and Henny, just four.

Other family units included Tom and Daphne, both in their fifties, and thirteen-year-old daughter Pen. Harry and Candis stood with Harry, Liz, and Hanna, ranging from twelve to eight. Scipio and Beke huddled with Frank, then seven, toddler Charles, and infant Milky. Tom Lloyd, the only slave with a last name, and Patt, "Mullattotress his wife," clutched Alia, five, and her younger sibling Peggy.

Some couples had only themselves to look after. Most were young adults. Among them were twenty-year-old Phil and teenaged Moll, Ephraim and Elsie, and Dimbo and Catt. Ginnie, at forty-five, was a dozen years senior to her husband Jess.

The group included two single-parent families: Doll, mother of five-year-old Rose and toddler Rany; and Ben, father of similarly aged off-spring Lucy and Betty.

Kate was an elder at sixty-five, possibly holding a place of honor by virtue of her life experience and long service. George too was sixty-five. Single women included Tamer, thirty-nine, five teenage girls, and the pre-teen Flora. Adolescent boys included Moses, Point Jack, Apollo, Abram, and Tom. Nineteen-year-old Peter was the sole unattached young adult male.

The enslaved, embarking together as the property of one person, were a larger group by almost tenfold than was typical for Monmouth County plantations. "General Forman purchased some more [African Americans], who had intermarried with his own, so as not to separate families."

Surveying the enslaved pioneering party awaiting departure, Samuel S. Forman observed, "They were all well fed and well clothed." His assertion that "he knew the most of them" suggests prior familiarity with the enslaved individuals and families living on farms owned by David Forman and members of the extended Forman family. Later Samuel S. would matter-of-factly recall, "They were the best set of blacks I ever saw together. . . . All were well-behaved, except two rather ill-tempered fellows."

*

Six wagons lurched forward that late November day. Some sat in the wagons atop barreled and boxed supplies. Others walked alongside. Overseer Benajah Osman and Samuel S., mounted on their own horses, rounded out the wagon train to over threescore souls.

Four four-horse teams pulled the larger wagons. Two-horse teams pulled the smaller ones. The large wagons likely were boxlike utilitarian affairs, fashioned from New Jersey white aspens, tall, strong, and straight. These were the kind of wagons farmers and traders employed to move produce to markets, salt works, and small workshops.

Two larger wooden-spoked wheels were affixed to each rear axle, while the smaller front wheels could rotate sideways a few degrees for making turns. Iron hoop tires, annealed to the wood rims by skilled wheelwrights, promised durability on unpaved roads. There was nothing to cushion against a bone-rattling ride. Utility boxes containing tools, jacks, grease, and ropes were affixed to the sides of at least some of the wagons. Likely all of them sported a friction brake for use on Pennsylvania hills and mountains.

"The first night we camped on the plains near Cranberry, having accomplished only about twelve or fifteen miles." Encamping under a waxing full moon seemed a pleasant prospect. Samuel S. and Osman devised a bed with canvas curtains to put under one of the wagons. But the elements made a mockery of their plan. A torrential downpour arrived unannounced during the night. The flat New Jersey ground prevented drainage and runoff. "The colored people mostly slept in their wagons" several feet above the soaked earth, rendering them a lot drier than their overseer and expedition supercargo.

Samuel S. doubtless became the object of mirth as his fine new "handsome buckskin small clothes" became soaked through. "The rain spoiled their beauty, and the wetting and subsequent shrinkage rendered them very uncomfortable to wear." Buckskin breeches, much like those worn by Saugrain and Pierce, were a prestige product of Indian hunters and tanners, tailored to European styles and American tastes. The preferred attire for endurance riding, the deerskin was luxuriant to the touch, durable and beautiful. Most importantly it minimized chafing from long miles in the saddle. Now shrunken and discolored, Samuel S.'s buckskins, from virtually the outset of the trip, were rendered an eyesore and deeply uncomfortable. If Samuel S. had any pretentions to styling himself as a frontier equestrian dandy, dressed in dapper deerskin breeches, the rain had dashed those hopes.

CHAPTER 4

The Ladies of Lancaster

BRACING AIR MUST HAVE TINGLED AND HUMIDITY HUNG LOW AND COLD over the Delaware River, transecting the former Indian ancestral realm of the Lenni Lenape, who had adopted the settlers' name for the river for themselves.

This year the current ran steadily. There was no need to run the gauntlet of floating ice shards and piercing freezing sleet, as George Washington's Continental troops had done a few miles upriver at McConkey's Ferry on Christmas Day 1776. The Forman band's river crossing would be in the other direction.

During that fateful episode thirteen years prior, Benajah Osman participated in the campaign as an enlisted New Jersey militiaman. He had dodged bullets on the front lines at the battles of Trenton and Princeton and had twice been taken prisoner during the eight long years of war. He had often served under the orders of General David Forman. Now he and so many other veterans were seeking their places in the uncertain aftermath of the Revolutionary War, the muddled Confederation, and the postwar depression.

While the river would have seemed familiar to the Indians of two centuries before, the land had changed with the succession of European settlers—Swedish, Dutch, English, and now American. With each passing decade, Americans brought in still more people to swell the populations of New Jersey and Pennsylvania, including enslaved Blacks brought in early by Dutch traders, and later by the English, to provide labor on farms like David Forman's.

Osman and Samuel S. Forman could not have dwelt for more than a few moments on the Washington's Crossing episode. They did not commemorate that audacious victory over Hessian mercenaries in any way. At other times Samuel S. reveled in such wartime tales. But this retrograde westward crossing of the Delaware by the Forman's enslaved Blacks posed practical issues demanding their immediate attention. It was their charges' responsibility to work alongside the ferrymen to assure safe execution of the crossing soon to commence and certain to take hours. Part of the six-wagon train awaited on one shore, while another made its way across on the flat-bottomed ferry boat to the Pennsylvania landing.

These ferry boats were flat barges, often called *bateaux*, each capable of carrying one heavy Conestoga freight wagon and its six-horse team. Two of the Forman's smaller, boxy farm wagons and their four-horse teams could fit aboard in place of one Conestoga. To prevent the horses from bucking or becoming unruly, each equine team would be unhitched from their harnesses. More likely, all animals were untethered, lest one agitated beast jump or fall into the river and take an entire wagon into the cold, surging waters.

Experienced teamsters, working their hired freight wagons and horses as one well-honed unit, would not have harbored such concerns or suffered overcautious delays. In contrast the Forman train provided their own teamsters from among the enslaved. They were unaccustomed to some of the newly acquired vehicles and draft horses. Since departing Monmouth, the group had only traveled together on the sandy lanes and plains of New Jersey for a couple of days.

Under Osman's and Samuel S.'s nominal direction, and relying on coachman Philip's and the ferryman's advice, they would have unhitched the teams, led each wagon onto the ferry barge, chocked the wheels, and tied the wagons down for the crossing. Benajah and Samuel S. probably took positions during the crossing on opposite shores. Those were the best posts in the event something unexpected arose with the emigrants or vehicles, while the group was divided in the course of their passage.

The Delaware's deliberate current guided the first half of the crossing. Downstream currents carried the ferryboat toward the center of the river.

The ferryman easily assured control by handling the thick hemp rope rigged across the river. The remainder of the passage was more arduous. The barge required active heaving to finish the crossing from midstream to landing. Once the ferry boat bottomed on the gravelly shallows on the Pennsylvania side, the burliest among the enslaved men proceeded to unfasten the wagons and roll them forth along the gangway onto dry land. Then the ferry returned to the New Jersey side to repeat the process.

The majority of the slaves never had occasion to learn to swim, nor had they ever seen a river this large. Some, fearing a fall into the cold waters, or potentially being jostled overboard by a nervous horse, added urgency to put the Delaware River behind them.

As each rig and equine team came ashore on the Pennsylvania side, they reassembled animals, tethers, and vehicles. One by one, the emigrants readied the wagons to resume the trip. By the time the sixth wagon made it across, the others were all ready to move on.

*

Proceeding west on the Lancaster Road, and bypassing Philadelphia, the wagon train made its painstaking way. The enslaved group, cooped up and itching for distraction, might have made a game of who would be the first to spot milestones encountered along the road. Each stone mile marker was emblazoned with a numeral and the coat of arms of the Penn family. Those who could read the numbers might have kept that to themselves to avoid uncomfortable questioning by their white overseers as to how they came by such literacy. Some probably did read, perhaps knowledge encouraged for reading Biblical passages and singing psalms at the Old Tennent Church back in Monmouth.

A good day's trek of over twenty miles would take them as far as Miller's Tavern at the Tun, having passed by the White Horse at mile 26, Downing's near mile 33, and the Shipp Inn just two miles further.

At the inns, Samuel S. and Benajah Osman might spring for a pint of beer at three-pence while gleaning news of the road conditions ahead, scan the newspapers for useful tidbits on commodity prices and exchange rates further west, and anticipate what they might expect of their reception in Lancaster. As the Formans rolled westward they observed the many neat farms and Pennsylvania Dutch log-built houses, which were often roofed in distinctive rust-colored pottery shingles.

By the time the six wagons and mounted leads beheld the Wagon Inn at the mile 41 stone, horses and humans would have grown accustomed to the road, though its rigors induced muscle aches and calloused feet. Most of the servants walked alongside the wagons, laden to overflowing as they were with goods intended for trading and tools for eventual settlement. Mothers with suckling infants like Beke and Doll may have been afforded a wagon seat if they grew excessively fatigued. But the jostling of wheels, and axles with rigid suspensions, communicated every rut and rock in the road. A seat might offer little comfort.

Along the road the group encountered the large and graceful schooner-like Conestoga wagons, guided confidently in both directions by seasoned teamsters, each carrying up to 11,000 pounds of freight. On a muddy road, the Conestogas left deep ruts that could easily mire the pedestrian emigrants. The big freight wagons would overtake and pass the Forman pioneers, by negotiation between teamsters and Osman if that occurred at a narrow stretch. The Forman wagon train, straddled on both sides by African American pedestrians, progressed more slowly than Conestogas powered by muscular, sweating six-horse teams.

To minimize costs Osman and Samuel S. gained permission to camp out of the wagons in nearby pastures along the way. The group fell into a daily routine in the course of a week on the road. House slaves prepared dinner from spartan provisions they brought along. Field hands did the hard work of individually jacking up every axle—all twelve of them— removing each of the twenty-four wheels, inspecting the oak spokes and their iron hoop tires, greasing wooden axles, and finally replacing the necessary wheels. Care of wheels and axles had to be performed at the close of each day's travels. Others unharnessed the teams, fed the horses, assured their horseshoes remained serviceable, and kept an eye on them in pasture.

In addition to two-way freight traffic, the emigrants would have encountered the fast stagecoach that had recently begun service between Lancaster and Philadelphia. Unencumbered by the mass of people and goods of the Forman party, the stage offered reliable passage over the

SOUTH WEST VIEW OF LANCASTER, P.ª

Lancaster, Pennsylvania, as it appeared in 1790. In early December 1789, the Forman pioneer wagon train passed through on the way west from central New Jersey. Ladies of Lancaster tried to convince the Formans' slaves to free themselves and take domestic positions in welcoming local households. Nineteenth-century engraving.

sixty-two miles to Lancaster, all the way from the Indian Queen Tavern in downtown Philadelphia, in just three days. It could be seen on the Lancaster road twice weekly.

Back on the road the next morning, the Forman emigrants reached the sign of the Red Lion. The almanac revealed that Lancaster Court House was just six miles further. First there would be an easy crossing of Conestoga Creek at mile 64 just east of town.

At last the wagons rolled into Lancaster, situated on a plain between two gentle ridges running east to west and delineated by neat fields and cow pastures. Unlike so many towns in America, Lancaster was primarily an offspring of the road. Most others followed Indian usage, where rivers and navigable streams served as highways through mountains and heavily forested wilderness, providing a watery road for travel and commerce.

American Army and militia contingents passing through Lancaster town remained a constant presence on the highway and at roadside inns. Local businesses served the soldiers. The town's tidy main street presented an inviting choice of taverns. Businesses offered robust wheat and fresh flour from the recent harvest, preserved meats and cheeses aplenty in both English and German styles, prized hardware for use or trade in the West, and the finest rifles crafted anywhere in North America.

Lancaster was then the largest inland town in America, gateway to the West, boasting over 3,000 souls in town and tenfold as many in the entire county. Among them were 348 slaves, all Blacks or mixed-race people. Inhabitants also included over 500 free people of color, both free Blacks and a few remaining Indians. The white community was predominantly bicultural, English speaking and German. It was also religiously diverse, encompassing congregants of Lutheran and Mennonite churches and the early and avowedly abolitionist Quaker meeting.

The town was cosmopolitan enough to host its own social scene and itinerant popular entertainments. Despite cultural and religious differences, the community managed to thrive as a whole. But a certain wariness persisted, and its local militia continued to meet and drill, with several battalions, each meeting on its assigned day. The frontier had moved west to Fort Pitt and beyond in the decades since the French and Indian War. But if hostile Delaware Indians or their allies dared raid into their former homeland, armed Lancastrians would be ready for home defense.

Just seven years prior, a force of natives and British Ranger allies had destroyed Hannah's Town, on the Forbes Road southeast of Pittsburgh. It was the last skirmish of the Revolutionary War directly involving British combatants. Since then, there seemed no end to Native American hostilities in the contested Ohio country further west. But that was on the far side of the Alleghenies. Militia training days in Lancaster tended to principally provide a happy excuse to socialize at the town's inns following the martial drills.

During the late war Lancaster was far enough removed from East Coast hostilities to serve as a Continental Army military supply center and prisoner of war camp for captured British and Hessian mercenary soldiers. Among those in such critical support functions were members of the Hubley family. One of them, John Hubley, Jr., would go on to study law, represent Lancaster County when the time came to ratify the US Constitution, and represent Lancaster in the state legislature. Now the course of events might come full circle to challenge the Forman enterprise.

Late in the war one John Asgill, a hapless British lieutenant and POW imprisoned in Lancaster, was selected randomly by lot for death in the Continental Army's retribution for the execution of a New Jersey militiaman by British Loyalists. John Hubley, Sr. was Asgill's jailer. General David Forman had never been to Lancaster, but he had persuaded George Washington to initiate the proceedings that ensnared young Asgill.

As chance would have it, the aristocratic Asgill family had connections to France's Queen Marie Antoinette. Despite the state of war, the French queen successfully pressured the American commander-in-chief to commute the execution of the British lieutenant, then in General Forman's hands and nervously awaiting his fate in New Jersey.

After Asgill was released months later at the prompting of America's French ally, he publicly alleged shocking abuse while in the custody of Forman's militia. An international incident resulted. General Forman had an abrasive affinity for causing or being associated with such controversies.

Now the Forman sojourners were about to encounter family relation Bernardo Hubley, Jr. in his role of high constable. Samuel S. recalled the incident vividly. Hubley stopped the train, demanding to review their papers as "we rather expected they would." General David Forman had "furnished me with all the necessary vouchers according to the laws of New Jersey and Pennsylvania relating to the transfer of slaves through those states."

While Hubley was examining the documents, "the servant women informed me that the women of the city came out of their houses and enquired of our colored women whether they could spin, sew, knit or do housework and whether they were willing to go South, so that if the authorities should stop us they would soon all have places and homes."

The townswomen gathered around the wagons while Benajah Osman and Samuel S. answered Judge Hubley's questions. Whether or not the judge knew that those in transit were associates of one at the center of that former drama, this was Samuel S.'s critical moment to which he had to rise as business agent for the venture's cargo, both of the inanimate and human varieties.

Samuel S. recalled what followed as a humorous anecdote, although he did not explain the levity. He implied that the proposal for the enslaved women to free themselves, or perhaps agree to self-limited indentured servitude as domestics in Lancaster households, was ridiculous. And perhaps it was so.

That is because the offers of the Ladies of Lancaster involved a fateful contingency. They made promises for employment *if* the African Americans were legally halted. But Lancastrians were unwilling at that point to defy the law and openly encourage the slaves to free themselves. Even to informed observers of the time, it still may have been legal for out-of-staters to apprehend slaves who had run away to Pennsylvania. If a New Jersey slave had decided to escape in Pennsylvania, in the presence of his owner's representative, it would have been an unprecedented and potentially ugly scenario.

A tense, brief, but consequential confrontation must have occurred. After conferring with his counselors, Judge Hubley decided he had no grounds to detain the wagon train further.

Would the Ladies of Lancaster have welcomed the runaways? Would the disaffected enslaved just run, perhaps encouraged by free and enslaved Black residents of Lancaster, and hope for the best?

"But our colored women laughed at the Lancaster ladies, who seemed mortified when they learned that we could not be detained." The wagons departed west from Lancaster into the cool afternoon sun. Among the onlookers were the ladies themselves, variously quizzical and perplexed, their offer having been dismissed as a joke by the very people they had hoped to rescue from bondage.

The story, however, is even more bewildering. In fact, the ladies' plan was betrayed to Samuel S. by unnamed Black women among the Forman emigrants. We are left with many questions about the informants' motivations. Was it to keep their families intact? Did they want to curry the master's favor? Did they distrust or disbelieve the strangers' offer? Were they wary of their fates if perceived as colluding in the escape of other bondsmen? Benajah Osman might punish the remaining slaves indiscriminately.

We will never know if any of the African Americans had second thoughts. In the long journey ahead, we can only wonder if any dwelled on what could have been had they decided, in that unexpected window of opportunity, to forsake their families and their masters for the vague promise of freedom among strangers in a Pennsylvania town they had never before seen.

CHAPTER 5

Two Ill-Tempered Fellows in
the Colony Made in Hell

SAMUEL S. AND BENAJAH WERE UNDOUBTEDLY RELIEVED TO BE DONE with Lancaster. The pioneer wagons lurched forth. Each driver in turn shouted and tugged his huffing equine teams into action. Twenty-two horses, six wagons, and threescore African Americans, from babes-in-arms to the elderly, combined to make an unintended parade and spectacle for the townspeople. Osman may have taken up the rear to assure none of the servants decided at the last moment to take up the Lancaster ladies' surprising invitation. In any case, the sparsely populated frontier, and its unsettled affairs with the Indians and Spanish, would offer the slaves new opportunities for freedom on their own terms, rather than at the whims of strangers.

Under arrangements orchestrated by General David Forman, whose commanding presence was felt even in absentia, the wagon train had been outfitted to be almost wholly self-sufficient, and the enterprise henceforth made a good pace of twenty miles per day. There was no requirement for stops at any inns they passed as the wagons continued to camp each night and their meals, prepared by house servants expert at preparing far better fare, created additional savings of time and cash. Perhaps Osman and Samuel S. might stop briefly to buy hay and feed for the horses when the supplies they had brought were consumed.

Nor did Benajah and Samuel S. have need to inquire of road conditions ahead. There was only one craggy road west. The old Forbes Road had been hacked out of the forests by the British Army decades before as part of the campaign to take Fort Duquesne from the French. Regardless of its state of disrepair, it was the only way to proceed. Come what may, they would overcome any obstacles with ingenuity and muscle.

Never before having led the movement of goods and people over mountains and for such distances, and having no teamsters and drovers in their employ experienced in mountain terrain, Benajah and Samuel S. improvised. They relied on their collective experiences: Osman's in the army, Samuel S.'s as a trader shipping grain to markets in South Carolina, and on the advice of those African Americans previously entrusted by the general and his overseer to deliver farm produce to market within New Jersey.

Their observations of others on the road must have confirmed their suspicion that their group was unusual in several aspects. The Forman wagon train was the largest enterprise, with the furthest intended destination, of any single group of pioneers making their way west across Pennsylvania in the first years under the new federal government. It was a year of war, terror, and uncertainty on the frontier. They would need to adapt to unaccustomed situations and unforeseen necessities.

After a wearying day, the hours of sunshine shortening day by day with winter's approach, the party encamped in wooded areas along the road. They selected spots that had good drainage in case of rain and offered nearby firewood that the enslaved could gather. Evening tasks included kindling a large fire, and as before, tending the horses and inspecting and repairing their conveyances. They also "turned the tails of the wagons all inward, thus forming a circle" as a measure of protection.

Continental Army strength by this time was little more than 1,000 soldiers for the entire United States, a shadow of its wartime strength of but a few years before. Most of that paltry number was deployed across a dispersed string of forts in the West. They depended on Carlisle, Fort Pitt, and the vagaries of Ohio River navigation for sending them soldiers and supplies.

A waning moon and intermittent cloud cover made for ever-darkening nights. The emigrants may have wondered about the presence of a vacant, floorless cabin they encountered on a succeeding night. Had the occupants been squatters, chased off of the land by agents of absentee

East Coast land speculators, or perhaps lured further west by the promise of better farmland? Indians would not have been expected to raid, kidnap, and murder on the eastern side of the mountains in lands formerly occupied by Delawares or allied tribes. But if their imaginings included lawless criminals chasing off the inhabitants, then the explanations for a perfectly serviceable abandoned cabin were legion and unsettling.

Osman and Samuel S. were not about to dither. In the absence of anyone from whom they might ask permission to stay the night and with temperatures plunging, they made the log cabin a place of refuge. They ordered a large outdoor campfire, whose crackles and radiant coals warmed and illuminated them. "All who chose took their bedding and slept in the cabin, some remaining in the wagons." Pleased and grateful for this respite, the vigilant leaders spread their own blankets before the fire and slept out in the open.

By Saturday, December 12, the group approached Fort Loudon. They were nearly 100 miles west of Lancaster, on the slow ascent toward the Allegheny mountain passes. Samuel S. was apprehensive of camping yet again in the woods. Fort Loudon's stockade and cabins were long gone, its timbers claimed by settlers for building materials. This same fate had befallen all the French and Indian War forts between Lancaster and Pittsburgh.

Samuel S. galloped ahead of Benajah and the others, hoping to find suitable commercial quarters for the night, despite his general aversion to the costs involved, perhaps with the luxury of a roof and fireplace. It was growing dark, and the shadows urged him to settle on the evening's plans.

Riding up to the first log house he encountered, he rapped on the heavy plank door. Before he could describe to the tall, lean resident what he desired on behalf of himself and threescore enslaved sojourners, the man unexpectedly gathered up Samuel S. heartily into his arms. "Mighty souls! If this is not little Sammy Forman!" With hugs and kisses on both cheeks, he added, "Why, don't you remember Charley Morgan? Yes, you can have anything I have, and we will do the best we can for you." Samuel S. recalled the gentleman as having served in the war with his older brother Jonathan, saying "This was a fortunate occurrence" because "bread and meat for the colored people was getting low."

Morgan offered what hospitality he could muster for so large an assemblage. The stop proved fortuitous for all. Staying for over two days, Samuel S. and Benajah replenished supplies. They bought wheat and sent it to be milled. The kitchen servants confidently butchered and prepared a fat steer that Samuel S. acquired. The sojourners "were all well provided for, for a while."

Their host regaled them with war stories. Samuel S. and the others crowded around the fireplace, hearing how "Charley could ape the simpleton very well, and was sent as a spy into the British Army in New York City, and returned safe with the desired information." Charley disguised himself as a civilian in the occupied city, a hazardous assignment reminiscent of the one that led to Lieutenant Nathan Hale's losing his life at the end of a hangman's noose.

Samuel S. and Benajah were surprised to have met Charles Morgan in this far-off foothills region. The New Jersey veteran may have been one of the many squatters eking out a living a step or two ahead of an absentee landlord's agents. This would not be the first time Samuel S. Forman and Benajah Osman would unexpectedly encounter friends or foes, succor or deadly peril, along their quest for the rich alluvial soils of Spanish West Florida.

Back on the Forbes Road, they continued westward. Ascending Tuscarora Mountain at Cowan Gap, they trundled past the ruins of Fort Loudon. Abundant wild pasture grasses around the old fort fed the horses even when they had eaten through their oats. Threescore hungry human mouths and their own growling stomachs were not as forgiving.

Just west of Fort Loudon the wagons and travelers forded Conococheague Creek, surrounded by hemlock, oak, and poplar trees, some of whose branches reached over the banks into the flow. Wheels and shoes unsteadily sought footing against the rushing waters on the smooth-stoned creek bed. As many as could clambered onto the laden wagons, or mounted the calmer horses, to avoid soaking woolen trousers and dresses.

The descent from Tuscarora Mountain was a steep, ear-popping, seven-degree grade. Everyone who was able pitched in to handle ropes lashed to trees and to each wagon to ease them down the slope. Such contrivances were required to counter the massive momentum of laden wagons from pressing on horse teams from the rear and losing control of the rigs. Visibility at the fog-enshrouded summit could be as little as fifty yards, obscuring the next sharp turn, serpentine bend, or rut to be overcome.

Finally, having crossed Tuscarora, the travelers continued west, across tilled farmland interspersed with meadows. Farmers and their families were rarely seen outdoors. The season was cold and damp. Harvested fields lay brown and furrowed, awaiting the imminent winter.

Next was the site of Fort Littleton, its 100-foot-square stockade and bastions at the four angles, long since stripped of its lumber. They beheld a knoll with meadowlands all around, a commanding position in this otherwise hilly region. The fort had been in its heyday three decades before during the French and Indian War.

General David Forman's master plan was for Ezekiel to depart from Philadelphia, catching up to the lumbering wagon train on its route west. But his brother's departure was delayed for a few days. Samuel S. noted to Benajah that their wagon train was running low on cash money, more of which Ezekiel was expected to bring. The sojourners, once committed to the road and in the midst of crossing the Alleghenies, had no choice but to proceed.

Their instinct was to push forward faster, anticipating succor at Pittsburgh, since Ezekiel would now meet them there. But they were capable of traveling only so fast on treacherous and unkempt mountain roads. They must proceed cautiously to guarantee safe passage of people, wagons, cargo, and horses on the arduous ascents and deliberate, controlled descents. When they reached the tiny crossroads at McConnelsburg, they availed themselves of the town's tavern and store, stocked with a variety of goods calculated to appeal to pioneers and area farmers. Having just descended from the highest of the Allegheny peaks, their provisions thinning, Benajah and Samuel S. enjoyed a hot meal indoors, though they could ill afford it.

Although they had conquered the most challenging mountainous barrier and the roughest going, Pittsburgh was still a long way off. If roads remained firm and heavy snows stayed away, and given the generally downward slope of the land, they could resume making twenty or more miles in a day. They would arrive in Pittsburgh in less than a week. Then again, if the snows arrived early, or if they encountered other unforeseen barriers, the emigrants and beasts of burden would find themselves starving, their progress impaired.

Samuel S. decided to take matters into his own hands to assure sustenance to his charges for the remainder of the trip. He offered to sell the inn's proprietor his mare at an attractively low price and to barter a few of his own dry goods at distressed prices, items he had hoped to sell to advantage further west. Benajah Osman could beg to be excused from horse trading, as his horse was the general's property and his role as overseer required him to be more mobile. Samuel S. would walk the rest of the way to Pittsburgh alongside the house servants and field hand families, if it came to that.

Asked by the innkeeper why he was willing to part with his horse for so low a price, Samuel S. admitted that he was out of money. His older cousin Ezekiel Forman, listed owner of General David Forman's African Americans, was overdue to join up with the wagon train.

It turned out unexpectedly that the innkeeper knew Ezekiel personally from prior business dealings. "I will lend you as much money as you need, and take your order on him [i.e., Ezekiel Forman's account], as he will stop here on his way. Now, step with me to the store." Pointing to a large pile of silver dollars on the store counter, he said: "Step up and help yourself to as much as you want, and give me your order." This was a happy and timely favor.

Ezekiel settled the advance when he passed through along with his wife and children several days later. Additionally, Samuel S. did expend some of his personal funds in order to avoid depriving the enslaved immigrants of necessities on the last leg of the overland trek across Pennsylvania.

The purchased provisions were timely. "The weather began to grow very cold, the roads bad, and traveling tedious." The immigrants returned to the road west, no longer threatened with running out of money and food. After overcoming the Sideling Hill summit and a moderately steep descent, the 20 miles more to Bedford passed smoothly. According to their almanac, they were 150 miles west of Lancaster and 100 miles from Pittsburgh.

*

Westmoreland County, a land cursed by disputes of several kinds, posed a different kind of challenge. The American colonies of Pennsylvania and Virginia, now part of the United States, jockeyed one another for influence in the area. Many independent, self-reliant settlers paid scant allegiance to any authority, and were deeply suspicious as to whether the emerging federal government to the east truly had their interests at heart.

One was liable to travel all day during the winter and encounter no one, or one could meet someone who hailed from Virginia perhaps transporting enslaved African field hands, or recent Scotch and Irish immigrants coming by way of Philadelphia or the Chesapeake, or settlers who had obtained land grants at the close of the French and Indian War, or some free Blacks who'd prefer you not ask too many questions. And, in the absence of reigning authority, some of the settlers, but also minor officials, could assert their own versions of the law and what they deemed permissible. No wonder that one commentator, reflecting Eastern leaders' aspirations to order, aptly labeled Pittsburgh and its backcountry "a colony sprung from hell."

For one Westmoreland Irish justice of the peace looking to stir up trouble and some free Black neighbors, it was simply not right to transport slaves through their county. It may have been legal, even according to the strictures of Pennsylvania's Act for the Gradual Abolition of Slavery, but it was not something they would abide. If swords and pistols issued to the enslaved were required to force the issue, then so be it. There was no advance notice of the wagon train passing through, nor time to mobilize for these impromptu Westmoreland friends of abolition.

For their part, the enslaved Forman pioneers produced two "ill-tempered fellows" willing to take up arms. Further participation might have been tempered by kinship among the enslaved and familiarity with the Forman masters. The "ill-tempered" two might simply have freed themselves by declaring their personal declarations of independence, fading into the forest, and eluding capture with the help of their newfound allies. But they did not do that. Perhaps they planned a more widespread fighting mutiny to break up the wagon train and free all of its involuntary travelers.

Because of an informant, however, "a faithful old colored woman," Osman intervened to defuse the situation. The plot did not proceed. Most likely he applied persuasion, and the thinly veiled threat of punishment, just as effectively as he had during the intervention of the Ladies of Lancaster. There was no resorting to violence, iron cuffs, chains, coffles, or whips. There is no evidence that the Formans' "two ill-tempered fellows" were severely punished. Nor were they "sold downriver" later. The wagon train lost no time, continuing their way west.

*

Who could the "faithful old colored woman" have been? That remains unrecorded and unknown. In one of Samuel S.'s manuscripts, she is described as someone "who had lived in our family some time." Sixty-five-year-old Kate fits the demographics of sex and seniority. A rare emigrant traveling with no close relatives, she may have attained a favored position with General Forman's family, perhaps as a senior house servant of long and faithful service. General Forman would not have placed a high dollar value on old Kate. Yet she must have been a robust soul to have been considered capable of embarking on the frontier trip and remaining with the owner's family rather than being sold before departure.

I suspect it was another, Ginnie, who inserted herself familiarly between Osman and Forman one evening, prior to confrontation with the justice of the peace:

> Here the [black] hands soon had a fire [kindled], the Captain's [Osman] and my bed nicely made before the fire and the [enslaved] people all stood before the fire. Mammy Ginnie, always providing for us, had her berth next to me and the Captain. And on [occasion] the Captain had some of the [black] people next to him, all in good spirits. Nothing occurred, but poor Ginnie apprised me of [the overture].

Thrust into an important position by virtue of gaining advance knowledge of trouble, whoever the informant was, she must have identified more with the master's interests than the possibility of freeing herself and fellow slaves. She stood in marked contrast to the two, presumably young, "disaffected" and "ill-tempered" fellows, who were ready to brave the consequences of raising armed Black hands to slave owners.

*

The wagon train proceeded across the swollen Juniata River, thoughts of the latest aborted resistance thrust aside in favor of the mechanics of getting families, wagons, and cargo across the swollen stream. The green-brownish water, as darkly shaded as nearby spruce trees, cascaded heavily. Hills on either side hovered closely to the roadbed at times, as the trail tracked along the left side of the creek in its narrow valley. Opening to a vista of low hills swathed in evergreen pines and seasonally leafless deciduous trees, the scene gave way to level, open meadows. They made good time.

On and on they went. Mountains loomed to their right in the distance, marked by a flecked gray barely discernible from similarly monochrome mist and sky. After ten miles of gently increasing elevation, the horse teams commenced straining and snorting as they began traversing switchbacks, where the road folded back on itself. Even the old and the tired would be on foot to relieve the beasts of some of their load. The higher elevations were often shrouded in fog and mist this time of year. Some days were clearer and brisk, permitting majestic glimpses over the tree-lined passes and Mount Ararat. The pilgrims' almanac noted abandoned fortifications among the Laurel Highlands, all in ruin.

Once over Bald Knob Summit, they passed isolated farmsteads and were propelled onward by a noticeable downward trajectory. After Laurel Ridge the road commenced an eight-degree grade downward for three miles. Ears popped as teamsters closely attended their wagons to assure teams did not lose their step and cadence as their burdens pressed behind them.

Finally, they reached the Susquehanna River, ferrying across its eddies. Pittsburgh lay ahead, a town of 370 souls in 77 households, built outside Fort Pitt. Here the Monongahela and Allegheny Rivers joined forces to form the Formans' highway into the interior—the Ohio River,

Elevated view of Pittsburgh as it would have appeared in 1790. The Monongahela River on the right merges with the Allegheny, seen on the left, to form the
Ohio River. Fort Pitt, built over the remains of the old French Fort Duquesne,
dominates the confluence of three rivers. The commanding location cemented
Pittsburgh's emerging role as gateway to settlement and commerce in the contested trans-Allegheny West and South. From a nineteenth-century engraving.

La Belle Rivière. They would have agreed with George Washington, view-
ing Pittsburgh almost four decades previously:

> *[I]t has the absolute command of both rivers. The land at the point is
> 20 or 25 feet above the common surface of the water; and a consider-
> able bottom of flat, well timbered land [is] all around it, very conve-
> nient for building.*

And yet, a guidebook written a few years after the Formans arrived,
intended for travelers like them about to embark on long river journeys,
remarked that Pittsburgh presented strangers with "rather a gloomy
appearance, arising from the smoke of the stone-coal. . . ." "The place,"
remarked a visitor, "will never be very considerable." Indeed, since Chief
Little Turtle's campaign against settlers in Ohio had commenced by 1785,
demand for Pittsburgh industry and trade goods stagnated.

The Forman pioneers, arriving in Pittsburgh about Sunday, December 20, 1789, nearly three weeks after setting out, must have been exceedingly pleased to note Ezekiel's arrival with his family by coach three days after. But there had been a mishap with the enclosure over their fine conveyance, which "got broken by a leaning tree" on the way into town. The damaged vehicle would be retrofitted as an open chaise (matching, as it happened, the latest style) to be taken to Natchez.

Getting situated in Pittsburgh precluded a festive Christmas observance. Years later, Samuel S. recalled minute details of their busy layover, but nothing of a holiday celebration of any kind. Fortunately, a Mr. Turnbull, a former Philadelphian now resident in Pittsburgh and known to Ezekiel, offered the group "use of a vacant house and storeroom" for "our numerous family." He added that "The colored people were all comfortably housed also," but did not record further details.

Samuel S. set up a temporary retail store at Turnbull's property to barter and sell items he brought from home in exchange for the equipment and supplies they would need for "our long river voyage" ahead. "We had a large quantity of dry goods, and a few were opened and bartered in payment for boats and provisions." Samuel's inventory included fine imported cloth from Persia suitable for tailoring into fancy suits and dresses. Meanwhile Ezekiel commissioned a flatboat and keelboat to be built at a local shipyard by selling "the horses and wagons . . . at a great sacrifice," to do so. He retained only "his handsome coach horses and carriage."

Travelers contemplating ventures downriver, be they settlers heavily laden with farm equipment and animals, farmers taking their harvest to distant markets, or traders accompanying their wares, could choose the type and size of boat to suit them. If one were traveling alone, with few items, one would sign on as a passenger or extra hand on someone else's large boat. Scheduled river boats did not exist.

Ezekiel could choose among several boat builders serving settlers and military contingents commencing their river journeys in Pittsburgh, and as the pair visited various boatyards, Samuel S. was impressed by the maritime construction enterprise. "These boats were flat-bottomed, and boarded over the top, and appeared like floating houses." Ezekiel shortly ordered a flatboat seventy feet long and about fifteen feet wide. He reserved a second "keelboat, decked over, with a cabin for lodging purposes, but too low to stand up erect," and ordered oak-planked interiors "to prevent the Indians from penetrating through with their [musket] balls, should they attack us."

Flatboats were built to be expendable. Once arriving at their destination, which could be as far south as New Orleans, they would be dismantled for construction timber. Keelboats, with their decks and gunwales, were capable of being poled upriver against the current. They took more skill to build than flatboats and were more durable. Though trading imported goods upriver on keelboats made for a fraction of the profit of merchandise going downriver, other merchants executed a broad circle: when the Spanish opened the Mississippi to American commerce they would purchase manufactured goods in Philadelphia; transport them overland to Pittsburgh; boat them downriver, seeking favorable trades and markets all the way to New Orleans; sell the boats for timber; sail back from New Orleans to the American East Coast with a strongbox of cash; and repeat the cycle.

While the boats were being built, Samuel S. prepared as best he could for the Ohio River phase of the trip. He purchased a new pair of shoes and hired a tailor to make a suit. The traveling businessman found a furniture maker to fashion him a trunk "made of remarkably handsome dark cherry," and equipped with cubbies and a secret compartment for important papers and accounts. Samuel also paid gunsmith Hugh Ripley two shillings sixpence to recondition Ezekiel Forman's guns.

The Forman party would have huddled indoors before hot coal fires as snow, wind, and cold temperatures buffeted Pittsburgh throughout early January. On clearing, a hard freeze followed. All the while they were aware that, "It being an Indian war time, all boats descending that long river, of about eleven hundred miles, were liable to be attacked every hour by a merciless foe, oftentimes led on by renegade whites." Disappointingly, intelligence about Indian raids on travelers and settlers was sparse. In those that did appear, there were few specifics as to the most hazardous geographies and which Indian nation might be behind the raids. Ezekiel and Osman assured that, "Both boats were armed with rifles, pistols, etc."

Suddenly in mid-January 1790, the icy encasements on the rivers fractured and gave way, seemingly all at once. The grating fractures emitted a sound new to the pioneers. The roaring cacophony was nevertheless welcome as nature's signal that the much-anticipated next stage of their journey was about to commence. The urgent flow soon propelled the jagged ice chunks downriver and out of sight.

The boatyard completed both boats. Ezekiel fixed the third Sunday of January, a Sabbath, as the date of their departure. He asserted that the Sunday departure was customary and would bring good luck.

The pioneers moved aboard the vessels, moored in readiness along the town's Monongahela waterfront. The day was remarkably pleasant for the time of year, "the river very high and the current rapid." A large local crowd gathered to see them off. Samuel S. estimated the number, including those departing, "reached very nearly a hundred." It was a big event for a small town. Citizens covered the entire wharf. The Forman pioneers were among the first groups to descend the river that season. News and rumor of Indian raids added interest and genuine concern among the townspeople at the group's departure.

Samuel S. joined Ezekiel on the keelboat along with his wife Margaret; their four children Augusta, Margaret, Frances, and little David, ranging in age from eleven to two; Margaret's housekeeper and companion; ten house servants; and two mechanic employees. They arranged their blankets directly on the floor, and belongings and household items in every nook. The one large enclosed cabin required taller people to stoop while standing.

Benajah Osman commanded the flatboat. Its wooden cabin stretched fully across the beam. The general appearance was of an oversized box on a huge raft, Ezekiel's dismantled coach and ploughs lashed incongruously to the roof. Two men were hired to help navigate and, if the need arose, defend the boat.

The field hands and their families clambered aboard. Ezekiel's two fine coach horses, the only livestock retained from the wagon train, had a manger reserved for them at the boat's stern. Farm implements—ploughs, hoes, shovels, saws, yokes, harnesses, and the like—vied for space with dozens of people. The trade goods entrusted to Samuel S. were probably distributed between the two boats to lessen the risk of losing all, should a mishap befall one cargo boat.

Ezekiel decided that it was prudent to travel in convoy with others. William Wyckoff and his brother-in-law Kenneth Scudder, both late of Monmouth County, agreed. Wyckoff, now an Indian trader, was on his way to Louisville on his own small keelboat with a shipment of merchandise. The presence of yet more Jersey men, though ones not previously known to Benajah and Samuel S., must have injected an easy familiarity into what could become a dangerous passage.

It was January 17, 1790, the first day of a new moon. The bastions of Fort Pitt came and went from view. So too, the slanted slate roof of its stone block house, the most imposing edifice of the largest US fortification in the West. None of the Forman immigrants would ever again behold the majesty of the three rivers at Pittsburgh. As they passed Fort Pitt at the point, swept up into the current at the headwaters of the Ohio River, all eyes focused downriver to novel sites and the mastery of unfamiliar navigation tasks. For now, their fates lay in the watery embrace of *La Belle Rivière*.

CHAPTER 6

Running the Ohio River Gauntlet, 1790

As the Ohio River coursed westward toward its confluence with the Mississippi, over a thousand circuitous miles distant, it undulated in serpentine twists and turns. It flowed away from Pittsburgh to the northwest for its first score of miles, then traced a broad and gradual arc west, then southwest. In places tall rocky hills and bluffs alternated on one side of the river and then the other. Along most of the way dense forest reached all the way to water's edge. Even without foliage in winter, one could peer only a few yards into the forests. Here and there settlers' fields appeared, sometimes on picturesque bottomlands at the mouths of streams and rivers. As each new tributary added its flow, the Ohio River imperceptibly but relentlessly broadened.

Having been warned many times how treacherous the high waters of the Ohio could be, the emigrants commenced their journey in a state of hypervigilance and perhaps dread. The tranquil, barren winter river scenery only heightened anxieties. The Forman men and hired hands additionally kept rifle and pistol flints at the ready, muzzles loaded with powder and ball. Ezekiel Forman's girls, and possibly some of the reliable enslaved men, may have been coached to reload the guns while under attack. Thus, the menfolk could hand off their discharged weapons in immediate exchange for loaded ones, achieving a formidable fusillade in the event of an Indian ambush.

Benajah probably sized up the situation with the eye of a soldier. He knew from his Continental Army and New Jersey militia field tactics that a firearm was useless while executing the dozen steps of the manual of arms to prepare a muzzle loader for firing. A battle-hardened veteran like himself could reload a smoothbore musket over twice a minute while standing in open order, as he had done at the Battles of Germantown and Monmouth. But he would surely be slower while crouching behind riverboat gunwales or cargo barrels, or handling the temperamental patched bullets and tight bores of a rifled musket. Like the disciplined British Regulars, Indians who sensed that an ambushed foe had discharged all their firearms at once could rush and overwhelm such hapless defenders with knives and tomahawks before they could reload.

The river itself could conspire to distress the immigrants, quite aside from any war parties Chief Little Turtle and his allies of the Delaware, Miami, Shawnee, Wyandot, and Ojibwa might dispatch against them. The pioneers had no quarrel with the natives, other than their posing deadly barriers to their faraway goals. Samuel S., Ezekiel, Benajah Osman, and the hired hands had their hands full, both for readying defense and for navigating a swift river in unfamiliar, untested, cumbersome boats.

Not surprisingly, the Forman party's leaders intended to stop as little as possible in this disputed territory. It seemed as if they were in the middle of a hostile world of elemental water, earth, and black sky, inhabited by wild beasts and unseen humans bent on their destruction. But as evening approached that first night out, with only the cold stars as their witnesses, the inexperienced boatmen decided to weigh in along the forested shoreline. They judged proceeding on the moonless river to be too hazardous.

Osman ordered the flatboat lashed to trees along the shoreline. William Wyckoff did the same with his smaller keelboat. The flatboat, though by far the largest of the three-boat convoy, could come closest to shore. The keelboat required deeper water lest it hit bottom. Ezekiel ordered the servants to drop a stout iron anchor, and together the three boats put in for the night, the flatboat closest to shore and the keelboats some yards farther out.

The immigrants could only discern the rustling of wind through leafless branches, the unceasing murmur of river eddies, and the occasional snorting of the horses. *Were these night sounds disguising skulking Indian warriors?* The sleepless among them may have shuddered.

Before sunrise, the keelboat caught a shifting side current. But the anchor held fast on the murky bottom before the straining line heaved

Flat and keelboats on the Ohio River. The Forman pioneers' flatboat, captained by Benajah Osman, transported dozens of enslaved African Americans. Forman family members and enslaved house servants traveled together on the seventy-foot-long keelboat. From an early nineteenth-century engraving.

and suddenly "tore away all the frame-work around the deck, causing a great alarm." The splintered structure splashed audibly into the river, leaving the damaged boat rocking violently and edging from the shore toward the open river. All was gloomy darkness.

Quick-thinking Black hands gathered an unused line and hastily lashed it to one of the other boats, itself tethered to shoreline trees. Adults, bestirred from the keelboat cabin by the ominous splintering, scurried on deck, holding candlelit lanterns aloft.

"Several little black children were on deck at the time, and as it had now become quite dark, it could not be ascertained, in the excitement of the moment, whether any of them had been thrown into the water." The enslaved mothers would have rushed to the deck as well, holding each child closely to identify the little ones they had nursed, while fearing one precious little face might not be not among them. The jostling bodies clamoring to get on deck were probably met with warnings to stay away from the boat's perimeter, lest they too fall into the water, and to maintain silence should Indians be lurking.

Thankfully within minutes—it must have felt like hours—all the children were safely accounted for. Samuel S.'s empathy for the distressed mothers, and perhaps his unhestitating readiness to dive into the dangerous waters himself if need be, may have enhanced his reputation among the enslaved as a relatively humane young man among the masters. As the servant mothers and their little children now settled down from their ordeal while the men surveyed the damage, all the sojourners who survived—masters, enslaved, hired hands; black and white; young and old—would agree with Samuel S.'s recollection years later that "it was the most distressing night I ever experienced."

*

Setting off again, Ezekiel and his young cousin Samuel S. modified their keelboat's regimen. Ezekiel placed a chair, intended to furnish their future home, on the now-exposed forecastle. He asserted himself as the boat's captain and pilot, who constituted its brains and eyes. Samuel S. took position as helmsman on the rudder. As the boat recaptured the current, Ezekiel shouted, "Port your helm," to maintain course midstream. "Starboard!" meant bear to the left. "Larboard!" meant move to the right. Samuel recalled his experience with real sailors when he had served as business agent a few years before, accompanying a shipment of flour from New York City to Charleston, South Carolina, and during a harrowing return trip. The nautical nomenclature he recalled from sailors who negotiated the open sea. He didn't know where cousin Ezekiel had picked up the lingo.

Diminutive Samuel S, now managing the helm, asked a hired hand to assist him, the two of them pulling this way and that. The river had made a long arc to the west and was flowing south. It is doubtful they made any recourse to a compass. One simply followed the river's current "downriver."

"Ours was a perilous situation till we landed at Wheeling," a larger town beyond the Appalachian Mountains portion of Virginia. Wheeling was rated at ninety-six miles downriver from Pittsburgh. There the pioneers paid to replace the missing keelboat gunwale and bartered for a large steering oar to improve the navigation of the keelboat.

Returning to the river, Ezekiel, Samuel S., and Benajah must have felt more confident, as several days' veterans of *La Belle Rivière*'s caprices. Courtesy of Wheeling's shipwrights, the damaged keelboat had been repaired and was better equipped than before.

Meanwhile, though, the regimen of salted meat and porridge meals grew tiresome. The travelers observed abundant game—deer, bear, squirrel, raccoon, and turkeys—ambling about in the woods near the shore. If one of the bigger species could be killed, the sojourners could enjoy fresh meat and perhaps bag a valuable animal skin for later trading.

The hired blacksmith convinced Ezekiel to set him ashore in pursuit of a flock of turkeys. Accordingly, the little boat was removed from the keelboat deck and placed into the water. The hunter departed, musket in hand, pet dog at his side.

"But he had not been long on shore, before he ran back to the river's bank" and gestured silently but urgently for the boat to return and whisk him to safety. Back among friends on the keelboat, he breathlessly declared that he had come upon a large campfire. "From appearances, he supposed a party of Indians was not far off." Panicking, he hastened back to the shore. "He had lost his fine dog, for he dared not call him," alerting the Indians.

The Indians, by years of unpredictable strikes on pioneers and boatmen, had so terrorized the Ohio Country that even the thought of them could induce someone to cut and run. The frustrated hunter's unseen campfire hosts could as easily have been a group of pioneers, as afraid of him as he was of them.

The flotilla proceeded past the site of another abandoned outpost, Fort McIntosh, then in ruins, its lumber picked clean. In this part of the river valley, bluffs fall away from the river, being quite steep in places. They are bare layered stone, fiery red in places, unlike most of the area, which has tree cover. Melting ice runoff accumulates into small rivulets. Waterfalls emerge from place to place, tumbling down the exposed rock toward the Ohio River. Here the river's course straightens.

The flotilla reached Fort Steuben. For veterans of the war, hearing the name von Steuben conjured feelings of national martial confidence and competence, both then in short supply along the Ohio River, in the Northwest Territory, and along the entire American frontier.

In 1787 it was the fort's mission to dispossess American squatters, who threatened peaceable native factions and the interests of for-profit Eastern land speculators, and to protect official land surveyors from Indian attack. In the first instance, the small US Army contingent largely failed as squatters remained attracted to the region garrisoned with a rare US Army fort whose military protection they expected. In its second task, the oversight of land surveying, the fort's garrison had completed its mission by the time the Forman boats passed by.

Laying out the verdant forests, meadows, and connecting streams into marked, delineated, and cartographically documented charts comprised an essential first step in the transition from communally held Indian hunting grounds into parcels that could be commodified, subdivided, and sold. They were then combined into townships and counties, and subdivided into retail lots for towns and farms, making the land subject to distant owners, speculators, and the federal government—to everyone, it seemed, except the natives and their traditional, communal lifestyle of hunting and farming.

It was little wonder that Chiefs Buckongahelas and Little Turtle and the Northwest Federation tribes, though their principal towns like Kekiongo were hundreds of miles distant, sent their war parties with special vigor against the land surveyors. The wielders of compasses, transits, and levels may have been slowed, and some terrified of the raids, but they were not stopped. The benign-looking surveyors' tools were more disruptive of the Indians' ways than batteries of heavy artillery.

The Forman flotilla leaders would not have divined all the implications of the abandoned Fort Steuben site, beyond its purpose of deterring Indian raiders.

*

The group landed at Marietta, where there was an American garrison at Fort Harmar and a settlement, just a year and half old, of the Ohio Land Company. The palisaded town presented on favorable level ground at the mouth of Muskingum Creek across the stream from the fort. The fort's sharp rectangular symmetry reflected the surveyors' hands, imposing abstract order on the wilderness.

On arrival, Samuel S. was pleased that "Some of the officers were acquainted with the family" and invited the Forman pioneer leaders to dine as guests of the Marietta settler families and soldiers from the fort. "It was a very agreeable occurrence . . . Governor St. Clair had his family here. There were a few other families, also; but all protected by the troops."

The Formans just missed meeting thirty-six-year-old Winthrop Sargent, an army colonel and secretary of the Northwest Territory. He was just then traveling to Fort Vincennes, far to the west in the Illinois Territory, to meet with Indians in that quarter. Sargent traveled with an armed escort of dozens of soldiers, for such were the times. Marietta itself was too formidable to have been attacked by Indians, and American leaders there took pains to be on good terms with natives living in the vicinity. Still, there had been atrocities inflicted on outlying settlers and squatters. A siege mentality prevailing, Marietta settlers did not get many visitors that winter.

Winthrop Sargent's influence was nonetheless felt even in his absence. As he towered almost six feet tall with a painfully erect carriage, Sargent's broad nose and quizzical brow suggested the man's New England Puritan severity. A historian noted "his lack of tact and diplomacy, this want of sympathy with the prevailing tone of society . . . as a result he became extremely unpopular." A coarse and unpleasant voice did not help matters.

And yet, Sargent believed in the redemptive and fruitful promise of the frontier. Speaking of the West and South, he "anticipated a future establishment in this country, where the veteran soldier and honest man should find a retreat from the ingratitude—never more to visit the Atlantic Shore." It was never clear what ingratitude he was referring to, but the same enthusiasm about the promise of the West enabled him to sell an impressive 154 shares in the Ohio Company to investors and prospective settlers from Massachusetts and New York. His successes in raising capital helped him land simultaneous appointments as secretary both of the company and the entire Northwest Territory. And as long as Chief Little Turtle's warriors terrorized settlers and scared off newcomers, the Northwest Territory settler population remained tiny, rendering the American government in the region a de facto military dictatorship.

Thus Sargent exercised his authority by issuing edicts that most frontiersmen, who were generally more rustic and suspicious of government than the transplanted New Englanders and easterners populating Marietta, found onerous and needlessly strict. Feelings of disdain between the Puritan-inspired proponent of the West and ordinary frontiersmen and settlers were mutual.

*

That evening visitors and hosts spent an enjoyable time together. Ezekiel Forman's musically inclined daughters entertained the officer hosts by singing familiar songs a capella.

The two groups shared striking similarities and differences, representing divergent strains of American pioneering and settlement on the frontier. Both were intrepid, entrepreneurial, and willing to take great risks to realize their visions of productive and permanent settlement. The success of both groups depended on developing market economies on lands long claimed by indigenous nations. Interest in developing public education and building civic institutions, an aversion to slavery in the Northwest Territory, and a belief in the redemptive value of the pioneering experience in the West were more pronounced characteristics among the Marietta denizens. The Forman pioneers were willing to leave the United States to assume Spanish allegiance for economic opportunity, were more interested in acquiring and enjoying consumer goods, and had no problem with building their agricultural enterprise by the sweat of enslaved African Americans.

That night, the sojourners "felt secure in sleeping away the fatigues of the journey" and safe within Marietta's formidable palisades. Back on the river the next morning, they were, however, reminded that safety and repose went only as far as the fort's bastions. The flotilla passed the nascent village of Limestone (Maysville) on the Kentucky side, and noted a few other parties sharing the Ohio and headed for destinations downriver. Just above the French settlement at the mouth of the Scioto River appeared a canoe paddled energetically by three frontiersmen who easily overtook the Forman flotilla of flatboat and keelboats. They could just as easily have encountered less friendly natives around the next bend.

Chapter 7

Fort Washington and Cincinnati

Finally Fort Washington presented its rough-hewn wooden bastions. Its boxy two-story, five-sided corner blockhouses were dotted with rifle ports shuttered to the cold. Those windows would open soon enough if the Indians were to have the temerity to attack, a possibility that generated constant vigilance.

Although the Forman pioneers' recent mishap was fresh in all minds, an American flag crisply flapping in the winter wind beckoned a respite from danger. Yet safety was more perceived than real, as Indian war parties preferred to ambush pioneers and soldiers alike just far enough away from the fort to preclude rescuers from arriving in time. Much to the natives' irritation, the embattled American pioneers continued their cycles of surveying, speculation, and settlement. War on the frontier, especially north of the Ohio River, slowed the influx of pioneer settlers, but had not as yet stemmed the flow.

Despite the ever-present Indian threat, a few intrepid pioneer entrepreneurs initiated settlements and businesses in the area. Ezekiel knew how Judge John Cleves Symmes's 20,000-acre charter from the Confederation Congress in 1787 along the nearby mouth of the Great Miami River had veered into the scandalous. Symmes had a penchant for promoting, subdividing, and retailing land to pioneers before he himself had clear title to it. He often sold the same property to more than one person. His party of twenty-six New Jersey and Pennsylvania settlers in late 1788 would soon merge with a nascent settlement in the shadow of Fort Washington, to become the frontier town of Cincinnati.

*

Fort Washington in 1790 at the future site of Cincinnati, Ohio. From an original late eighteenth-century sketch by Jonathan Heart.

The Forman emigrants lashed their boats at a landing and were invited into the stockade. They were surprised to meet General Josiah Harmar himself, recently appointed by the president to subdue the Miami, Delaware, Shawnee, and other allied Indian nations.

Harmar, tall, balding, and with bright blue eyes supporting a martial demeanor, betrayed no anxiety over the disordered state of the frontier, though perhaps he should have. His presence within the armed enclave, clinging to the Ohio River's shore, could be read as evidence that the natives dominated and contested every acre of land beyond pistol shot of the fort. The traveling party, in turn, put aside their own skepticism and were instead flattered by the general's invitation to join his table at dinner. By the standards of their porridge and salt pork while on the river, the roast bison and tea served them made for "a most sumptuous dinner."

At the soldiers' encouragement, the expedition leaders moved their little fleet to a mooring directly before Fort Washington "so that all should be safe under military guard." It seemed that their original choice, just a hundred yards' distance from the fort's main gate, was judged unsafe to both visitors and the US Army. Most likely the African Americans, who remained on the boats and at the mooring while the whites were being entertained, were also relieved to sleep under the protection of the fort's sentries and cannons.

At the landing they now shared, Samuel S. recognized the canoe and three *voyageurs* who had overtaken them upriver above the Scioto. The plainly frightened men explained that Indians had ambushed them on the river, seeming to materialize out of nowhere, perhaps from a hidden shoreline lair. The canoeists barely escaped with their lives but for paddling faster than their pursuers. One man had been shot through the shoulder, another through the calf. The third escaped unharmed. Their cargo intact and wounds attended by the post doctor, the three determined to press on and be done with their ordeal.

Samuel S. and Benajah may have wondered how they would fare if Indians attacked them. Their ponderous flatboat and keelboats could not have outrun a marauding Indian war party coming at them in canoes.

General Harmar extended an invitation for another social call the next day. "The company consisted of Mr. and Mrs. Forman, their three daughters, and [young] Master David Forman, Miss Church, Captain Osman, Samuel S., Colonel Wyckoff, and his brother-in-law Mr. Scudder—eleven in all." The visitors must have been a welcome relief at the isolated outpost during the early February gloom. Samuel S. sat beside the general, an eager audience for his tales of exploits during the late war. Notably, there was little talk of roving Indian war parties, who seemed to be the post's constant shadowy companions and nemeses.

No one recorded the experiences of the African Americans at Fort Washington and Cincinnati. Most were probably as relieved as anyone for a couple of days off the river and under the protection of uniformed American soldiers. Some may have bartered small items with the enlisted men, perhaps flour shaved from their cargo for a gill of whiskey, while overseer Benajah Osman was seeking out his old army acquaintances in the fort. Had the two "disaffected fellows" calibrated their prospects for absconding, an unknown reception by hostile natives and the ever-daunting prospect of permanent separation from family likely dissuaded any overt moves.

Following their sociable two-day layover, the Forman and Wyckoff boats were back on the river "floating rapidly down the *La Belle Rivière*." Bolstered by hard-won experience in boat handling, and good fortune in not encountering Indian war parties, the group traversed hundreds of miles of river without incident.

*

When the pioneers reckoned that they had descended almost 400 miles from Cincinnati, they urged all the boats' sojourners to increase their vigilance for their next challenge. Scanning the shores, lined with massive cottonwoods and sycamores, they anticipated reaching the Falls of the Ohio. An absolute impediment to continuous river travel, the Falls could only be traversed with care and skill.

Only William Wyckoff, who had run the Falls in both directions on his previous business forays, knew what to expect. For the uninitiated, white and Black alike, the Falls appeared "very tremendous at first sight, and startled our people much" as the barely hissing murmur gradually increased on proximity to a deafening roar. Oarsmen shouted and gestured to one another since they could no longer share orders as they had in leisurely conversation.

The Falls were not a single cataract, but rather a series of rapids dropping the Ohio River twenty-four feet in the course of two miles. In low water seasons, the water babbled and rippled through three distinct channels across sedimentary flats almost a mile wide. Running the rapids at low water risked wrecking boats, losing cargo, and drowning people. The keelboats, though more strongly constructed, sat deeper in the water than the flatboats, and presented added risk. Prudent boatman would lay in short of the Falls to hire a river pilot from Louisville to assist their passage.

At low water in spring and summer, the preferred chute of the three was just eight feet wide, presenting a test of skill and strength of the widely variable products of upriver boat builders. While hazardous to craft as small as canoes, the shallow waters, until just a few years prior, had permitted herds of buffalo to migrate from Ohio over the fossil-encrusted riverbed flats into the great salt licks of Kentucky and back again. That annual migration had prevailed from remote prehistory. The advent of flintlock muskets, ramping up the efficiency of native hunting, the international trade in furs, and now the Kentucky settlers' appetites, had made the annual migration and soon the buffalo themselves extinct in the Ohio Valley.

General David Forman, prime mover of the pioneering expedition, carefully timed the arduous winter wagon train crossing of Pennsylvania and the Alleghenies, in order to float the Ohio and its Falls at high water. The general no doubt was aware of travel accounts discussing the Falls and how best to negotiate them. Some boasted that descending the Falls of the Ohio during the winter could be executed "very safely, by keeping well over on the right or northwestern shore, for these falls are by no means dangerous." But wrecks were known to occur regardless of the season, and opinions were often predicated on whether one was a booster for settlement or had been personally wrecked on the rocks. "The tortuous channels" offered three "chutes"—the Kentucky, the middle, and the Indian or northernmost channel—and were each craggy, crooked, and dangerously fast.

By virtue of experience and navigating a smaller boat, William Wyckoff and Kenneth Scudder probably ran the rapids first and without incident. Benajah Osman followed with the seventy-foot flatboat. He probably disembarked the Black people and horses at Fort Steuben, at the head of the falls, before shooting the rapids. Lessening the boat's draft considerably, the precaution smoothed the passage and precluded danger to his human and equine cargo, should there have been a mishap.

Osman may have retained several strong hands on board to help manhandle the oars. Staying in the main current was the chief challenge. Likewise, Margaret Forman, her children, and some of the house servants would have been invited to disembark while Ezekiel and Samuel S. guided the lightened keelboat over the Falls.

Having braved the Falls without incident, their Forman flotilla's collective sighs of relief might have been heard over the roaring waters. They floated the remaining short distance, as lightly and effortlessly as a pebble skipping over a pond, to the Louisville, Kentucky, landing or perhaps mooring at the calm shoreline at the mouth of Bear Creek.

Once ashore they could take a moment to look back and appreciate being safely delivered from peril. They may have wondered at the petrified plant and animal life arrayed on the rough surface of the rapids' platelike rocks, which they had just crossed. Surely many settlers perceived the West as a land closer to Creation, a place of wonder that demanded that adventurers prove their mettle against the elements, strange beasts, and fiercely proud natives.

Wycoff and Scudder continued almost at once to their business destinations downriver from Louisville.

The enslaved Forman pioneers likely developed different perspectives, though we can only speculate on what those were. While on the river, the field hands were largely confined to the crowded flatboat's communal cabin. It was a little world permeated by the pungent scent of hewn and sawed pine, oak, birch, and poplar, competing with the odors of unwashed people and of horses huddled together. They were not chained or shackled. Nor did they have much leisure to contemplate the strange and novel vistas, or walk about freely, as did some of the Caucasian pioneers. Their lot was onerous, to be sure, enmeshed in the clutches of a cruel institution. Yet it was not as overtly awful an experience as had been borne by earlier generations of Africans making the notorious Middle Pasage, or later generations of enslaved antebellum African Americans. The latter would be characterized by violently enforced shackling, families rent asunder, and traveling by steamboat on a "river of dark dreams" as they were sold downriver.

Samuel S., Ezekiel, and Benajah did not share the curiosity of so many others. They were more intent on filling their account books with speculative trades for items on which they hoped to turn a profit in Spanish West Florida, and with moving their venture forward. They had come thus far over 1,100 miles, but it was still less than halfway. They faced 1,300 miles more, and barriers both human and natural, before arriving in Natchez.

But for now, Louisville, a town of perhaps 200 souls, by situation and appearance would not fail to make an impression. As one visitor remarked, "I saw numerous houses of two stories, elegant and well painted, and, as far as the [remaining] stumps of trees would permit, that all the streets were spacious and well laid out."

He could have spoken for the entire Forman team. Samuel S. guessed that there were sixty dwelling houses in town. Some were unusual. James

Patten's cabin at 8th and Main Streets was built into the side of a gargantuan sycamore tree. The town was laid out like a trapezoid, with its longest side facing the river, planted atop a bluff parallel to the river. The Indian threat had since receded to the suburbs but remained a constant concern of townspeople. It was in fact here that William Wells, the alleged red-headed captive of the Miami "gone native," was abducted at Bear Creek only eight years before.

All agreed that the town "is rather unhealthy, particularly in August and September when a kind of fever and ague rages and makes the countenances of all the people appear yellow and wan. . . ." Illnesses, likely including malaria, yellow fever, and later smallpox, plagued the town seasonally and in periodic epidemics. Louisville would become known to many as "the Graveyard of the West."

Within days of the Formans' arrival in the latter part of January 1790, the weather grew "so severely cold" that the river again became as blocked with ice as it had before the thaw back at Pittsburgh. "Here we laid up, disembarked, and took an empty house in the village, the front part of which was furnished for a store, which exactly suited us." From this space Samuel S. "opened a store from our stock of goods, and took tobacco in payment, which was the object in bringing the merchandise." It "was remarkably fortunate" that the party found shelter for themselves, the African Americans, their supplies, and their remaining two horses, along with a retail store—all in the dead of winter.

Samuel S. found what they considered "the Southern people" to be remarkably friendly to strangers. He distinguished those, mostly Virginians, who had come with their slaves to settle new plantations, to be recognizably different in origin, customs, and outlook from what he was used to. Though Samuel S. tended to attract friends who like himself hailed from the East, he and Ezekiel's family were delighted to be welcomed by, and do business with, everyone.

The young visitor was practically adopted by a Mr. and Mrs. Ashby, whose plantation lay just outside of town. The couple were "as kind to me as though I had been their own son." The enslaved Forman African Americans, on the other hand, had fewer opportunities to interact with the locals. At the time both free and enslaved Black Kentuckians were rarities within the little town. Only five free Black townspeople were counted in Louisville's 1790 census. Most African Americans were residents of the plantations being established in the hinterlands of the county.

It is possible that Ezekiel or Benajah Osman worked out a bartering arrangement to exchange the field hands' labor during their stay for use of a vacant house and for a store in town for Samuel S.'s merchandise. Even in winter, the farms and plantations of Jefferson County had an insatiable need to repair rail fences, tend farm animals, clear fields, chop firewood, and complete countless other agricultural tasks demanding labor and attention. Such cashless reciprocal transactions reinforced the web of commercial interests up and down the Ohio and Mississippi River corridors from Pittsburgh to New Orleans. Moreover, from a security viewpoint, should they have thought about it, the Forman's human capital would find few opportunities to escape. Unlike some places they encountered in Pennsylvania, there were few free Blacks in the area and no avowed abolitionists in Louisville and the surrounding Jefferson County willing to assist or harbor them.

If the Black Forman pioneers did talk with local slaves or freemen, though, they might have heard that African Americans had been integral to the region from its first settlement by Americans. The Black soldier Cato Watts served in George Rogers Clark's 1778 western frontier campaign and went on to help wrest Fort Vincennes from the British the following year. Watts's story would have been shared in hushed tones, because he also had earned another, dubious distinction. He was the first person convicted of murder in Kentucky in a court of law—for allegedly killing his master.

More poignant, perhaps, was the story of enslaved Bob, brought into Jefferson County by the Floyd family of Virginia. Bob was assigned to clear the land of primordial hickory and sycamore trees, the first and most arduous task in creating a plantation. The very first tree Bob set upon with his ax teetered, "slipped back on the stump, and tore off his right foot, or at least all the skin and flesh from his ankle down." His owner Mr. Floyd nursed Bob personally as best he could, but to no good outcome. Bob died in early February 1780, probably from gangrene or septicemia. He was put to rest in an unmarked grave, so far from Virginia, and so far from Africa.

*

Samuel S. found himself in his element. Kentucky plantation families had earned a reputation for their jolly, fun-loving ways. A previous visitor to Louisville, when the town was even smaller and more rustic than it was in 1790, was struck with the spectacle of a community barbeque on Corn Island, the site of the earliest settler cabins of Louisville:

> We . . . saw the genteeler sort of people in numbers coming in from the country, each with a young girl behind them or woman on the same horse, the way of riding in this country, to a great barbeque . . . and to conclude with a dance in town in the evening.

"We had scarcely got located" before the Formans and their associates were invited to subscribe to a ball. Samuel S. anticipated however that entertainment could turn raucous if the spirituous "produce of the country" were involved. He learned that truth some weeks before when a similar ball was held. As the hour grew late and the ladies departed, the young men "had a row, and destroyed the most of the breakable articles that the house afforded." Such "instances of rudeness," however, "occurred only when no ladies were present."

When any notable person visited the town—these might range from the governor of the Northwest Territory to the First Lady's nephew—it was the custom "to get up a ball in their honor." Such pretexts for merriment served both social and commercial interests. Even Ezekiel successfully negotiated a deal with a vineyard owner outside of town to purchase tobacco intended for sale to the Spanish in New Orleans.

James Wilkinson, the former Revolutionary War general who would manage to sow controversy wherever he turned up, was a fixture on this social circuit. Wilkinson was just then a civilian. He had relocated from Virginia to Kentucky in 1784, making his mark trading Kentucky produce with the Spanish in New Orleans. He busied himself seeking opportunity and found one, displacing the aging and now frequently inebriated George Rogers Clark for popularity among many settlers, businessmen, and plantation owners.

In addition to young men and women in attendance that night from the surrounding plantations and from the town, many of the officers of Fort Steuben came from across the river as well. They brought military musicians with them, making for the best music anyone had heard in some time.

The ball opened with the minuet, an elegant dance rarely seen on the frontier. Ezekiel and a southern lady led. Margaret sat it out, Samuel S. recalling that "Aunt Forman did not dance."

Samuel S. drew a dancing partner who had emigrated from Maryland. She happened to know Ezekiel Forman's oldest adult son by his first marriage, General Thomas Marsh Forman. That coincidence "rendered our casual meeting all the more agreeable."

After the initial dance, Ezekiel Forman and James Wilkinson became acquainted, though the older folk did not stay long. The "young blades" and their female counterparts "were disposed for a frolic." Thankfully in this instance the "articles that the house afforded" remained intact. Samuel S. was gratified by the social scene, having never before experienced the like.

CHAPTER 8

A Bachelor in Louisville

AT THE END OF FEBRUARY, WHEN THE ICE AGAIN GAVE WAY, EZEKIEL and the Forman pioneer party departed Louisville. As before, Ezekiel's family and house servants resumed their places on the keelboat. Osman accompanied the field hands on the flatboat, joining two other flatboats in a convoy departing for downriver destinations. Only Samuel S., moving over to Captain Thomas Patten's boarding house, remained behind to barter the remainder of the merchandise they had brought over the Alleghenies.

For a time, Samuel S.'s festive life as a Louisville merchant was tempered by anxiety for the travelers. "There subsequently came a report, that when they reached what was called the low country, below the Cumberland and Tennessee rivers, they were captured by the Indians." Samuel S. and town residents were convinced that the Formans had become victims of an elaborate trap. There were rumors that Caucasian spies for the Indians operated with impunity within Louisville, and that seemingly ordinary river men and tavern patrons could be traitors with deadly intent.

> *It appears a white man there . . . learned the names of Ezekiel Forman and Captain Osman, their place of destination, and all about them. This fellow was a decoyer, who lived among the Indians, and whose business it was to lure boats ashore for purposes of murder and robbery.*

This was the dastardly role Chief Little Turtle's son-in-law William Wells would later be accused of. Known by his Indian name, Apekonit, meaning carrot and evocative of his red hair, Wells would have possessd physical characteristics perfect for the role. But his alleged activity as a decoyer has never been verified; nor is there evidence that Samuel S.'s belief in a plant within Louisville was true rather than a paranoid invention. But there were incidents of ambushes on the river, so the fear that the Forman pioneer party had fallen to one was realistic.

Just the previous July, Richard Chenoweth's family suffered multiple fatalities, including three children, during an Indian raid on their plantation just east of town. Peggy Chenoweth was felled by an arrow, scalped, and left for dead. She somehow managed to survive, thereafter "covering her hairless scalp with a dainty cap." The year before, when Dr. Saugrain was recovering from his wounds at Fort Steuben, a Delaware Indian war party perpetrated a similar atrocity. The Ballard family, who dwelled just south of Louisville, found themselves on the wrong end of the Delawares' arrows, guns, and tomahawks.

Samuel S. "was in a painful suspense for a long time" concerning the Formans' fate on the Lower Ohio River. At length he received a letter from Ezekiel with instructions for liquidating their store. With no regular mail service, Ezekiel had to have found a reliable northbound traveler who agreed to hand-deliver his letter. This was good news indeed, though a close call involving a decoyer would await.

Meanwhile Samuel S. looked forward to the next dance while, more importantly, tending to his goods and trading them for good-quality tobacco from any willing plantation owner.

In recent years the Spanish were paying generously for high-quality tobacco, which fetched as much as ten dollars per hundredweight in New Orleans. Even with the 15 percent tariff that the Spanish levied on imports from the United States, American traders could anticipate large profits for delivering their tobacco downriver. General James Wilkinson's success was due in large part to his being able to finesse Spanish restrictions on Mississippi River navigation, to his own advantage.

Following King Carlos III's decree of free land grants to settlers in Spanish West Florida, the situation became even more favorable for expat Americans to trade with Spanish domains as resident citizens because the import tariffs no longer applied to them. The river remained open to them regardless of strictures on American trade. There were no limits on the amount of tobacco one could bring into New Orleans for sale at high, subsidized Spanish government prices.

General David Forman's master plan was for a Forman family member—Ezekiel—to establish permanent residence and Spanish allegiance in Natchez. When Ezekiel moved on, Samuel S., as his cousin's agent, assumed the task of bartering for all the tobacco he could gather in Louisville. Then Samuel S. would follow with the commodity, which Ezekiel—as a newly minted Spanish subject—would sell duty-free to the Spanish in New Orleans. Ezekiel would realize windfall profits on the tobacco paid in Spanish silver hard currency—a great boon in that it would be an entire season before he could grow his own tobacco and other cash crops in Natchez.

By clever trading in Kentucky tobacco, Ezekiel could rapidly raise "hard money" capital to finance the purchase and development of new plantations in Natchez. This capital would magnify the venture's footprint well beyond the original Spanish grant of 800 acres of free prime agricultural land that the general had obtained by document in New York City from the Spanish envoy Gardoqui. The general wrote letters of credit for Ezekiel as a financial cushion, should the tobacco trading scheme go awry.

Samuel S. succinctly described the business model: "Here I opened a store from our stock of goods, and took tobacco in payment, which was the object in bringing the merchandise." He kept an eye on his retailing and trading competition, but did not think much of it. His stock, including high-end bolts of cloth, dry goods, and ribbons, must have been unlike anything hawked by other merchants. Regional gentry wanted their women to show off the newest and most stylish gowns at the numerous balls and barbeques. It was the savvy Formans' pleasure to assist in that.

The young shopkeeper-tobacco agent enlivened his store's retail experience with the endearing antics of a furry pet he named Cuffey, a month-old bear cub. With the rest of the group departed, and finding himself completely on his own, it must have been gratifying to take on a cuddly companion. He kept Cuffey chained in the store to the delight of customers.

Samuel S. also befriended a young fellow his own age, a Mr. Smith from New York. "Smith and I agreed to let each other know when a dance was in agitation, and they were very frequent." But Samuel had a problem preventing him from attending. "I apologized for not being able to go, as I had no suitable pumps." Smith proposed a solution. "You have purchased a parcel of elegant moccasins for your New York ladies. You don a pair, and I will another." So they attended the ball decked out in the unusual footwear, and introduced a new fashion! "It was something new to appear in such an assembly . . . but they were much admired, and, at the next dance, almost all appeared in moccasins." Supple deer skin, tanned and fashioned into footwear, produced by Native American women from those tribes at peace with the settlers, enabled the celebrants to step lively on the dance floor.

Mrs. Ashby visited the store frequently, fussing over Samuel S. with respect to his lodgings as his own mother might. She examined his clothing "to see if any repairs were needed." She dispatched on-loan bedding from her plantation "and had a kind old woman examine my trunk, taking out all my clothing, first airing and then nicely replacing them, and kindly did all my washing during my stay." Mr. Ashby and the rest of the family came as well.

A similar kind turn was offered by Captain Thomas, who assigned a little Black youth gratis to the store for the duration of Samuel S.'s stay. The boy's mission was to "do my chores, tote water, sweep my store, clean my shoes, etc." One of the errands Samuel S. assigned the boy was to fetch milk for Cuffey and to feed the young pet.

Contrary to his East Coast experiences, Samuel S. discovered that Kentuckians considered billiards a "genteel and healthful amusement" for young women. As he recalled for his only daughter years later, "During the morning hours a few ladies used to honor me with a call, when I would spend a little while in that pleasant recreation." He discovered that time spent at the billiards tables with the ladies allowed him to improve "in manners from their refinement."

Other incidents in Louisville suggest that amusements, at least those involving resident and visiting menfolk, could be considerably coarser. Already alerted to their proclivity toward drink, Samuel S. seemed to acknowledge that frontier reality in carefully avoiding the even more undignified amusements. Those were pursued on one hand by visiting boatmen, frontiersmen, and enlisted soldiers, and on the other by what he called "young blades" and "Virginians"—wealthy settlers' sons, "gentlemen" looking to raise hell in town at their leisure, of which they seemed to have plenty.

Vulgar would be a generous label for these groups' whiskey-fueled antics. One visitor was appalled to witness "the barbarous custom of gouging, practiced between two of the lower class of people." The quarrelling men, rather than settling their differences by boxing or dueling according to widely honored unwritten rules, preferred to "seize each other, and . . . twist each others' thumbs or fingers into the eye and push it out from the socket till it falls on the cheeks."

Samuel S. had more benign experiences with aggressive behavior among the Kentucky blades and their social circle. Yet they were still troubling. One night he was jarred from sleep in his room at Patten's by thuds of stones being thrown against his storefront and window shutters by some inebriated hooligans. "At first I thought it might be Indians." The fusillade continued, punctuated by the smashing of all the glass windows. Not only were Samuel S.'s windows shattered, but "his store door was broken open by the pelting of large stones." The inebriated troublemakers similarly vandalized another property belonging to the landlord that night.

Fortunately, Samuel S., acting on the landlord's behalf, reached an accommodation with "these gentlemen" and the damage was repaired. Samuel S. only mildly chided the culprits, "situated as we were on the frontiers in time of Indian warfare." It was good business for him not to press charges so as to maintain positive relations with the locals. Some of them were doubtless the sons and neighbors of plantation owners whose tobacco crop he hoped to acquire. He did not press the matter further.

In mid-March 1790 Samuel S. sent a letter downriver to Ezekiel, asking for instructions. Ezekiel received the letter a month later and replied promptly, though it took another month for Samuel S. to receive the letter from Natchez.

Ezekiel counseled liquidating the remainder of the dry goods stock at whatever value the market allowed and gave his agent a list of desired cargo best suited to market conditions in Natchez and New Orleans. Not surprisingly tobacco headed the list, followed by "furs, tallow, whiskey as much as possible but good strength, flour, corn, and butter." Flour was fairly low on the list because, as Ezekiel noted, a boat of New Englanders brought a cargo of flour to Natchez, depressing its demand and price.

Tobacco remained the priority—but Samuel S. was reminded only to acquire the best quality. Ezekiel heard that Spanish buyers in New Orleans had refused some merchants' tobacco leaf as inferior. And he complained that one source did not come through with the sale of tobacco in a deal that they apparently concluded in Louisville two months before. The seller seemed to be holding out for new, better terms than he had agreed upon. Such was the nature of dealings in the highly valued commodity.

Unbeknownst to Ezekiel, now arrived in far-off Natchez, on March 29 a delegation of Chief Little Turtle, or one of his allies, violently inserted themselves into that transaction by visiting the tobacco grower's settlement and plantation at Cassania. Samuel S. heard in town that "one day Indians visited it, killing his people, and destroying his vines." The commanding officer at Fort Steuben sent a detachment to the rescue. The soldiers arrived too late. One settler among the group, which included fourteen children, was killed. The rest took shelter at the fort "and thus the station was, for a time, broken up." The surviving planter was left in no position to negotiate over tobacco under any terms.

*

In late May four flatboats arrived at Louisville on their way to New Orleans. One boat had suffered damage going over the Falls. Pulling into Louisville for repairs and hearing the owner's story, Samuel S. seized on the opportunity to close out his business, prepare his boat and shipment, and join their convoy on its departure.

His most important deal was with a Mr. Buckner for his entire tobacco crop. "After spending the night in conversation" the two came to terms. Samuel S. traded his remaining stock for the tobacco, apparently inspected, casked, and ready for transport. Buckner threw in a flatboat big enough for the entire shipment. Samuel S. was responsible for hiring the crew and captaining his newly acquired craft, which he grandly christened the *Nancy*.

He hurriedly hired boatmen from among men loitering along the wharf seeking such engagements. An "old sailor," William Wishant, agreed to team with Samuel S., who would serve as captain of his own boat. Northwestern frontiersman William Carroll and a Jersey man rounded out the crew as a second twelve-hour shift.

All got to work stowing cargo. It included ten casks of tobacco, each weighing 1,000 pounds, six barrels of tobacco, each a half cask, and a variety of wild animal skins. All required careful placement into the flatboat to distribute the tons of cargo equally. The containers were heavy and unwieldy and thus required precise and gentle handling so as not to loosen the *Nancy*'s pegged lumber and oakum water proofing.

Departing in late April, two months after Ezekiel's group, Samuel S. bid hasty goodbyes to his newfound companions and friends. He recalled wistfully his farewell to the parent surrogate Ashbys, "I never parted with briefly-made acquaintances with so much regret."

With his boat and convoy now ready, he, Cuffey, and his crew embarked as part of a convoy of Kentucky boats. "The bear was about a month or two old when I got him; and when I went down the river, I took him along to Natchez."

With the confidence gained from their travels on the Upper Ohio between Fort Pitt and the Falls, the boat captains guided their vessels back into the current. The river gradually widened as it consumed each of its tributaries, lessening the vigilance and concentration required of the boat captains and crews.

*

And what of the reputed episode involving Ezekiel, Benajah Osman, and an Indian attack? It had indeed been a close call.

Where the Tennessee River joins the Ohio, Benajah and the keelboaters heard and soon fixed their eyes on a plaintive figure ashore. He shrieked, gestured, and implored the boaters to stop and save him from Indians.

As Ezekiel ordered the broad oars to slow the boat to maneuver toward the north shoreline, the man called Ezekiel by name. He beseeched "on bended knee" to be taken aboard, that he would serve as a free hand all the way to Natchez if need be—anything to extricate him from imminent danger. He called out to Ezekiel's hired boatmen, who had signed on in Louisville, by name—Christian Hartlock, George Robbins, and George O'Connor.

Ezekiel reflexively empathized with the man's predicament. He likely conferred with his boat hands, and perhaps a trusted servant. Did anyone know this oppressed man? Perhaps he was a settler like themselves, a person who had heard of the Formans' intended destination during their weeks in Louisville, and who now had fallen victim to some Indian raid. How could they ignore a fellow white settler whose life seemed in imminent danger?

The keelboaters decided to effect a rescue. They maneuvered toward shore.

Benajah Osman on the flatboat followed some hundreds of yards upstream. His unwieldy craft remained under the influence of the current. From his vantage point he spotted armed natives lying motionless in wait among the trees along the shore. The winter's scant vegetation had not fully concealed an ambush! Late winter sun glimmered weakly on steel musket barrels and tomahawks.

Osman, recognizing the trap, shouted ahead to Ezekiel to regain the current and to keep well clear of the dangerous shore. Already suspicious of falling prey to a "wily decoyer playing his treacherous part," Ezekiel readily complied.

In an almost comical coda, "an old Indian, finding that his plot was exposed, ran down to the beach, hailing the boats, shouting: 'Where you go?'" As the pioneers steered clear, the Indian war party's leader could not help but express his disapproval. Did he really think that his admonishments would induce his intended victims to return to the trap?

"But for the circumstance of Captain Osman being in the rear, and discovering the exposed Indians screened behind trees, the whole party might have been lured on shore and massacred."

Such had been the fate of other Ohio River travelers in the late winter and spring of 1790.

CHAPTER 9

Mississippi Wide and Wild

SAMUEL S. WOULD NOT LEARN OF THE TRAVAILS OF THE MAIN BODY OF Forman pioneers for months, until Ezekiel wrote him from Natchez, "It is with much pleasure I take up my pen to tell you of our safe getting to this place—through innumerable perils and difficulty!" Details could wait. "I wish it was in my power to take the time to detail them to you, but it is not finding much [time to write], [there is] very much to do." There were as yet no taverns or inns anywhere in the Natchez district. "I have been on horseback almost every day since I came." Billeting was not a trivial task for his large captive labor force. He endeavored for days "to place my people but have not [yet] succeeded."

Formans Ezekiel and Samuel S., under the long reach of General "Black David," were all about business.

*

Departing in late April, two months after Ezekiel's group, Samuel S. in turn completed the Ohio River run and met the wide Mississippi. He had chosen to stand the evening watch with the "old sailor" he'd brought on, Frederick Wishant, since the seaman possessed the muscle and nautical experience Samuel S. lacked.

But Samuel S. shortly came to regret this choice of crewman, later describing the sailor as "deranged." Whether that was from an overfondness for distilled frontier spirits or intrinsic mental demons is not clear. And adding to that misfortune, Samuel S.'s newly hired hands were unused to the rig. The *Nancy* broke "from her fastenings and went a mile or two down-stream before they brought her to."

The trip began inauspiciously. Mr. Bayard, commander of one of the boats in the convoy, often invited Samuel S. to dine and sleep on his flatboat when they anchored for the night, as Bayard's conveyance was the more commodious. One evening Wishant paddled the *Nancy*'s canoe over to fetch the young man, huddled in his blanket against the evening chill. "The sailor, it seems, had taken a little too much whisky," rocking the craft violently as he pushed off, swamping the canoe. "My arms being entangled with the blankets, I was totally helpless." Bayard's boatmen observed the mishap, "jumped into their small boat, came to my rescue, and saved me from a watery grave."

Cuffey's mischief provided comic relief. The adolescent bear got into a barrel of ham. Discovered by the hired boatmen, who could not restrain him, Cuffey "jumped off and hid behind the hogsheads of tobacco." Enraged that some of the market produce was ruined, Samuel S. lost his composure and threw the bear overboard. "This he liked." Cuffey thought his impromptu soaking was great fun and swam about. "Had he not been chained, he would have deserted." On subsequent hot days, the bear jumped into the river without prompting. Samuel S. was the only person from whom Cuffey would accept direction or discipline.

After 200 uneventful miles progressing down the Lower Ohio River, the convoy reached Fort Massac, abandoned by the French decades before. The magnificent scenery and remaining ramparts invited investigation. All six boat captains determined to look around the site, offering to take along a few of the curious boatmen. They unlashed one of the small boats and paddled ashore to the seemingly deserted fort. The remaining hands anchored the flotilla in a tranquil spot offshore.

On landing, the travelers separated into several squads, each taking off in a different direction to explore the extremes of the sprawling five-pointed fort's remains. "It was in the afternoon, just after a refreshing [spring] shower."

Fort Massac must have been a formidable structure in its time. Hundreds of yards of earthworks separated the corner bastions although little remained of the palisade and blockhouses hewn from surrounding forests. Some features had been reclaimed by bushy thickets and adolescent trees. The groups rapidly lost sight of one another.

The first to arrive at the entrenchment soon "espied a fresh moccasin track." As the three groups converged on the spot, scrutinizing the footprint for themselves, they recoiled to a man, as if they had encountered a parcel of slithering rattlesnakes.

"We all looked at it, and then at each other, and, without uttering a word, all faced about, and ran as fast as possible for the little boat." Each man varied his direction according to his idea of what constituted the most direct route back to the beached boat, which was now out of sight. Samuel S.'s group came to the shoreline in an overgrown stretch some distance from the boat, whose location they could not discern. "Those of us who missed our way concluded, in our fright, that the Indians had cut us off."

Scrambling willy-nilly along the shoreline during a few moments that seemed like an eternity, the tourists eventually regained their places aboard the flatboats moored safely offshore. Now reassuringly huddled behind the thick plank gunwales, firearms in hand, they "recovered our speech" and "pieced together what each had seen and felt during our flight to the boats." The travelers collectively constructed an explanation that rationalized their falling short of their own conceptions of manly heroics. They concluded that the presumed Native American, whose moccasin track had put them to flight, was some lonely Indian "travelling on an overland trail between Louisville and St. Louis; and, judging from its freshness, the one who made it was as much frightened from our numbers as we were at our unexpected discovery."

*

The rivers continued to present navigational hazards Samuel S. could scarcely have imagined. One afternoon, with his boat leading the convoy, he noticed one of the other boats suddenly pass. "We observed by the woods that we were standing still—evidently aground, or fast on something below the surface." He tried various means to float free of the obstruction. Each failed before he asked that a rope be tied from his boat to a tree along the shoreline.

While rigging the line, "We heard a whistle, like that of a quail . . ." despite there being no such birds in these woods. "We felt some fear that it might be Indians [signaling]." Samuel S. and the boatmen redoubled their efforts at the rope and freed the *Nancy* without damage. Afterward they discovered that "we were fast upon a planter—that is, the body of a tree firmly embedded in the river bottom."

Later observers gave names to additional river hazards. "Bayous" occurred during high water season, where tributary streams "sally forth from the main river with astonishing rapidity" and where boats, once sucked into them, were next to lost, "it being almost impossible to force so unwieldy a machine as a flat bottomed boat against so powerful a current." And "wooden islands" were places where "quantities of drift wood [have] through time been arrested and matted together . . . the bed of the river not having had sufficient time to form" a bar or gradual ascent. Instead, a deadly "current will carry you . . . unless you use timely exertion."

The convoy's boat captains finally reached the end of their Ohio River travails and met the great Mississippi. At the confluence, the clearer blue-green Ohio River waters took more than a mile before subsuming their lighter hue into the chocolate brown, muddy Mississippi waters. As one wit described it, "they look like putting dirty soap-suds and pure water together." Another observed that the Mississippi River waters were "too thick to drink and too loose to plow."

The travelers, not being forewarned, were initially taken aback by the Mississippi's forbidding turbidity. They rummaged through their boats for pots and crocks, filling them with clear Ohio water while they still could for fear of running out of drinkable water. Even so, their small store of Ohio waters ran out within days, but they discovered the Mississippi "was very good water, when filtered" by allowing the silt to settle in a bucket overnight.

*

While Mississippi waters may have been murky, the pioneers' prospects brightened overall. The travelers realized that the Northwest Indian Federation had not stirred up trouble in the Spanish sphere or among most of the Cherokee, Chickasaw, and Choctaw. The first day they entered the Mississippi, the boatmen on all six vessels "discharged all our rifles and pistols" in a ragged celebratory volley, "as we were then out of danger from the hostile Indians."

Vigilance for real and imagined Indian threats now gave way to more fraternal pursuits. On the second day, the six boat captains agreed to dine together on each boat in rotation. The exchange of pleasantries and sharing of viewpoints "rendered our journey more pleasant" and created an informal society of men with shared business interests. Some discovered that they also shared distant ties of kinship, common East Coast origins, Revolutionary War military service, or Masonic membership.

Returning to the river the group found themselves slowed by a strong opposing wind and ominous lightning. White-capped waves chopped and splashed up to the tops of the gunwales. "The waves ran so high that we felt in danger of foundering." When the forward boat reflexively pulled for shore, the other five boat captains immediately followed.

Samuel S. could make out Indians in a canoe darting out from the shoreline and paddling hard for the lead boat. Wondering what to do, he called to his hired hand William Carroll, the northwestern man, trusting his experience. But Carroll returned a "wild look," as flustered as his questioner. Samuel S. directed his hands to heave to midstream and scramble to load their rifles and pistols, while he kept "an eye upon the suspicious visitors."

Proving friendly, the Indians were peaceably received by the lead boatmen without "hostile demonstrations" being made by either party. Judging the river conditions more threatening than these friendly Indians, all the boats now turned toward making their landings, which they accomplished "after much hard work." Instead of aggression, the Indians "lent a hand in the rowing" and nudged the unwieldy flatboats out of the main flow and toward dry land.

These Indians may have been Delawares, from a band independent of the Northwest Indian Federation, who had obtained permission from the Spanish to settle near New Madrid.

It was Samuel S.'s turn to host all the captains to dinner. Having ample fresh beef on hand, "I invited three of our copper-faces [a racist term for Indians] to dine with us." After dinner he offered the entire company mixed whiskey and water "in the only glass I had," refilling it and handing it to his guests in succession. "When I came to the [Indian] leader, he took the offering, and reaching out his hand to me in a genteel and graceful manner, shook mine heartily; and then repeated the cordial hand clasp with each of the others, not omitting his own people." Everyone was quite pleased with the meal and reception. The evidently ranking Indian "drank [to] our healths as politely, I imagine, as Lord Chesterfield could have done."

After the dinner, the boatmen "asked leave to visit the opposite, Spanish side of the river, where these Indians had a large encampment." The Indians objected to the men going armed with rifles. The chief addressed the boat captains with enough English to be understood as, "We came among you as friends, bringing no arms along." The captains agreed and all went unarmed.

When they returned, the boatmen reported that there were a good many Indians there. By some means, some of the visitors brought and treated the Indians to *la tafia*—a rotgut rum—and everyone "became very much intoxicated." An Indian woman, sensing the possibility of trouble, secreted all their men's knives such that "the Indians could not fight." The next morning, the captains were relieved to bid goodbye to "our new acquaintances."

The following day, the flotilla continued on its way, passing through the little village of *L'Anse à la Graisse* or, as Americans knew it, New Madrid. The multicultural community there, with its Spanish commandant, left a favorable and lasting impression for its fine food and hospitality.

Now entering the wide Mississippi, the six flatboat captains adopted a signaling system necessary to keep in touch over the broad separations that occurred among boats during a day's travel. "We agreed that the foremost boat should fire a gun as a token for landing, if they saw a favorable spot after the middle of the afternoon. It was not possible to run in safety during the night." Each afternoon a thunder shower swept across the river and a headwind would slow progress.

The flotilla pulled in at Bayou Pierre to visit Peter Bruin, an American Revolutionary War veteran expat, now a successful planter, merchant, and Spanish magistrate in the region. Bruin was one of the first Americans to gain a Spanish grant of free land in an arrangement similar to what General David Forman had negotiated. Bruin's land grant was in the Nogales (later Vicksburg) area of Spanish West Florida's Natchez District. "That section of country is remarkably handsome, and the soil rich. The colonel's dwelling-house was on the top of a large [prehistoric Indian] mound, and his barn on another, nearby."

Natchez was just sixty miles easy sailing downriver. Samuel S. Forman, Mr. Bayard, and the convoy captains soon sighted the bluffs over which the town hovered, topped by the Spanish fort and a fluttering Bourbon flag.

The *Nancy* was one of six boats logged into the port on Tuesday, June 22, 1790. Ezekiel, who had asked Spanish officials to be on the lookout for them, hurried to greet his cousin. He would want to learn how much tobacco and other cargo Samuel S. had brought on his behalf, and assure that the shipment would be afforded the favorable treatment he expected as a new Spanish colonial national.

CHAPTER 10

Wabash Cannon Ball

BEFORE THE REVOLUTION THE BRITISH COLONIAL GOVERNMENT HAD set a line of demarcation at the Allegheny Mountains as the furthest extent of Anglo-American settlement permitted along the western frontier with Indian lands. Memorialized at the Treaty of Fort Stanwix in 1764, the line was modified in 1768 to set the Ohio River as the boundary. Anglo-British settlement would be permissible south of the river, while the lands to the north would remain the domain of resident Indian nations.

This placated some of the natives, who following the conclusion of the French and Indian War were at first unsure of the British assertion of sovereignty that had replaced the French. But the initial high-handed British administration immediately perplexed Indian tribes. Only after Pontiac's Rebellion laid waste to several forts and the British suppressed the revolt did the Indians of the northwest and British arrive at a more peaceful, symbiotic relationship.

During the late colonial era, this détente frayed. Virginia settlers and land speculators pushed against the Fort Stanwix limits, imposed under King George III's authority. While the Fort Stanwix Treaty involved opening Kentucky lands south of the Ohio to settlers, hunting rights remained with the Indians. Further complicating matters, Shawnee and Delaware Indians did not subscribe to the treaty and simultaneously rejected the Iroquois' audacity to give away what they considered to be Shawnee and Delaware lands. In turn, encroaching Virginia settlers in the Upper Ohio Valley directly challenged any Indian claims to the region.

The Delawares' Buckongahelas lost his only son Mahonegon to ensuing frontier violence in trans-Allegheny Virginia when Captain William

White, a native of Frederick County, killed the young man in a skirmish. That same year, further west in the Kentucky region, Daniel Boone lost his teenage son James to a tortuous death in another action involving the Delaware, Shawnee, and Cherokee. These dissenting tribes, by rejecting the Iroquois' Fort Stanwix Treaty, prepared to violently oppose settlers, whom they considered interlopers on their ancestral hunting grounds. The gruesome deaths at the hands of these Indians were meant to deter all comers. Such raids and massacres led to Virginia's Royal Governor Lord Dunmore's declaration of war against the Shawnee and Mingo in 1774.

Dunmore's War fanned anti-Indian sentiment and buoyed acquisitive land speculators. Dunmore's policies played on racial tensions and prejudices but also, somewhat cynically, attempted to divert and confound the emerging Patriot cause.

The following year, as Loyalists broke openly with American Patriots, Dunmore famously proclaimed freedom for slaves who enlisted to fight against American Patriots, seizing upon an expedient that both filled the thin ranks of Loyalist soldiers in Virginia and undermined the interests of the colony's slave-owning Patriots. He was no more fundamentally anti-Indian in his 1774 war against the Shawnee than he was a proponent of universal abolitionism. Both were pragmatic, self-serving moves.

All through the Revolutionary War, as Americans pushed pioneering and settlement claims into the trans-Allegheny West, conflicts pitting the English, the Loyalists, and their Indian allies against American militias and some Continental troops raged. Compared to combat along the East Coast, conflicts in the West were fought by far fewer people over great and sparsely populated distances. But the ferocity of the conflicts and their implications were immense. Neither side was able to win a clear-cut strategic victory.

Both the Seneca, who broke with the majority of the Iroquois Federation, and Piomingo's faction of the Chickasaw, were exceptional among Indians as consistent allies of the Americans. Their warriors often served as fighting scouts for the Americans. But the majority of Indian nations fought as allies of the British or endeavored to remain neutral.

*

Virginian George Rogers Clark's surprise victory at Fort Vincennes in 1779 in the far-off Illinois Territory conferred on the Americans leverage that induced the British to concede the entire Northwest Territory and lands east of the Mississippi River to the Americans at the Peace of Paris that concluded the Revolutionary War.

Nevertheless, the English were slow to turn over strategic forts in the Northwest, and the Indians had their own ideas about sovereignty over those lands. The British maintained a mutually profitable fur trade and readily supplied Indians in the region with arms and high-quality trade goods. This dynamic encouraged a proxy struggle enabling Indian dominance in the Middle Ground, where Indians informally allied to the British checked American expansionism. During the 1780s settlers in Kentucky and Tennessee were almost continually harassed by deadly raids by Indian bands, while settlement north of the Ohio River remained restricted and potentially deadly for any pioneers who dared to establish farms there.

It seemed that whatever position one desired to assert, one could find Indian factions willing or able to be browbeaten, or seduced with gifts, to accede or impede treaty agreements and surrender land to the American government. British imperialists, and Spanish in the South, could find Indian factions amenable to their proposals through comparable means. American diplomatic interactions with Indians during this period were distinguishable from European colonials' more by their aims, rather than their means. Land cessions and settler expansion were the constant themes of the Americans. Spheres of influence for trade (particularly animal pelt and deerskin), rather than land acquisition, were more characteristic of the English and Spanish colonials.

Most Indians were not opposed to the presence of American or imperial trading posts. They welcomed the firearms and gunpowder that so enhanced the efficiency of hunting, and coveted the durable manufactured goods that they had no tradition of making themselves. Their networks enabled adaptable native nations to play off competing foreign interests to obtain the guns, iron, steel, and lead required to hunt and wage war.

Traders, however, brought other practices into Indian Territory that were not as welcome. They took Indian women as wives and consorts, bringing mixed-race progeny and cultural admixtures into traditional homelands and families. Whiskey intoxicated or addicted natives unused to strong alcoholic beverages. Christian missionaries introduced a foreign, monotheistic religion that often condemned long-standing indigenous beliefs and practices.

Colonial settlers were the most troubling of all. The enclosure and cultivation of farmland, animal husbandry, and competition in hunting game on the diminishing ranges rendered the settlers' ways incompatible with seminomadic hunters and smaller-scale Indian farming.

Individual Indian tribes within nations often conducted their own foreign policy, adding to the complexity. For example, as Buckongahelas led some Delawares in warlike defiance to American expansion north of the Ohio River, other Delaware converted to Christianity and actively adopted European-style agricultural ways, such as the ill-fated Gnadenhütten settlement. These Christianized Delawares had aspired to neutrality in the Ohio country. Still other factions of the Delaware voted with their feet, moving further west at Spanish invitation to New Madrid on the Mississippi River or into Northern Michigan and Canada.

British agents, traders, and interpreters captured key Indian leaders' sentiments at a 1784 conference held near British-occupied Detroit. Chief Joseph Brandt, a notable Mohawk diplomat and Iroquois Federation representative, counseled an accommodative approach to the Americans. He proposed setting the Muskingum River in Eastern Ohio as a realistic place to delimit American settlers, with Indian lands protected to the west. Brandt had allied with the British during the Revolutionary War, only to see his people suffer from punitive Continental Army campaigns into Upstate New York—actions, incidentally, in which Samuel S. Forman's brother Jonathan participated. Yet Brandt's was an isolated voice at the Detroit conference. The Miami, Delaware, Shawnee, and other tribes sought to put teeth into the earlier Fort Stanwix divide at the Ohio River between Indian lands and American settlement.

Three broad groupings of Indians emerged in the 1780s with that common goal. The most militant were led by Little Turtle, a war chief of

Chief Little Turtle (Miami) from a nineteenth-century engraving of a lost portrait by Gilbert Stuart. Courtesy National Anthropological Archives, Smithsonian Institution.

the Miami; Blue Jacket, a Shawnee war chief; and Buckongahelas of the Delaware. Brandt asserted a more accommodative stance on behalf of the Iroquois nations. The third grouping's homelands were farther distant from the most hotly contested areas, but they were vitally interested in keeping large-scale settlement from their lands. Among these were the Ojibwa, Ottawa, and the Potawatomi.

Influenced by eloquent leaders operating in a consensus environment, an Indian coalition emerged that was willing to stand firm against settlers and fight if necessary. Thus, the Northwest Indian Federation was formed. The principal tribes that anchored it were the Miami, Delaware, and Shawnee. A recent historian described it as "a loose and fragile coalition of villages," with each Indian nation having its distinct experiences and aspirations. Another historian recognized the chiefs' "collaborative coalition leadership, collective vision, and intertribal consensus politics," conjured in the common defense of the Indians' Middle Ground.

Among the dozen or more Indian nations residing in the Northwest Territory, it is extraordinary that strong leaders emerged and allied so effectively, under such trying circumstances, to defend a threatened way of life over so vast a territory.

While Little Turtle is best remembered as a figure who eventually made peace with the United States, that pacific conception diminishes his impressive abilities as one of the most energetic, resourceful, and skillful defenders of Eastern Woodlands, Algonquian-speaking natives' interests in American history.

Mishikinaakwa, Little Turtle's name in his native language, was born in what is now Indiana about 1750. His father was a Miami chief and his mother a Mohican. He experienced a modicum of European-style education from Jesuit missionaries, but he appears not to have acquired fluency in English or other European languages. He relied on multilingual traders or bilingual family members to communicate with the British and Americans.

As a British ally at the time, he led a 1780 attack that annihilated a French frontier detachment. That experience taught him that colonial powers were not invincible. At six feet tall, "sour and morose" at times, bedecked with sparkling silver ornaments on his ears and clothing, he presented an "impressive, if foreboding" appearance. Nearly legendary throughout native villages in the Ohio Territory by 1790, he was revered for his wisdom and courage.

In counsel Little Turtle achieved consensus by words and dramatic action. In October 1788, for instance, a Wyandot leader urged him to attend peace talks aimed at coexistence with the Americans. The Wyandot diplomat ceremoniously draped a large wampum belt, likely artfully constructed of white beads, to embody peaceful intent, over Little Turtle's shoulder, "recommending to them to be at peace with the Americans, and to do as the [Iroquois Confederation] Six Nations and others did." The chief said nothing in contradiction, but stooped just enough to let the belt drop to the ground. The Wyandot got the message. Little Turtle would maintain respectful communications with the Americans, but he stood for Indian tribes uniting in war against a common threat.

Another notable leader of the Northwest Federation was Buckongahelas of the Delaware, or in their language, the Lenni Lenape. The Delaware nation possessed a tradition of diplomatically oriented peace chiefs and, of equal standing, war chiefs. Over a century of conflicts had led to the war chiefs asserting greater prominence in Delaware society. Buckongahelas likely came from a line of Delaware leaders, as his name, meaning "giver of presents," evokes a traditional prerogative associated with tribal chiefs.

Buckongahelas spent his early years in what is the modern state of Delaware. He married and, as the leader of his band of the Delaware, moved away from the tensions of the East to what is now Upshur County, West Virginia. There his son Mahonegon was killed in conflict with Virginia settlers.

Buckongahelas built close ties with Shawnee Chief Blue Jacket and relocated his band of Delawares near to his new ally in the northwest corner of the Ohio Territory. In doing so, Buckongahelas parted ways with Delaware Indians under Chief White Eyes, who assumed a neutral or pro-American stance.

Buckongahelas viewed with suspicion those Delawares who were converted to Christianity by Moravian missionaries and resided in European-style agrarian communities while endeavoring to be neutral pacifists. One of those missionaries met with Buckongahelas, and was impressed with the Indian's "gallant and generous" nature and mild-mannered demeanor. Nevertheless, Buckongahelas was wary of the Americans, who "will in their usual fine way, speak fine words to you, and at the same time murder you! . . . They enslave those who are not of their color, although created by the same Great Spirit who created us. They would make slaves of us if they could, but as they cannot do it, they kill us. There is no faith to be put in their words."

Blue Jacket, in his late forties, was the oldest of the three notable Indian Federation leaders. Virtually nothing is known of his early life. He first appears in a missionary's writings in 1773 as a full-fledged Shawnee chief, reigning over a village on the Scioto River in the Ohio Territory. Blue Jacket fought against the Virginia colonials in Lord Dunmore's War and became an ally of convenience with the British during the Revolutionary War. Faithful to his desire to uphold Shawnee claims to their traditional lands, he joined the Miami and Delaware armed resistance in the Ohio Territory.

A captive described Blue Jacket as a muscular man towering six feet tall with "open and intelligent countenance . . . the most noble in appearance of any Indian I ever saw." At that point he sported a scarlet coat, in the manner of a British officer, edged in gold lace and set off by British-made gold epaulets and a colored sash. More in the Shawnee manner were his red-dyed leggings and fine ornamented moccasins. He wore the silver gorget of a British officer, a King George III sterling silver peace medal, ornamental silver arm bands, and Indian trade metalwork.

Blue Jacket had adopted some of the Europeans' ways. It is said that he sent his son to British Detroit to be educated. At home he slept in a curtained four-poster bed, ate at a table with silver cutlery, and graciously offered a captive tea on her multiple visits to him and his French wife.

When Indians received news at British Fort Niagara of the Treaty of Paris, they vented their frustration to the garrison commander. They "could never believe that our King could pretend to cede to America what was not his own to give, where that the Americans would accept from him what he had no right to grant." Indians soon learned that the British would unofficially supply and arm them in their opposition to the United States in the Northwest Territory. Britain rationalized subversion of the

Treaty of Paris on the pretext of America's neither honoring prewar debts nor compensating Loyalists for seizures of their property.

Indians, though initially disappointed that the king's government did not consult them on the terms ending the Revolutionary War, could exploit the situation to their own advantage. An alliance of like-minded tribes might assert the Middle Ground for themselves by violently discouraging settlers and defeating the tiny US Army garrisons and any ragtag militias that might dare to oppose them.

The Americans asserted sovereignty over the entire Ohio Territory by right of conquest and formal cession by the Treaty of Paris. Demobilizing the Continental Army in 1783 except for 1,000 soldiers, the United States was in no position to evict the British from their northwest frontier forts, nor could they chase down and chastise all independent-minded Indians. Rather, the Confederation government expected the Indians to sign on to formal treaties recognizing US control over the region, and cede sufficient tracts to satisfy American land companies and settlers eager to bring commercial agriculture there.

Americans were willing to offer traditional gifts of valued trade goods to Indian tribes who would sign on peacefully. This approach was integral to retiring the national debt at a time when the American Confederation government had no other plausible means to pay off veteran Continental soldiers or the national debt that had financed the Revolutionary War. Individuals turned land developers like the scandalous Judge Symmes, and joint stock enterprises like the Ohio Land Company, would pay the government large amounts of money for prime tracts and in turn make a handsome profit by retailing those lands to settlers.

If any Indians were foolish enough to oppose the Americans' strategy and plan, a detachment of the regular army, augmented by short-term militia musters, hardy frontiersmen, and settlers would bring them into the fold. The official position was that Indian lands would not be confiscated. Their voluntary consent by treaty would be required for any cessions of land to the federal government, and ultimately to pioneer settlers. Indians would not be attacked except "in just and lawful wars authorized by Congress." Those treaty negotiations fell to the Secretary of War, Henry Knox, rendering the idea of voluntary Indian land cessions something of a farce.

Nevertheless, some Indian tribes met with American military representatives on just such grounds, and pursued the days and weeks-long customs of diplomatic speeches, games, and entertainments. A keenly observant American officer, Ebenezer Denny, took notes at the negotiations that culminated in the 1785 Treaty of Fort McIntosh. About 1,100 Indians were present, chiefly of the Wyandot and Delaware nations. In early December, assembled Indians staged an Indian ball game, the forerunner of lacrosse. This was probably a gesture meant for the edification of all present, and may also have induced the Americans to observe fit and agile Indian athletes, prepared to be warriors if their leaders deemed that necessary.

Seneca Chief Cornplanter arrived among the hundreds of warriors. Denny noted that the "Shawnees are the fellows the present treaty was intended for; they seem to hang back." Also attending were Chief White Eyes's faction of the Delaware, who had allied themselves with the Americans during the Revolutionary War.

Officer Denny was contemptuous of the Indians, describing them collectively as a "motley crew—an ugly set of devils all—very few handsome men or women." He was almost as disdainful of the American militia, "so irregular and mutinous that it took the best regiment to protect the convoys of provisions [intended as treaty gifts to the Indians] from the deserters."

Getting down to business, an Indian orator, probably through a translator,

> *denied the power which the United States assumed; asked if the Great Spirit had given it to them to cut and portion [Indian lands] in the manner proposed. The Ohio River they would agree to [as the boundary for settlement], nothing short; and offered a mixed [wampum] belt, indicating peace or war.*

General Clark, the senior American negotiator, pushed the belt off the table and "set his foot on it" to indicate his disregard for the warning it represented. The Indians "were sullen," but returned the next day to acquiesce after consulting among themselves: "After considerable difficulty, a treaty is signed to, but with much reluctance on the part of the savages."

Buckongahelas arrived a few days later on January 24, 1786. After the expected salutes, ten of his best warriors underscored this attitude, performing a war dance "quite naked, except for the breech cloth, [and] painted their bodies and faces to have a horrid appearance; armed with tomahawk and scalping knife."

Nonetheless, the "Treaty concluded at Fort McIntosh was explained to Buckongahelas and his tribe, to their satisfaction." Or so thought officer Denny.

Cornplanter, who had signed the treaty on behalf of the Seneca, conferred with his people, and in short order returned to rescind his signature. The American negotiators heard him out, reassured him, but did not allow the Seneca to revoke their approval.

Denny and the American delegation then declared success, as was expected by their superiors back at the capital in Philadelphia. Wrote Denny, "the Indians must now look up to the Americans, and ought to be thankful if allowed to occupy any part of the country, more perhaps than they expected would be done for them." As an aside, Denny wondered, "The Lord knows when we'll get rid of these creatures."

When General St. Clair arrived at Marietta, Ohio, as governor of the Northwest Territory, he met with 200 Indians at nearby Fort Harmar in December 1788. There, he signed a treaty with Seneca Chief Cornplanter and the Iroquois Six Nations. Cornplanter's rival, the Mohawk's Joseph Brandt, was tellingly absent. In a second treaty with a different native federation, the Delaware ceded more land, but negotiated hard-to-retain hunting rights. Unfortunately, executing such a provision practically guaranteed confrontations between Indian hunting bands and settlers.

Ebenezer Denny, present for these meetings too, noted in his journal, "This was the last act of the farce." General Arthur St. Clair found the negotiations "both tedious and troublesome." And, as with the 1785 Treaty of Fort McIntosh, many Indians quickly disavowed their approval.

The treaties of Fort McIntosh and Fort Harmar did nothing to lessen the murderous Indian raids on settlers in the Ohio Territory and Kentucky. New settlements planted along the north shore of the Ohio River

Battle of the Wabash or St. Clair's Defeat, November 4, 1791, as imagined by illustrator R. F. Zogbaum for *Harper's Magazine*, 1895.

at Marietta, Maysville, and Cincinnati emboldened militant raiding parties to strike at outlying settler stations; to prey, as Dr. Saugrain and the Forman party saw, on pioneer river traffic; and to rampage into Kentucky.

The Indian raiding parties audaciously targeted US Army soldiers. An army patrol in the Wabash River Valley of Western Ohio in June 1789 found the still-warm body of a comrade. "He was shot in two places with [musket] balls, had two arrows sticking in his body, was scalped, his heart taken out and his privates cut off."

Typically, after a raid, the Indians would vanish into the forests and return toward Kekiongo and their settled towns in northwestern Ohio. Random reprisals might follow. Here neutrals could just as likely be targeted as the avowed Indian enemies of American expansion. The dead spirits of the Christian Delaware men, women, and children executed at Gnadenhütten could attest to the fact.

Northwest Indian Federation war parties became so emboldened that even American Army garrison troops were regularly ambushed as they ranged just out of sight of their stockades, or when they came to the aid of embattled settlers. This was the situation the Forman pioneers encountered when entertained by General Harmar at Fort Washington in Cincinnati in early February of 1790.

Army leaders in the region, like Winthrop Sargent and others who also held stakes in the land companies, faced an inherent contradiction. On the one hand, they wanted settlers to stay within the tracts governed by treaties with Indians, and stood to lose if squatters settled elsewhere. But when they were attacked, in spite of the annoyance to the overstretched American Army, the military was loath to stand by as fellow Caucasian Americans were butchered by native enemies of the United States. Sargent's position was pointedly sensitive as he was the Northwest Territory Secretary in addition to his roles in the military and as a land company super-salesman.

Meanwhile, frontiersman and settlers viewed the army as ineffective in their defense, as indeed it was at this juncture. Its weakness posed immediate and deadly consequences for them personally. They came to view the federal government as an incapable, uncaring tool of the East Coast elites.

Aware of the mayhem on the western frontier, President George Washington ordered a military campaign in 1790 to destroy the principal Indian towns along the Maumee River and Kekiongo, stop the Indian depredations, and bring the Northwest Indian Federation to terms. General Josiah Harmar coordinated a nucleus of US regular troops and militia recruited in Kentucky to march north from Cincinnati. Their mission was to destroy Kekiongo, the principal town from which most Indian war parties were thought to originate, and to defeat the Northwest Federated Indians on the battlefield.

Now that the British were successors to the French in Canada, and the Spanish had taken over *Luisiana* and West Florida, Kekiongo, with its series of towns, remained an important Indian habitation. It was a welcoming region for Miami, Delaware, and Shawnee Indians opposed to American settlement in the Northwest. A visiting missionary was impressed with the extensive fields of corn, beans, and squash surrounding the settlement, and the hundreds of log cabins and dome-shaped wigwams, grouped into precincts for the several distinct allied Algonquian Indian nations. Another noted "good gardens with some fruit trees, and vast fields of corn in almost every direction." The entire vicinity was surrounded by dense forest teeming with abundant wild game.

Following European military battle doctrine, General Harmar moved his forces to attack Kekiongo and lay waste all Indian habitation, fields, and any hostile forces he encountered en route.

Fort Washington at Cincinnati served as the staging ground for the campaign. It was 1790, late in the same year as the Forman pioneers' visit. All summer long, militia recruits trickled in from across the Ohio River in Kentucky and from western Pennsylvania. Nonetheless, the Indians' terror campaign apparently dissuaded the ablest frontiersmen and settlers from venturing into Indian country north of the Ohio because doing so would leave their Kentucky homes and family members exposed to attack. The recruits who did come were a decidedly mediocre mob who appeared "to be raw and unused to the gun or the woods." Adding to the challenges, supplies were slow in arriving from the distant East Coast. Finally, Harmar sallied north at the end of September with some 320 US Army regulars and over a thousand militiamen. The force was organized into three battalions: one from Kentucky; one from Pennsylvania, a group of light mounted troops; and the rest regular US Army troops.

When General Harmar reached Kekiongo in mid-October, he found it abandoned by the Indians. Unlike Harmar, Little Turtle and his allies maintained good intelligence on his enemies' movements. Harmar's men set ablaze everything "that could be of use: corn, beans, pumpkins, stacks of hay, fencing and cabins, &c." By the general's account the destruction included the razing of five villages in addition to Kekiongo. It was "the next best thing to killing them." The *coup de grâce* was the utter destruction of "twenty thousand bushels of corn in ears."

Harmar divided his forces more than once as he led them north from Cincinnati. But now Indians under Little Turtle's direction struck back and defeated some of these contingents. At one point, officer Denny was appalled that the "greatest number of militia fled without firing a shot," leaving a detachment of thirty US Army regulars to be attacked where they "stood and were cut to pieces." One retreat was so precipitous that dead soldiers were abandoned on the field to victorious Indians, who promptly unsheathed their scalping knives.

News of the defeat reached the American capital on December 12, 1790, appalling Secretary of War General Knox and President Washington. Among the 180 Americans lost was the army doctor who had succored the sorely wounded Dr. Antoine François Saugrain only two years before at the Falls of the Ohio. In addition, half of the American force's pack horses, essential for mobility in frontier forests, were lost to Little Turtle's braves.

*

A deeply chagrined Washington replaced Josiah Harmar with Northwest Territory Governor Arthur St. Clair. The new field general's work was cut out for him. The entire trans-Allegheny American frontier now lay exposed, to the horror of American settlers and pioneers.

Investors in western lands perceived the threat not only to the settlers' lives, but also to the very rationale of their business model and its hoped-for infusion of cash to pay down the US national debt. Retired General Rufus Putnam, a leader of the Ohio Land Company, wrote Washington and Knox in January 1791 demanding more federal troops and a more effective campaign to quash the Indian threat. "I think it does not require the spirit of prophecy to foretell the consequence," he warned of inaction. "No more lands will be purchased but will probably [be] seized on" by private adventurers with no regard for "the laws of the United States or [for that matter] the rights of the Natives."

The laudable blueprint that the Ohio Land Company planned for the Northwest Territory, and eventually realized, was not much in evidence at this juncture. That vision of neatly surveyed townships, bountiful farms, institutionalized government support for public education, and the exclusion of chattel slavery from the region, could only be fully realized once the existential the threat of Indian war had been addressed.

In April Secretary of State Thomas Jefferson weighed in: "I hope we shall give them [the Indians] a thorough drubbing this summer, and then change our tomahawk into a golden chain of friendship." Jefferson hoped the hostile Indians could be dealt with without resorting to a permanent increase in the national debt. He told George Washington in April 1791 that he feared recurrent campaigns would lead to a standing national army and, as a predictable consequence, increase the national liability.

Congress granted Secretary Knox's request for an increase in the regular army and 1,300 militia volunteers for four months' service, and an appropriation of $100,000. General St. Clair was ordered to collect the expanded army at Fort Pitt, proceed to Cincinnati, and from there strike north for Kekiongo. And, at Jefferson's behest, President Washington implored Cornplanter to intercede to "render those mistaken people a great service, and probably prevent their being swept from the face of the earth." The peace overture never materialized.

Winthrop Sargent, now General St. Clair's military adjutant in the field, was hearing irksome things about the newly emboldened Indians. He wrote to St. Clair, "All those scoundrels . . . say, send their women to fight us and with sticks instead of guns." General Harmar's campaign, which had destroyed Indian houses and their cornfields, had done little to impair their will to fight.

The British encouraged the Indians with military supplies and ready access to trade goods, although they stopped short of a formal disavowal of the Treaty of Paris.

As the year 1791 dragged on, any hope of a prompt humbling of the restive Indians faded. General St. Clair established the headquarters of the American Army in the West at Cincinnati. Sargent, in his role of adjutant, did his best to whip the ragtag militia recruits into an effective fighting force. This increasingly appeared to be a thankless and impossible task. James Wilkinson, leading a section of the army from Kentucky, and preternaturally involved in self-aggrandizing intrigues, found subtle ways to subvert his commander St. Clair.

Meanwhile, supplies trickled in slowly, were poor quality, and fell far short of the needs of a larger force. Still, chided by Knox and Washington to get on with the campaign, St. Clair at length led his troops north. It was late Autumn, very late in the campaign season for a conventional army. Logistics would be further strained as the army proceeded into dense forests. Progress was slowed as a military road needed to be cut for the wagons, pack horses, and artillery caissons. The weather deteriorated into torrential rains and sharp nighttime frosts. On top of all this, St. Clair became ill and had to be carried at times in a litter.

The general's force was becoming drained of energy, plagued by desertions and food shortages. St. Clair and Richard Butler, his second-in-command, permitted the expedient of allowing a narrower road to be cut, the better to make forward progress, but at the expense of less visibility and maneuverability, should the enemy emerge from the forest cover.

Piomingo of the Chickasaw nation arrived with about twenty of his warriors as American allies and much-needed scouts to reconnoiter the hostile Indians. The Chickasaws later styled themselves the unconquered and unconquerable. Their formidable track record in war included humbling Hernando de Soto in 1540, and more recently, intermittent warfare with Choctaws and Creeks closer to their Mississippi homeland. Chief Piomingo immediately ranged into the wilderness in an effort to locate and track the Northwest Confederation Indian forces.

Morale wavered among the American forces. Noted Denny: "The trees and limbs falling around and in the midst of us, with the darkness of the night and in an enemy's country, occasioned some concern." Ominous surroundings, bone-rattling cold and wet, and empty bellies along with superficial resolve induced two artillerymen to attempt to desert to the enemy. They "were taken, tried and sentenced to . . . death"; though justified by military law, the prompt and lethal punishment failed to improve morale.

The Americans thought they had come quite close to Kekiongo, but in fact, they were dozens of miles away. On the evening of November 3, 1791, the exhausted Americans set up their camp in a position hemmed in by surrounding forest and low ground. They neglected to assign proper sentries or to clear a perimeter. Piomingo's scouts, with a huge range of unfamiliar Ohio forested terrain to cover, failed to detect the opposing Indian force, which was close at hand.

For several days, anticipating battle, Little Turtle's, Buckongahelas's, and Blue Jacket's warriors engaged in religious purification rites to prepare themselves for what lay ahead: abstaining from sex, imbibing the traditional purgative black herbal drink, and painting their bodies in designs associated with strength and war. The Indian leaders conferred on the deployment of their forces and tactics, invoking supernatural support from "our Great Father above." Fifty Potawatomi deserted on the eve of battle, but all else was in readiness.

At dawn on November 4, 1791, the Indians struck the American camp, emerging from their forest cover in a broad crescent-shaped front. The deployment is generally credited to Little Turtle and his forces, who occupied the center of their advancing front. Buckongahelas played a leading, some say superior, role to Little Turtle's on the battlefield itself.

The American force suffered numerous casualties. Indians surrounded the American camp, as both flanks of the crescent-shaped line of Indians surged forward to encircle it. Barely surviving the onslaught, officer Denny later reported that the American firepower "made a tremendous noise, but did little execution." The Indians "seemed not to fear anything we could do."

Little Turtle assigned his son-in-law William Wells to lead Indian riflemen in picking off the American cannoneers, which he and his fellow warriors carried out with devastating efficiency. Ironically, the Indian adoptee's older Caucasian biological brother Samuel Wells was among the Kentucky militia fighting in the American Army that day. He was one of the few to emerge from the battle unscathed.

As Denny put it,

> *The men being thus left with few officers, became fearful, despaired of success, gave up the fight, and to save themselves for the moment, abandoned entirely their duty and ground, and crowded in toward the center of the field . . . perfectly ungovernable.*

After three hours of relentless Indian attack, numerous failed American bayonet charges, and silenced artillery, the Americans broke into a disorderly retreat.

Many of the wounded were abandoned on the field, only to be killed in gruesome ways and scalped by Indians in close pursuit. Some women camp followers, fleeing from the overrun baggage train, also suffered such a fate. So did St. Clair's second-in-command, General Butler. Sorely wounded, he was abandoned at his request on the battlefield by two of his sons.

It was, by any measurement, a complete Indian victory. "The road for miles was covered with firelocks, cartridge boxes and regimentals." The Indians closely pursued the routed Americans for six miles, slaughtering the laggards. "Delay was death. . . . Numbers of brave men must be left a sacrifice, there was no alternative. . . ."

Some said Little Turtle, on account of his inherent humanity, called off the slaughter of the fleeing vanquished. The muddled retreat continued for twenty-nine miles all the way back to the nearest staging area at Fort Jefferson.

Colonel Sargent, St. Clair's chief adjutant, though himself twice wounded, "took upon himself the burden of everything, and a very troublesome task he had." He was called upon to tally the losses—630 killed and missing, of whom 37 were officers; 283 wounded, of whom 31 were officers. In battles of this era, as is the experience today, wounded usually far outnumber the dead and missing. In this instance, in the face of the Indians' execution and butchery of most of the wounded left behind, the opposite was true. Native American losses are thought to have been a tiny fraction of the American casualties—twenty Shawnee and fifteen Miami warriors.

Uncounted in Sargent's figures were the noncombatant camp followers who supported the army. Some scores of them died in the attack as well, and only three women of hundreds present as camp followers escaped in the retreat. Of those left behind, a quarter were killed outright and the remainder taken captive.

American material losses crippled the offensive capabilities of the army's remnants and strengthened the native victors'. Abandoned to the Indians on the field by the routed Americans were 1,200 muskets, almost 400 field tents, hundreds of pack horses ready to deploy with their harnesses, swords, medicine chests, traveling forges, blacksmith's and gunsmith's tools, and thousands of pounds of army field rations. Captured official papers provided granular insights into the Americans' campaign strategy and command structure.

It was a devastating day for American arms, the largest single defeat in proportion to its size of any American expeditionary force. Remembered variously as the Battle of the Wabash, St. Clair's Defeat, or the Battle of a Thousand Slain, it exceeded by threefold American Army casualties at the better-known Custer's Last Stand at the 1876 Battle of the Little Big Horn.

Officer Denny had the task of bringing the news to President Washington and Secretary Knox. It took him six weeks from the day of the battle to arrive at the capital in Philadelphia. His report sent the usually imperturbable president into a rare and brief rage, railing against General St. Clair. In the year to follow, Washington's administration would undertake a number of measures to limit the damage.

*

Winthrop Sargent returned to the battlefield, "this melancholy theater of our recent misfortunes," three months later to bury the dead and to look for abandoned cannon the Indians might use against American forts. Sargent and his contingent encountered snow-covered corpses "exposed to view, mutilated, mangled and butchered with the most savage barbarity." His return to the site likely dredged up personal memories of the sights and sounds of desperate combat, the abandonment of the wounded, the slaughter, and the infliction of his own battle wounds. It was yet another experience that would contribute to straightlaced Sargent's dim view of human nature.

St. Clair faced a court martial. Although he was exonerated of wrongdoing, most of the blame fell not on leadership but rather on the cowardly militia. When facing a congressional inquiry on the fiasco, Washington asserted the then-novel concept of executive privilege to shield some potentially embarrassing internal correspondence on the venture from congressional oversight.

Washington then called Revolutionary War hero "Mad Anthony" Wayne out of retirement to replace St. Clair. He dispatched two officers—John Hardin and Alexander Truman—to try to open a dialog with hostile Federation leaders. Both were murdered and scalped while on the errand. Meanwhile, the Iroquois Six Nations were invited to intercede on the Americans' behalf with Little Turtle and his allies.

Henry Knox sent General Rufus Putnam to Vincennes in order to assure the neutrality of Indians in that quarter. William Wells, reconnecting with his birth family in the course of negotiating to free Delaware Indian hostages taken by the Americans, agreed to accompany Putnam as a translator.

In the summer of 1792 the Northwest Confederacy convened along the Glaize River in northwest Ohio to consider their strategy with respect to the Americans. Washington and Knox had directed General Wayne to hang back and await the outcome of the Indian Federation's councils.

Thirty-six hundred Indians attended. Alexander McKee, a trader well connected to the British in Canada and trusted by the Indians, was the sole white man permitted to participate. Tribal observers came from as far as Mississippi, New York, Upper Michigan, and Canada.

Despite the recent overwhelming victory over General St. Clair, some voices expressed concern the Americans would be back. Chief Blue Jacket of the Shawnee spoke in favor of compromising on the line of settlement, moving it into Eastern Ohio at the Muskingum River, as Joseph Brandt had earlier advocated.

Buckongahelas settled the matter, "We are resolved to stick close by each other and defend ourselves to the last." He presciently asserted that the Americans intended to build more forts to "drive Indians entirely out of the country." The Northwest Indian Federation would continue to maintain the Ohio River as a boundary for settlement. They would continue the war on settlers, squatters, and the US Army.

CHAPTER 11

Establishing a New Home in Natchez District, *Luisiana*, 1790

SAMUEL S. FORMAN AND THE REST ON THE CONVOY OF FLATBOATS FIRST sighted the towering bluffs at Natchez from miles upriver. The Spanish fort, variously named Rosalie or Panmure by the previous French and English occupants, was enthroned at the crest of a steep path up from the river landing. Atop the fort, the Bourbon crested flag fluttered, a white patch against the sky.

The flotilla docked across from the cluster of wooden buildings gathered on a narrow stretch of bottomland just a few feet above the river. Such was Natchez on their arrival, a town of about 200 souls, with dozens of wooden structures crafted from logs and midwestern timbers salvaged from flatboats that ended their river voyage right there in Spanish West Florida.

Their arrival at first generated "a little alarm at the fort." The Spanish garrison could be heard beating their drum to arms, for the traders and settlers had been mistaken for amphibious attackers. There was good reason to be on guard for waterborne aggression. In 1778 the American Continental Congress had sent a ragtag flotilla down the Mississippi that briefly occupied the outpost. In 1781, Governor Bernardo de Gálvez, an American ally, conquered the region for the Spanish monarchy. Gálvez brought stability, although not invincible protection.

The latest concerns were based on well-founded rumors that George Rogers Clark, who had taken Vincennes on the Upper Mississippi from the British in 1778, was now eyeing this region. It was part and parcel of

Natchez as it appeared in 1793. Natchez-under-the-Hill was the lower town, where river commerce was conducted, the rougher sort congregated, and the Forman pioneers arrived. Atop the steep bluff were the Spanish Government House, Fort Panmure, and elegant town houses and plantations being erected in the growing town, as laid out by district Governor Gayoso. Eighteenth-century engraving by Collot.

the Yazoo Land Company's unilaterally staking claims to rich farmlands near Walnut Hills, only sixty miles upriver. Perhaps the American speculators had now turned their strategems for acquiring Indian and Spanish land into outright aggression.

In addition, there was the Georgia Legislature, scheming and acting as if they owned the place. Georgians showed the Spanish Natchez District on maps as their own new Bourbon County. At that time Georgia, quite independently of the nascent American federal government, asserted that its north and south state boundaries projected due west through tribal lands all the way to the Mississippi River. Neither the Spanish nor the Americans, nor the English and French before them, had asked the Indian nations, who called the East and West Florida interior expanse home, what they thought of the whites' territorial notions.

Chiefs Little Turtle, Buckongahelas, and Blue Jacket's Northwest Indian Confederation sent emissaries, carrying ceremonial belts and red tobacco, to tribal leaders among the southeastern native nations, seeking allies for their defense of traditional Indian homelands. America's nominal ally Spain desired no active role in the bloody conflicts transpiring in the Ohio Valley and opposed native expansion of that war. Rather, the Spanish sought to foster amity in the region and among native peoples in the Southeast.

For almost a decade, successive Spanish officials maintained Natchez as a peaceful district, although instability and expansionism lurked on the periphery. The Spanish District Governor Manuel Gayoso de Lemos, with remarkable tact and diplomacy, maintained a pragmatic administration incorporating the French, English, and Creole plantation and trade-oriented holdovers. He courted the Indians and welcomed American settlers willing to become His Most Catholic Majesty's subjects, while endeavoring to keep the expansionist cabals of others at arm's length.

No wonder the Spanish military garrison of Natchez stood ready to muster at the unannounced approach and "formidable appearance" of a half-dozen flatboats that carried no national flag. They perhaps misconstrued the signal gun fired by the lead boat to prepare for landing as a signal to attack. If Fort Panmure high above on the Natchez bluffs had unleashed their heavy cannon on the approaching flotilla, mayhem could have ensued.

Fortunately, the peaceful intent of the flotilla rapidly became apparent and the "affright soon subsided."

Samuel S.'s *Nancy* was one of six boats arriving at the Port of Natchez on that Tuesday, June 22, 1790. The fort garrison's commandant, Carlos Grand Pré, logged them in. Ezekiel, who had asked customs officials to be on the lookout, hurried to greet his cousin. As a two-month Natchez resident now and Spanish citizen, he owed no import tariffs for the arriving goods. American citizens on the other hand were required to pay a 15 percent or higher import tariff. Some, like the wily James Wilkinson,

Manuel Gayoso de Lemos. Charming and able military and civil governor of
Natchez and Spanish West Florida from 1789 to 1795, later governor of all of
Spanish *Luisiana*. 1942 photo of Pedro J. de Lemos' painting, courtesy of the
Frick Photoarchive.

might work around such rules while secretly being a paid Spanish agent. The circumstances of his later being the American Secretary of War seemed not to bother him one bit.

Ezekiel likely brought to the levee a work gang of his strongest male hands, such as Jess, Ephraim, and Toddy, to unload his cargo from Samuel. S.'s flatboat. He would have interrogated Samuel S. on the amount and quality of Kentucky tobacco he was able to acquire. At ten Spanish silver dollars per hundredweight, the ten 1,000-pound casks and six barrels, amounting to six and a half tons of choice Kentucky leaf, would fetch $1,300, a small fortune at the time.

Moving the cargo required stevedores' skills with block and tackle, dexterity, and strength. Selection for such a task could be viewed as a privilege for the enslaved, insofar as coming into town to perform work on the levee afforded plantation-based slaves brief but valued opportunities to mingle with other African Americans who lived and labored in town. The Forman slaves might also have been eager to greet the affable Samuel S., whom most knew from days back in New Jersey, on his safe arrival.

Samuel S. bid farewell to his traveling companions and fellow flatboat captains while his hired boatmen took their wages and sought ways to return to the United States. Returnees could scrounge for new engagements such as poling a keelboat upriver, meager and arduous work. There were more downriver boats than return traffic, since most of the flatboats were broken up for their lumber at their destination. It was far easier work going with the flow rather than upriver, against it. In fact, most boatmen discharged at Natchez made their 400-mile way back north on foot along the Natchez Trace. But, with cash wages in hand and far from anyone's law and order, and ranging north through Choctaw and Chickasaw lands, criminals and highwaymen routinely bedeviled these travelers. As it was, Samuel S. later heard that "the old sailor" Wishant, with whom he had such difficulty, "was found . . . in the woods, dead," possibly a casualty of the foul play victimizing those along the Trace.

Stepping off his flatboat for the last time, we can picture Samuel S. with Cuffey, the cuddly brown pet bear now a few months older and quite a rambunctious beast. The pet bear entered the port of Natchez without registering. But if the creature had arrived in the form of bearskin or demijohns of bear grease, *those* would have been duly noted as commodity imports. Samuel S. registered himself as "intending" to settle in the region.

On recalling his arrival in Natchez decades later, Samuel S. Forman claimed he never asserted a serious intention to settle in Spanish West Florida. Did he state his intention to settle simply to avoid paying the considerable Spanish import tariff? Or perhaps he simply wanted to keep his options open. He would have understood that swearing allegiance to Spain meant renouncing his American citizenship. Perhaps Samuel's equivocal declaration satisfied officials who anticipated the region's charms and promises of worldly success would win him over.

Ezekiel would have been curious to examine the additional items for trade that Samuel S. had acquired on his behalf back in Louisville. One hundred twenty pounds in iron bars might best remain in Natchez to stock a blacksmith's forge, but he would have to decide what to do with the two kegs of lard. The animal skins were already spoken for. The fine lot of pelts—beaver, wildcat, and otter, more valued than deerskins—were bound for a dealer in New Orleans, Philip Nolan, who would find international buyers for the furs. He likely also eyed the timber comprising Samuel S.'s flatboat; that too, could be repurposed, sold to provide the framing for wooden structures in Natchez town or nearby plantations.

As he began surveying his new home, Samuel S. would have been struck by the Spanish officials he met, who were so important to his activities as a sojourner in Natchez. Their language and accents perplexed the ear. Major Carlos Grand Pré, who had greeted them on arrival, sounded exotic to the Americans—a Francophone Swiss long in the Spanish service.

In contrast, Stephen Minor, Governor Gayoso's assistant and protégé, spoke in unexpectedly perfect English, accented with the Formans' own mid-Atlantic American intonation from where Minor hailed as well. This tall fellow with an easy and solicitous manner must have put Samuel S. at ease.

Among the older British colonial land grant holdovers, the Loyalist émigrés who had outrun the American Revolution, and the more recent influx of Americans claiming Spanish land grants, English had become the *lingua franca* of Spanish West Florida. Though English predominated now, Spanish, French, Choctaw, other Native American tongues, and African languages could be encountered at every turn along the dirt lanes of the small town.

Cosmopolitan in its way, with *Luisiana* and its French Creole population part of Spanish territory for almost two decades, along with West Florida since Gálvez's conquest almost a decade before, Iberian Spaniards were in the minority both in numbers and culture. Manuel Gayoso, the Spanish governor of West Florida, depended on small Spanish garrisons, a heterogeneous civil service of multinational origins, and outreach to the Indians to cobble together an effective administration in the service of Spain. Spanish West Florida was a huge buffer province, with ill-defined borderlands that separated the centuries-old Viceroyalty of New Spain from the restive English in Canada, Americans coming over the Alleghenies, and the fiercely independent indigenous peoples in the Southeast.

*

Ezekiel had arrived with his farm supplies and slaves two months earlier on Thursday, April 22, under more urgent circumstances than his cousin and his flatboats. Having narrowly escaped the decoy-led Indian raid on the Lower Ohio River, Ezekiel set about several immediate tasks as soon as he had set foot in Natchez.

First and foremost, he needed to present Gardoqui's land grant certificate, the most important single document entrusted to him by his brother General David Forman. Ezekiel also presented a letter of introduction from the well-connected James Wilkinson, which he had obtained during his sojourn at Louisville. Wilkinson's effusive words assured the Spanish of the good intentions of the Forman pioneers, though Wilkinson seemed to speak more of his own values in describing their venture as one dedicated to the "pursuit of wealth & happiness, the great objects of every intelligent being." Further, James Wilkinson effused that Ezekiel, having moved "his family & fortune from the United States to His Catholic Majesty's dominions on the Mississippi," demonstrates "a decided preference for your bounty & your [Spanish] Government. This circumstance gives Mr. Forman a more than common title to your patronage."

Once ashore, overseer Benajah Osman, who also declared his intention to settle and seek his future in Natchez, may have directed the dismantling of the seventy-foot flatboat. The rough-cut lumber would have been stacked and made ready to transport to their land grant, as soon as Ezekiel and the Spanish determined where that would be. The more substantial keelboat, on which the Forman family and the ten house slaves had lived, was probably sold to someone contemplating the arduous trip upriver. Meanwhile, the Forman party's people, animals, provisions, household goods, farm implements, and carriage needed shelter from the frequent spring afternoon downpours of the Delta.

The two month's separation between the arrivals of Samuel S. and Ezekiel had created an advantage of sorts. Samuel S. was welcomed by his own family members and retainers and could get right down to business. Nevertheless, for the entire Forman enterprise, the process of acclimating to this strange and alluring new land was just beginning.

CHAPTER 12

High-Stakes Ball Game, 1790

THE SOUTHEAST INDIAN TRIBES, DESPITE EFFECTIVE LEADERS LIKE THE
Chickasaw's Chief Piomingo, Choctaw's Pushmataha, and Creeks'
McGillivray, did not throw in their lot with Little Turtle and his allies.
Piomingo and his band of Chickasaw had already distinguished them-
selves by fighting as American allies *against* the Northwest Indian Fed-
eration during St. Clair's disastrous campaign of 1791.

Nor did the Creeks and their many component Muscogee tribes need
the eloquence of the Northwest Indian Federation emissaries to advocate
for pan-Indian resistance to the settler encroachments. Chief McGillivray
already aspired to Indian autonomy over traditional Creek lands. For him,
the best path was not pursuing a guerrilla war of terror against encroaching soldiers and settler families, but rather playing off one colonial power
against another to curry the Creeks' favor.

In 1790 McGillivray accepted an invitation to Philadelphia and met
with George Washington. The president offered to guarantee Creek territory within the United States, made the chief a colonel in the American Army, and granted him an annual cash stipend. With troubles in the
Northwest, Washington had no interest in offending the Creeks in the
Southeast.

The chief likely felt that if the Spanish later attempted a similar
approach to gain peace and favor with the Creeks, and offered larger emol-
uments, so much the better. Why not accept money and gifts from both?
Chief McGillivray's brand of Indian resistance, armed with modern guns
gained through the deerskin trade, and aided by deft diplomacy and negotiations, could make him and the Creeks sovereigns of the southeast interior.

Between the traditional Muscogee bandana set off by tufted feathers over his ears and the glint of a British officer's silver gorget, Alexander McGillivray cut a charismatic figure. His life experiences straddled the native and Anglo-American worlds. His manifest capabilities and presence rendered his ambitions plausible to many Indians and Caucasians.

McGillivray's Native American dress was in part theatrics intended for his own people. By ancestry he was three-quarters Caucasian, the child of a mixed-race Creek beauty, who was herself the daughter of a French colonial officer assigned to a frontier fort and a Creek mother. And while multiracial children were generally spurned by white settlers, Caucasian captives of the Indians, like William Wells, could acculturate to their new families yet still be pursued and invited by their birth families to reintegrate into the settler world.

Alexander McGillivray's childhood experiences were different from most. His British colonial father fully acknowledged the boy as part of the family and endorsed his education in both colonial and native societies. When the young man's father, a Loyalist, returned to England after the War, McGillivray retreated to his mother's Muscogee Creek people in the Indian backcounty.

By 1783 he had distinguished himself as a charismatic leader. He sought to unify diverse Muscogeans' actions and consolidate the political power of their tribal councils under him. In 1790 the Creeks numbered 20,000 across 50 towns. Tribal and clan affiliations distributed political power and decision-making. McGillivray's brand of a more centralized polity was unprecedented.

The Muscogeans' chief maintained a lifestyle quite unlike that of his Creek maternal uncles. He lived in a gabled house modeled after Georgian mansions in England and owned Black chattel slaves who toiled on his private plantation and served him at the dining table. His polygamous marriages, though, placed him more in line with traditional Muscogee Creek practices.

The Creeks now had to deal with an assertive Spain, successor to the English in West Florida. Forts now flew the Spanish flag at Pensacola on the Gulf, and Natchez in the mid-Mississippi Delta. Chief McGillivray—like Little Turtle, Buckongahelas, and Blue Jacket—was not about to play the passive pawn to the European and growing American designs on his traditional lands.

*

McGillivray's ambitions for the Creeks pressed against disputes with their native rivals along the Mississippi, the Chickasaw and Choctaw. Such disagreements were real and militated against what the Creek chief worked to achieve among his people. And for the rivals, defense of their own hunting and trapping rights was foremost. Luxurious, thick and silky-smooth beaver pelts commanded especially high prices. Indians eagerly exchanged them at the Pensacola trading post for imported guns, powder, shot, blankets, fabric, knives, and other desirable imports.

So when a territorial dispute between Creeks and Choctaw broke out, quarreling chiefs determined to settle their disagreement peaceably. They were following a practice common to Eastern Woodlands Indians ranging as far north as the Iroquois Six Nations, pitting their best athletes against one another in a competitive stick ball game. The game would determine which nation laid claim to hunting rights at the beaver pond.

No white traders or settlers were present for what became known as the 1790 Noxubee River ball game, be they Spanish, American, English, or French. Details of what transpired were related years after the fact by an aged native observer.

The Choctaw proposed the contest. As challengers, they selected and prepared the field. The date was set on a new moon to be three full moons hence. Preparations extended for weeks. Indians not directly involved in the dispute, on hearing of the game, came long distances to witness the spectacle. The assembly, including players, Choctaw and Creek villagers of all ages and both sexes, and Indian visitors, numbered in the thousands.

Players on both sides sported loincloths, colorful individual adornments, and silver trade trinkets. The scant clothing, set off by ornamentation and body paint, flaunted chiseled native bodies together with colors and traditional designs distinctive of their nations, towns, and clans. Choctaw athletes, for instance, could be distinguished by their collars and mock tails fashioned from colorfully dyed and flowing horsehair.

Ball Play of the Choctaw, by George Caitlin circa 1846, courtesy of the Smithsonian American Art Museum.

Onlookers would have dressed for the occasion too. Though far inland from Natchez, Pensacola, and the settlers' towns, some Choctaw women would have shown off long woven cloth dresses in the European manner, adapted with distinctive rickrack designs and aprons and highlighted by applied geometric borders.

Southeastern tribes maintained long traditions of wagering on the games. Individuals bet their private property in individually negotiated deals, made during a set hour prior to commencement of play. Some have asserted that items of barter in a wager could include intimate time with one's wife, or the bettor's own indentured labor. As game day approached, "ponies loaded with skins, furs, trinkets, and every other imaginable thing that was part and parcel of Indian wealth . . ." could be observed to converge from every direction of the compass. The wagered physical items were set aside in an area specifically for the purpose. Losers were expected to surrender their goods without so much as a murmur. If these involved land and hunting rights, the winning side promptly assumed their geographic prize.

Essential implements of the game for each player were two identical *kapucha* sticks, six to ten feet long, fashioned from strong, smoothed, and polished hickory wood. Each long stick was bent back on itself forming a palm-sized hoop at the far end, and lashed together into a single long arm, which the athletes wielded. Sinews were tied across the hoop, forming a small cup. Holding a stick in each hand, the players caught, carried, and launched the ball—called a *toli*—from one of the cups toward goalposts, much as in modern American football. Even more accurately, the game could be viewed as the untamed predecessor of modern lacrosse.

On the morning of the game, the opposing teams would have marched forth from their encampments in the surrounding forest. To the pounding and rhythmic accompaniment of ceremonial drums, the scene unfolded with as much circumspection and hushed seriousness as if the athletes were departing for war. In fact, a synonym for the contest is "Little Brother of War."

As the Choctaw and Creek drummers each beat out their distinctive cadences, echoing from distant hillocks, the columns neared one another from the sidelines. The discordant cacophony must have heightened anticipation.

The athletes entered the field, and some split off from their columns to assume positions arranged in advance. Contestants' agility and strength had been honed by years of hunting, athletic competition, and occasional raids and warfare against neighboring tribes or settler encroachers. The ball game exalted individual prowess, rather than an elaborate cooperative offensive. The players most confident in their ability to intercept the ball congregated near their own team's goalposts, the better to defend them. Those capable of flinging the ball as accurately as a spear congregated near their opponents' goals. Those fleet on their feet and confident of catching the opening ball toss in their cups marched straight for the center of the field. The player who could move the ball downfield and project it between the opposing team's goalposts scored a point.

Other aspects of play were never enunciated and regularly sparked hot disputes during the game. While weapons were not permitted on the field, rough handling, wrestling between opponents, fisticuffs, bone-breaking tackles, kicking, pushing, and the like were frowned upon but not forbidden. The dense hickory *kapucha* sticks doubled as formidable clubs.

The rule was that there were no rules regarding bodily contact between players. A broad and forceful arc of the long pitch, a catch on the run, and attempts at interception, when pursued by dozens of players converging on the ball, practically guaranteed collisions. Injuries of varying severity were inflicted at every turn, both accidentally and deliberately. The Indian ball game was indeed a full contact sport.

Spectators closely followed the game's twists and turns, always focusing on the ball, and running toward the action to get a better look. This might well have involved the intermingling of Choctaw and Creeks. Disputes triggered by ballfield antics, injuries, or taunts could easily degenerate into insults, verbal disputes, and physical abuse. Linguistic differences exacerbated friction. Anxious anticipation of the next controversial play could goad aroused fans to the brink of mayhem.

By all accounts the players on this day were equally matched in skill and stamina. The names of the athletes and their ballfield feats are lost in the clouds of time and memory. But the game itself was recollected as hard fought, the outcome in doubt from beginning to end.

First one team, then the other, took a narrow lead, as the game continued hour after hour. There were no time-outs, fouls, or timed quarters or innings. Play proceeded continuously until one team's player flung the *toli* to the goalposts for the score. The exultant player and his friends would call out *illi tok*, meaning "one down, and one less to win." Others might utter a turkey hunting call in triumph and derision. The two medicine men from the opposing tribes officiated as best they could by whipping opposing players who wrestled with their counterparts on the field.

After four hours of sweat-drenched play, a Creek scored the winning goal. He immediately faced a barrage of complaints from the vanquished Choctaw, answered by the exuberance of the winning team and its onlookers.

Insults and altercations broke out as the Choctaw and Creek mingled into the evening hours, and the victors came to claim their winnings. One such interaction resulted in blows and the drawing of blood. A Choctaw is said to have flung a taunt, only to be denigrated by one of the most offensive provocations among Indians. The Creek athlete grabbed a nearby woman's petticoat, perhaps from among the pile of wagered items, and flung it at the feet of the Choctaw. Despite the matrilineal nature of Creek society, any implication that an athlete or warrior deserved to be clothed as a woman constituted a most demeaning public insult.

In the waning daylight it was hard to discern who struck first. The disputants and onlookers promptly produced fists, knives, bows and arrows, and tomahawks. Matching mutual contempt with physical force, mayhem quickly spread throughout the camps. Warriors from each tribe "commenced joining in the fight until all were engaged in bloody strife." An orgy of violence proceeded for many hours into the night.

When the elders finally restored order two hours after sunrise, the playing field and surroundings were littered with hundreds—one account asserts 500—dead, including women. Many others from both tribes writhed in agony.

Tribal elders and chiefs united to confer on what to do next. They wisely sought additional advice from village chiefs further afield. A general council mutually decided that, though the Creeks had won the athletic contest, the subsequent slaughter was an affront to the forces of nature and to the sacred nature of the ball game. They agreed that no advantage should be taken by either side of territory or wagered items. Dead athletes would be buried on the spot. They would enter the spirit world in their full regalia, as they had played and witnessed the game. Creek tribesmen withdrew east to their territory, leaving the Noxubee beaver to contend with Choctaw hunters.

*

The great Noxubee River ball game was but one example of the intertribal warfare and rivalries within Spanish West Florida, in the region now comprising Mississippi, Alabama, and western Georgia. Their warlike focus and numbers might better have been channeled into resisting settler encroachments. By reducing the number of warriors available to resist, inter-Indian rivalries in the region indirectly enabled the rapid

Alexander McGillivray (Creek), 1790 sketch by John Trumbull. Fordham University Library, Charles Allen Munn Collection, New York, New York.

influx of new settlers, who brought slave-based plantation agriculture into the Natchez District. While Chief Little Turtle and his allies sprang to resistance to the north, there was no concerted armed native opposition in Spanish West Florida's Mississippi region.

The Northwest Indian Federation continued to terrorize American pioneers, having already twice badly defeated the US Army—at General Hamar's disastrous raid on Kekiongo in 1790 and General St. Clair's defeat at the Wabash River in 1791. So long as the Northwest Indian War raged, George Washington and the fledgling United States could do little to assert sovereignty over the largest part of West Florida, to which Americans felt entitled by the Peace of Paris. Nor could acquisitive adventurers—domestic, foreign, and freebooters—be kept from hatching schemes to profit by, and acquire pieces of, Spanish West Florida, and to exploit American weakness in the Old Southwest.

Creek Chief McGillivray may have envisioned pan-Indian autonomy in the Southeast, but only under his personal leadership. Creek aggression toward other Indian nations resulted in Indians fighting one another at this critical juncture. The fight over the Noxubee River ball game was one especially murderous example of those rivalries. It played out with no Caucasians apparently even aware of its occurrence at the time.

The diplomatic Manuel Gayoso de Lemos, working from his seat at the Natchez District, meanwhile played peace broker among regional native nations. Inter-Indian conflict in the region arguably helped Spain assert itself as an honest broker to achieve peace among them and, not coincidentally, to advance Spanish colonial influence in the region.

In this stew, the Forman plantation enterprise would flourish. In Natchez, as the expatriate-friendly Spanish administration nurtured the slave-based economy, Gayoso maintained the district as a tranquil bubble, while competing forces buffeted the borderlands at the margins. Indians slaughtering one another over ever-diminishing hunting grounds added to long-standing woes. Internecine strife precluded indigenous peoples from asserting themselves more forcefully against the burgeoning settler plantations anchored at Natchez.

CHAPTER 13

Sword and Olive Branch, 1791 to 1793

GEORGE WASHINGTON TOOK HIS CHARGE AS PRESIDENT SERIOUSLY. THE loss of life, instability on the frontiers, and tarnished reputation of American arms added to his woes. The defeats of Generals Harmar and St. Clair affected him deeply. Tests to US sovereignty, and to the viability of the nation, seemed to be coming from every quarter.

Though he personally had invested in western lands, as did many of the founding figures, the actions he would soon take were not as directly self-interested as those of some other prominent leaders. The same could not be said of Arthur St. Clair and Winthrop Sargent, or even his own Secretary of War Henry Knox, each of whom had invested substantially in the Ohio Land Company, and whose interests in taking possession of this territory from the natives exceeded patriotism, romantic visions of agrarian settlement, and the calculus of shrinking the national debt. Chief Little Turtle and his Northwest Indian Federation posed the most immediate threat. Miamis, Delawares, Shawnees, and their allies must be contained, a general Indian rising across the entire western and southern frontiers prevented, and the Indian Federation ultimately defeated. British and Spanish colonial adventurism, in lands ostensibly ceded by the Treaty of Paris, needed to cease. And private adventures in the West, and those of a state like Georgia, needed to be subordinated to federal jurisdiction.

The finances of the United States were inadequate to these tasks. Interest on the national debt, left over from the Revolutionary War, needed to be paid, as well as growing military expenditures for the war in the Northwest.

Revolutionary France wanted the United States to involve itself in its ongoing European wars, including against Spain, as a military ally, and stood ready to interfere directly in American politics to further its interests. The Haitian slave revolt threatened southern slave interests. Geographic isolation from the travails of Europe by the Atlantic Ocean made for rhetorical flair but did not capture reality. Like it or not, the United States was involved in international trade and shared numerous interdependencies with European colonial powers. Meanwhile, its population at home grew restive. They feared continuing Indian depredations, were disgusted with an army demonstrably incapable of defending itself, and chafed at a federal government keen on taxing them in novel ways.

Nor was the situation complementary with Washington's view of himself as a military leader. In important ways he emulated the Roman General Fabius, who lost most battles against the sophisticated army led by the legendary Hannibal. However, oftentimes Fabius fell back from the fray, avoiding battlefields but keeping his forces intact. So too had Washington lost more frequently than he won in battlefield contests during the Revolutionary War against experienced British generals and well-supplied opposing armies. As Americans, we celebrate Washington's great tactical victories at Trenton and Yorktown. But the list of lost battles where he personally commanded and lost is longer—Harlem Heights, Kipps Bay, Brandywine, and Germantown among them. Washington had cooperated with unlikely allies—monarchical France and Spain. He had outmaneuvered and outlasted domestic naysayers. But now he faced a new set of challenges, most stemming from the unfinished business of the Revolution.

So, Washington summoned General "Mad Anthony" Wayne from retirement to lead a revitalized army. Wayne was one of those individuals who excel in military feats and leadership, but struggle with bad personal habits that served him poorly in civilian life. Alternate explanations explained his "mad" moniker. One credited his impetuous and successful exploits during the Revolutionary War, including the audacious capture of British fortifications at Stony Point on the Hudson River in 1779. Others praised his "mad" ability to hone young unruly soldiers into a disciplined fighting force.

A Pennsylvania farmer before the war, Wayne had tried to return to that vocation after hostilities ceased. But fondness for strong drink and women probably contributed to troubles at his farm north of Philadelphia. He fared no better at a Georgia plantation, nor at running for Congress. Elected as a Georgia representative, campaign irregularities promptly disqualified him. Purportedly, he had run for office as a way of eluding his debts.

James Wilkinson wanted to lead the Western Army. Instead, Washington appointed him as second-in-command. Gladhanding but disloyal Wilkinson, then ensconced in Kentucky as a leading advocate of separation from Virginia, was a surprising choice. Washington and Knox could have scrutinized a résumé pockmarked by scandalous intrigues. Those included Wilkinson's involvement in the Conway Cabal, which had sought to replace Washington as commander-in-chief with Horatio Gates during the Revolutionary War; a falling out with Gates that led to a ludicrous pistol duel; and a controversial army stint as a supply officer. More recently, some suspected Wilkinson of promoting more than Kentucky's separation from Virginia. Why stop there? Why not an independent Kentucky run for the benefit of himself and his cronies?

By putting his trust in Wayne to lead the resurgent army, Washington knew that he would single-mindedly address the enormous challenge that he faced. Although Wayne had been accustomed to shortages of all kinds plaguing the Americans during the Revolutionary War, he still managed successes. If such shortages were to recur, with logistics stretched and supply lines unreliable from East Coast contractors through a forbidding and hostile country, Wayne would somehow find a way.

Wayne specified every aspect of his new Legion of the United States. It would consist of four sub-legions, each containing light infantry, riflemen, cavalry, and field artillery. He would drill his soldiers arduously not to be intimidated by Indian guerrilla surprise tactics—so arduously that his troops were said to be more afraid of him than of the Indians.

Going on the offensive into the Ohio Territory, he commanded that staging forts be erected in clearings far from forest cover, and built stoutly. They featured blockhouses, palisades, and lookout perches. His choice of names and some of the organizational structures echoed Roman antiquity and were meant to inspire citizen soldiers. He was particularly drawn to Lucius Quinctius Cincinnatus, the Roman general called out of retirement to mobilize and lead a highly effective army against Rome's invaders. The tale may have resonated with Anthony Wayne's conception of the moment. He moved the headquarters of the Western Army from Fort Pitt to Fort Washington, and formally renamed the surrounding frontier settlement Cincinnati.

Wayne added technological innovation to his strategies and tactics. He ordered infantry muskets to have their touch holes widened and their cartridges filled with an especially fine-grained gunpowder. While this was less accurate, his musketeers could reload faster, increase their firepower, and let more lead fly at the enemy at short range. Riflemen would also be equipped with a collapsible defensive spear, the better to keep Indians at bay during the vulnerable times when the flintlock rifles required careful reloading.

He improved intelligence gathering by enlisting an unlikely spy. Following St. Clair's November 1791 defeat, where the Wells brothers had fought on opposing sides, William Well's white birth brother had succeeded in making contact with his little brother, now Little Turtle's son-in-law. Appealing to filial ties and emphasizing the Americans' inexorably recovering strength, he persuaded William to become a double agent on behalf of General Wayne and the Americans. Wayne's success at tracking and anticipating enemy movements led the Indians to name him "Black Snake," on account of his uncanny awareness of his surroundings. Wayne's troops could not be effectively surprised in the field, as were General Harmar's and St. Clair's.

*

Washington ordered that peace overtures be made to the Indian Federation in parallel with military preparations. He strengthened ties with friendlier Indians to prevent unrest from spreading. It became a common if exotic sight to observe tribal delegations in the capital, going to and from meetings with ranking cabinet officials and the president himself. He participated in the dignities and ceremonies of Indian diplomacy, involving handling wampum belts and listening attentively to formal speeches delivered through interpreters. Only the yellow fever epidemic that afflicted Philadelphia in 1793 interrupted the steady stream of visiting native delegations.

He further directed Henry Knox to address specific nations' concerns. With respect to the integrity of Indian lands, Native Americans who were allies or neutral to the United States indirectly benefited by Little Turtle's resistance. This is because American military weakness in the embattled Northwest generally encouraged George Washington and federal leaders to mollify visiting Indian leaders from other regions and to grant their requests.

The Seneca and Chickasaw, consistent America allies, were among the delegations who visited Philadelphia during these years. Other visitors included chiefs whose peoples had struggled against the Americans during the Revolutionary War, like the Iroquois Chief Brandt and Upper Creek Chief McGillivray. Skillful diplomacy, and implied competition from English and Spanish colonial interests, provided Indian diplomats opportunities to gain guarantees limiting previous land cessions, gaining gifts for their tribes, and sidestepping any new demands.

Although the discussions involved fundamental differences in worldview and the use of disputed Native American lands, George Washington's decorum, stateliness, and respect for the visitors never failed to impress. Chief Piomingo of the Chickasaw treasured his interactions with Washington and they are celebrated in tribal lore to this day. But other courted leaders, like the Iroquois Chief Brandt, remained effectively neutral. Muscogee Creek Chief Alexander McGillivray accepted American favors but remained open to later and better Spanish offers.

Still, Washington's intercessions, as well as intertribal and international dynamics quite out of American control, conspired to prevent an outright Indian conflagration across the entire northern, western, and southern borderlands.

*

Washington invited northwest Indian tribes to a treaty conference at Sandusky, Ohio, in 1793. Unsurprisingly, both sides could not find common ground. The most militant among the Federation's tribal leaders, flush with victories over Harmar and St. Clair, felt little incentive to accede to American terms. Meanwhile General Wayne welcomed additional time to whip his Legion of the United States into a formidable fighting force. Unlike the ill-considered orders from Henry Knox in 1790 and 1791 to Harmar and St. Clair to move against the Indians despite the lateness of the campaign season, Washington allowed Anthony Wayne to determine his own timetable.

The final Indian offer at Sandusky was made to the American commissioners after two weeks of mutually frustrating talks. Instead of waging a costly war in blood and treasure, they proposed the Americans buy off their own settlers and leave in "peaceable possession" the Northwest Indian Federation and their lands. Chief Brandt of the Iroquois subscribed to this more aggressive stance, but Chief Little Turtle, his scouts in the field busy observing Wayne's meticulous preparations, and possibly gaining insights into the Americans' determination through his son-in-law William Wells, advocated for moderation. Little Turtle nonetheless went with the consensus of allied Federation leaders, which was the militant stance.

To no one's surprise, the Americans dismissed the proposal out of hand. The Moravian missionary John Heckewelder, who was present at the negotiations, generally had the confidence of both sides. He judged the Indians' stance "impertinent and insolent." The "treaty business" ended promptly.

General Wayne was soon at work deploying his forces northward from Cincinnati to the rebuilt fort sites along the military road, cut earlier during St. Clair's campaign. Symbolically, he ordered the most advanced fort to be built directly on the battlefield where the Indians had routed St. Clair's forces in 1791. He christened it Fort Recovery. With it, a cacophony of drums, bugles, practice live gun firing, construction of new buildings and battlements, and clattering cavalry patrols rang through the Ohio wilderness. And if Miami, Shawnee, and Delaware scouts were observing and reporting back to their leaders about their formidable foe, so much the better.

Meanwhile, the fruitless treaty discussions at Sandusky ran their course. Likely remembering St. Clair's ill-fated autumn campaign start,

Wayne decided to go into garrison duty rather than to attack the Indian Federation during the unpredictable 1793–94 Ohio winter. More time in garrison meant still more drill and preparation for General Anthony Wayne's Legion of the United States.

*

Native Americans with grievances were not the only ones to challenge federal authority in the trans-Allegheny West. A new revenue measure, passed by Congress and signed into law in 1791, placed a federal excise tax on distilled spirits. It was the first-ever internal tax by either the Confederation or new federal constitutional government.

The new tax rankled western settlers. Whiskey had become the region's favored product. Much of the economy rested on the production, barter, sale, and imbibing of whiskey distilled from the bounty of recently cleared fields. A large part of harvested surplus "amber waves of grain"—rye, barley, wheat, and corn—went into the local production of the distilled spirit.

Whisky could be transported east for profitable sale, while within the West, a barter economy prevailed. Hard cash was scarce. The spiritous brew was used as currency to pay workers and, as was the case with Samuel S. Forman when he set up shops briefly when passing through Pittsburgh and Louisville, accepted readily in barter by traders.

The excise tax on whiskey thus irritated western settlers in distinct and grating ways. The tax was to be collected locally by newly appointed revenue collectors, right at the production still. Small producers along the frontiers were at an immediate disadvantage compared to their bigger eastern competitors, who did not bear westerners' additional cost of hauling the whiskey from an often great distance to market. Adding to the slight, westerners accustomed to taking wages in whiskey regarded the excise as a tax on income. Those sending their whiskey downriver would be double taxed—once by the new federal excise and again by Spanish import duties collected at Natchez or New Orleans.

Though dislike of the new tax was widespread, resistance assumed an especially pugnacious tone in Western Pennsylvania. Protestors, most of whom were Revolutionary War veterans, applied the rhetoric of popular sovereignty to subvert the tax collectors. So-called Whiskey Rebels convened meetings, signed petitions, and mobilized militias to oppose arriving federal tax collectors. Authorities in Philadelphia reduced the tax by a penny a gallon, but that was not enough to placate angry protesters. All of this would stoke an already incendiary situation in the Ohio Territory—even as General Wayne positioned his drilled and ready contingents to defend embattled settlers stationed along America's frontier.

CHAPTER 14

A Year in Spanish West Florida, 1791

EZEKIEL FOUND NATCHEZ A DISTRICT OF CONTRASTS. THE TOWN WAS quite small, but it bustled with activity. There was a gaggle of wooden buildings readily flooded by the great river coexisting with dignified two-story residences and a Spanish fort on the heights. The upper town commanded a magnificent view up the breeze-swept Mississippi. Still, most of the inhabitants lived and worked on plantations in the suburbs of the town and for miles inland.

The indistinct borders of the entire Natchez District, at least by Spanish reckoning, ranged to the north beyond Vicksburg all the way upriver to Chickasaw Bluffs at Memphis, east into Choctaw and Creek Indian Country toward the Americans' far-distant Georgia, and south toward Baton Rouge and the more ethnically French portions of Spain's *Luisiana*. The Indians, Americans, English far to the north, and even the French might have harbored different notions of the extent of West Florida and of Spanish influence east of the Mississippi River. No one, however, openly doubted Spanish dominion in *Luisiana*, and its expansive territory on the far side of the Mississippi River from New Orleans to the Gulf of Mexico. From this wide expanse, Ezekiel was most eager to claim a specific attractive delta tract for himself and his family, where he could put his African Americans to work.

The region's population had almost doubled since the most recent census. Now at about 4,000, whites were still a slim majority, since the eponymous Natchez Indians had been practically eradicated by the French decades before. And the Forman immigrant pioneer party, with its sixty Blacks, had raised the entire population of the Natchez District by several percentage points on arrival. Ezekiel's group was precisely the kind of set-tlers the Spanish sought to turn their new territory into a vital, productive borderland and bulwark for the ancient Viceroyalty of New Spain. Gover-nor Manuel Gayoso de Lemos thought in just those strategic terms.

While Ezekiel Forman searched for land on which to plant his first crop, he rented a large house halfway up the steep hill between the upper and lower towns as a temporary base of operations. He had a keen eye and observed at the wharf that "the New England people" who had made up one of the boats in Ezekiel's downriver convoy, "sold their flour here at five & a half dollars, six to nine reales. Superfine [flour] at [New] Orleans, beef, pork, corn, etc. in proportion." Such real-time insights were invalu-able in discerning opportunities to cut arbitrage deals in upriver country commodities imported to Spanish cash markets, and in deciding on how best to develop his future plantation.

Within a week of Samuel S.'s arrival, Ezekiel increased his cash and credit on hand by selling off fifty dollars in goods to Natchez resident Charles King. He held in reserve as well thousands of dollars in letters of credit from General David Forman, for potential large purchases of land and farm animals. With the prompt acquisition of free Spanish land, judi-cious use of farm tools, labor, and livestock imported on the pioneer boats, and planting a large tobacco crop, Ezekiel hoped to create his plantation with a minimal use of hard money and credit.

He bought outright 500 acres along St. Catherine's Creek, about five miles from town, a move he regarded as "temporary" until "he could become better acquainted with the country." He immediately set Benajah Osman to organize the African American men into work gangs, some tasked to enlarge and build dwellings, the others to clear land for planting.

The workers also built a commodious log cabin for the short term that featured a pleasant dining and reception hall, foreshadowing Eze-kiel's aspiration to live like a country squire. Samuel S. described it as making "a good and comfortable appearance."

As lumber was scarce, flatboat timbers may well have found their way into the framing of the cabin. Osman and the enslaved workers had brought saws and carpenter's tools on the long trek. They probably con-gratulated themselves on their foresight and good fortune in arriving with their cache of tools and farm implements intact. Save for the purchase of a strong ox team or two, the settlers were virtually self-sufficient, fully capable of rapidly establishing a plantation.

In addition to tools and provisions, the Formans brought with them large and experienced agrarian and household workforces. Reinforced by the shared experience of their epic trek and decades of previous association with the Forman family, the group was primed for the tasks ahead. Familiar ties, mutuality, and perhaps affection among some, bound the masters, overseer, and the enslaved into a well-oiled machine that succeeded in producing cash crops for market in just one season. If the cycle could be repeated on new, generous Spanish grants and purchases of prime land, the owners could practically count in advance the bags of Spanish silver dollars to be made.

*

While the Forman family house was taking shape, the enslaved workers built their own shacks in a cluster along the banks of St. Catherine's Creek. Likely also built with recycled flatboat timber, the shacks were "in range" of the big house, but still "some distance off" and "made quite a pretty street." Their shacks also included little plots for whatever they could grow for themselves to supplement their allotted staple food rations of corn meal, leftovers from the main house, and the unmarketable pork and beef by-products of cattle raising.

Mississippi land was so fertile that the African Americans' garden plots, typically tended on Sunday Sabbath, were capable of enriching the slaves' diets with varied greens and vegetables. Masters usually looked the other way when some enterprising slaves found opportunities to sell or swap a surplus in Natchez.

Osman continued his role as overseer, much as he had done for General David Forman back on the Monmouth plantation. Samuel S. recalled Benajah's approach to directing "his" laborers as particularly mild. He "was a kind-hearted man and used them well" while sharing the owners' self-congratulatory views on the treatment of their enslaved African Americans as "well fed, well clothed, well housed, each family living separately, and . . . treated with kindness." Certainly, *[t]hey had ocular proof of their happy situation when compared with their neighbor's servants. It was the custom of the country to exchange work at times; and, one day, one of our men came to me, and said: "I don't think it is right to exchange work with these planters; for I can, with ease, do more work than any two of their men;" and added, "their men pound their corn overnight for their next day's supply, and they are too weak to work." Poor fellows, corn was all they had to eat.*

No information is known concerning how the "two disaffected fellows," who found allies in Western Pennsylvania for an abortive slave revolt, had fared here. Were they sold downriver to the draconian sugar cane plantations, or did they become inured to slavery on the Forman plantation, deferring their dreams of freedom for future generations to realize? Perhaps they succumbed during the first years of settlement to the rampant fevers that so decimated unacclimated white settlers, though surviving evidence documents no African American deaths in the early years of settlement. Margaret Forman's companion and manager of the household Elizabeth Church, for example, "was taken with a fever, and died in a few days." Her role seems to have been taken over by an enslaved servant—perhaps Ginnie. We do know, by way of General David Forman's close and continuing interest in "his" property, and Samuel S.'s detailed travel journal, that the "two disaffected fellows" had safely completed the trip to Natchez with the rest.

Forman plantation slaves were never implicated in the regional slave revolts of later years, advertised as runaways, or involved in any recorded resistance or proscribed activities. Ezekiel Forman owned a few irons and whips, but these seemed to have remained in storage; the enslaved needed no more than "chains of the mind"—limited expectations, dependency in a strange land, family bonds, and perhaps a charming overseer's manner—to keep them in thrall. Outrageous abuses often recorded in antebellum escaped slave narratives, such as forced separation of families, lynchings, whippings, starvation rations, and rape, appear not to have been in the Formans' playbook as plantation masters.

*

Samuel S. learned of the American Army's defeats in the Ohio Territory and of continued Indian Confederation attacks on settlers. "I think it was in the autumn of 1790 that General Harmar was defeated by the Indians, and most of these brave officers [he had met at Cincinnati] were killed." But some news coming to Natchez was wildly inaccurate. Samuel S. heard that "Harmar's defeat caused a French settlement [Gallipolis, downriver from Marietta] . . . to be broken up." The Indians had indeed attacked Gallipolis, killing some, but did not destroy it. The French settler colony, which by then included Dr. Saugrain as a leading citizen, survived, even if it did not thrive.

Meanwhile, as Osman and the enslaved were establishing the plantation, clearing land, and sowing the initial tobacco crop, Samuel S. made the rounds of Natchez society. He traveled most often in the company of Ezekiel. Margaret and her children came along on the more purely social calls.

The Forman carriage, now ingeniously refitted, must have made quite an impression on neighboring plantation owners, who were wont to outdo one another in acquiring and showing off prestigious goods. An early Natchez resident recalled the first carriage as a "very gorgeous affair" that was "painted yellow and had flaming red curtains"; people in fact "gazed at it with as much curiosity as though it had been a comet." At that time the bridle paths passing for roads were not wide enough for such elegant conveyances. Prior to a visit, hosts would make sure that "the cane-brakes along the trail [were] cleared away sufficient to permit the comfortable passage of the carriage." Most often it was simply more convenient for plantation families to get around on horseback.

The planters were remarkably hospitable to one another. Samuel S. recalled attending a "frolick" several miles distant from Ezekiel's country seat and, as there were no taverns as yet in the district, he "put up at the first house he came to." Here his horse feasted on "pumpkins and as much corn as you wish" and Samuel S. was treated as one of the family.

Social relations, not to mention good business, demanded that interactions with the gentlemanly and genial Governor Manuel Gayoso and his staff be cordial. A recent widower, the Spanish native grew up in a well-connected family on a consular assignment in Oporto, Portugal, a region known for its sunny outlook, fine wines and food, and international perspective. Though educated in London, Gayoso never strayed from loyalty to the Spanish monarchy. He served competently in an army regiment prior to being groomed for service in Spain's newest North American province—West Florida.

His practical leadership talents and personal magnetism make it difficult to imagine a man better suited to represent his country in this fraught borderland. In fact, Spain assigned some of their best leaders and administrators during this time period to *Luisiana* and West Florida. This reality defies the popular misperception of sinecures and incompetents fatally hobbling the centuries-old Western Hemisphere Spanish Empire. In fact, Gayoso and Bernardo de Gálvez were among the most resourceful, able, and culturally sensitive Spanish colonial officials ever to serve in North America.

Gayoso had a reputation "rare among Spanish officials for never having used his office for personal gain." He was warm and engaging, possessed a wide-ranging intellect, and displayed genuine curiosity and interest in people. He spoke and read Spanish, English, and French with equal ease. He shared the concerns of his subjects, including siting and building a plantation for himself, all of which uniquely reflected his aspirations for peace and cooperation in the region.

Samuel S. and others might wonder what such an urbane individual was doing there on the northeast edge of the Spanish dominions. If they did, they kept those speculations to themselves. Most were appreciative of Gayoso's personal qualities, support of liberal land grants, and mild administration.

Unlike the Viceroyalty of New Spain anchored in the capital at Mexico City, there was no Inquisition in *Luisiana* and Spanish West Florida. Gayoso wholeheartedly supported the official pronouncements of tolerance, both for the practical aspect of attracting American Protestant immigrants, and the fact that the policy seemed to embody his true nature. So long as the de facto religion of the district was settlement and cash crops, the religious schisms that had fueled bloody European wars for hundreds of years would be glossed over in Gayoso's eclectic Natchez.

He extended a warm, standing invitation to the Formans. "Governor Gayoso told us, after we moved out to St. Catherine [Creek], that there would always be a plate for us" at his Concord Plantation table—a mini-palace evoking the customs of Bourbon Spanish royalty—and at the Spanish Government House in town.

The name Concord captured Gayoso's aspiration for a peaceful and prosperous region of the Spanish borderlands. This grand residence, with its dual semicircular staircases of imported white marble, seemed to challenge his most prosperous residents to put still more land under cultivation, and, with their bounty, attempt to outdo Concord's beauty and ostentation. That would serve Spanish interests handsomely. The expatriate American landowning immigrants would view Spain as the source of liberal land grants, access to world markets, and luxury goods through New Orleans; and in short, the font and guarantor of their wealth and safety.

Samuel S. recalled his "family was much visited by the [district's] Spanish officers, who were very genteel men." Stephen Minor, the Pennsylvania-born Spanish official, who surprised and pleased the new immigrants with a commonality of language, regional background, and mutually extended hospitalities, was one such favorite. A widower, his second marriage to Martha Ellis, daughter of a wealthy planter, must have been a high point of the year's social season. John Ellis's White Cliffs plantation dated back to an English land grant. Ellis and many in the Forman's new circle had "large families, sons and daughters, very genteel and accomplished." When not in Natchez or New Orleans for business, shopping, and diversion, these elite family members resided on plantations within a dozen or so miles from the Forman plantation on St. Catherine's Creek.

Given the crude state of the roads and the fast-growing canebrake, calling on a neighbor by coach could take up an entire day or longer. Mixed-sex sleepovers were common. Samuel S. explained to friends back home that all proceeded "with the greatest circumspection and decorum. The extreme hospitality of the Southerners and the difficulty of travelling made it excusable." He recalled one ball where the guests stayed over, sleeping right in the dining room. The following morning, refreshments were presented and "irregular dancing kept up till noon."

Many of the Formans' new friends and acquaintances had been British Loyalists. They variously had immigrated to the Natchez District on English land grants early in the 1770s or fled the rebellious colonies during the war. Any lingering hostilities between former Loyalists and Patriots were hardly discernible in the Natchez social whirl and growing plantation economy. Under Manuel Gayoso and the Bourbon Spanish dominion contentious issues were glossed over and borderland controversies were kept at a distance. The eclectic oligarchy of Natchez planters wore the mantles of national allegiance and religion lightly, while taking seriously the acquisition of land, slaves, and conspicuous wealth.

William Dunbar was an Anglo-British holdover who thrived regardless of regime. Having immigrated to North America from Scotland with a load of goods to trade with the Indians, he had made the same demanding overland trip to Fort Pitt and then downriver to Natchez almost twenty years prior to the Formans.

Dunbar's first years as a planter were clouded by recently acquired Jamaican Black slaves igniting an incipient revolt. One captive committed suicide by drowning after capture, rather than facing discipline and a return to a life of toil. Dunbar sufficiently modified his approach over the years so that his growing slave-based plantations were never again the scene of armed resistance or multiple runaways. He also became a devoted and widely respected scientific botanist and surveyor who maintained like-minded correspondents in Europe and, eventually, the emerging United States. The Spaniards appointed him district surveyor, a critical post in a region whose economy depended on government land grants and the establishment and sale of privately owned plantations. Thus, Dunbar and his family were a part of the West Florida planter elite anchored at Natchez.

Also among the elite families were the neighboring Monsantos, who Samuel S. fondly recalled visiting at their 500-acre plantation along St. Catherine's Creek. Benjamin and Clara Monsanto "were the most kind and hospitable of people." No one seemed to care that they acknowledged, though did not practice, Judaism, which by a literal reading of the Spanish *Code Noir* was forbidden. The Monsantos' patriarch had in fact been forced to flee New Orleans for a time under an early Spanish colonial governor or face persecution under the Inquisition. King Carlos III's royal edict, however, inviting immigration into the Spanish West Florida

Natchez District and *Luisiana* signaled a more tolerant stance, and may have permitted the Monsantos and even Protestants, for whom the same strictures applied, to acknowledge their faith.

Emerging Southern Delta manners never failed to amuse Samuel S., whose jocular manner led most he met to invite him to join in. However, neither he nor the other Formans were privy to the entire social scene. Prominent plantation families numbered in the dozens among the district's Caucasian population of 1,100. Included was twenty-two-year-old Andrew Jackson, the future president, who had come in 1789, building a cabin north of town at Bruinsburgh, Bayou Pierre. Jackson traded in wine and "sundries" sent from his business associate in Nashville. Those sundries included enslaved Blacks imported into Spanish West Florida from Nashville. Establishing himself in the Natchez District, Jackson befriended and partnered with Thomas Marston Green, a scion of the Green plantation clan.

It was there that Jackson was joined by Rachel Donaldson and where the couple married in 1793. Unbeknownst to the newlyweds, her divorce from her previous husband had not yet been finalized. Technically, the marriage was bigamous. When the Jacksons discovered the discrepancy, they rectified the situation by remarrying in an unambiguously American jurisdiction. Such unions were not unusual on the frontier, where government officials and religious leaders were sparse. Later, controversy over the legality of Rachel's divorce and remarriage would embitter the newly elected president. He would forever claim that the merciless hounding his wife endured from his political enemies during the presidential campaign led to his beloved Rachel's death in 1829, just after the election.

*

Not all Samuel S.'s calls were social. Business always came first. He later recalled a successful trip to yet another former New Jerseyman to trade cloth for horses to work on Ezekiel Forman's plantation. After he had been resident in Natchez for some months, his cousin "asked me if I intended to apply to the [Spanish] government for lands." When informed in the negative, Ezekiel said that "he was glad of it unless I remained in the country." He hinted that one of the Spanish officers was intent on leaving the Natchez District and that Manuel Gayoso might make the "elegant plantation, with negroes for its cultivation" available as a gratis grant of the land, and favorable terms for the rest. Ezekiel advised that, if Samuel S. were to buy the plantation, then flip it at a profit, without any real intention of settling, Governor Gayoso would be upset and direct his ire at the older Forman. Thus Samuel S. should weigh the opportunity carefully.

As if on cue, William Dunbar, in his capacity as Spanish surveyor-general, called on Samuel S. unannounced with another, similarly tantalizing offer. "He brought the survey and map of my land, and presented a bill of sixty dollars for his services." Samuel S. protested that he had not solicited a gratis land grant, nor had Governor Gayoso ever said anything to him directly, "nor did I want any."

Dunbar replied that he was acting on the governor's explicit order, directing him "to survey for Don Samuel S. Forman 800 acres of land," and it should be "the best and most valuable tract . . . including a beautiful stream of water . . . well located, near a Mr. Ellis, at the White Cliffs." Dunbar urged the young man, "By all means take it." This was well beyond the 240 acres typically granted to single Caucasian male settlers, "so the governor showed much friendship by complimenting me with so large a grant."

Papers that Samuel S. had long forgotten have recently come to light. In spite of his later demurral that he was taken aback by the offer, they show that Dunbar had written him prior to his "unannounced" visit. There, Dunbar pointed out that excellent land in the district ripe for free granting was available to promising planters willing to settle and develop new plantations. Samuel S. was indeed a more active participant in these deliberations than he later recollected.

Nevertheless, Samuel S. had grown homesick for his elderly parents. He later claimed he had always promised his father "that I would return [north to the United States] if my life was spared me."

Frisky Cuffey, gone prematurely to his Maker, would not be a concern in the deliberations. When the beast became too troublesome in captivity, Ezekiel had Cuffey killed and butchered "and invited several gentlemen to join him in partaking of his bear dinner."

When it became generally known that Samuel S. had decided it was time to depart, Governor Gayoso asked him directly what he intended to do with the land grant. "I replied that if I did not return in a year or two, that his Excellency could do what he pleased with it."

His departure in 1791 after barely a year's residency in Natchez served as another pretext for a final round of social calls. Ezekiel Forman assured that these farewells took place in style. The frolicsome visits proceeded over a period of days. Samuel S. was to recall them wistfully as "by-gone days of happiness never to return." Accompanying him were Ezekiel's teenage daughters Augusta and Margaret. Perhaps their father calculated that these visits would gain the girls additional exposure to planters' sons, who might in their time pay court to the girls. Marriage, after all, was a business opportunity just as important, and potentially enriching, as land itself.

*

On Ezekiel's advice and that of Spanish officals like Stephen Minor, Samuel S. determined to depart by way of New Orleans, a river route of 300 miles of bends and bayous, "and thence by sea to Philadelphia." By comparison, a return upriver would be prolonged and dangerous. Caribbean and Atlantic Ocean swells were far preferable to Chief Little Turtle's northwestern Indian raiders.

Parting from the family "was most trying and affecting, having traveled and hazarded our lives together for so many hundred miles." He never expected to meet them again "in this life."

"Many of the poor colored people, too, came and took leave of me, with tears streaming down their cheeks." Whatever else Samuel S. may have meant to them, his departure was one less link to their earlier lives in Monmouth County, and the shared journey across thousands of treacherous frontier miles punctuated by scenes of unexpected, wondrous grandeur en route.

In June, leaving behind the Delta humidity and increasing seasonal heat, Samuel S. stepped aboard the brig *Navarre*, to make his way north to Philadelphia. He took with him a modest-sized cargo of tobacco, cotton, and furs that he thought might command a premium back East. In the rugged cherrywood travel trunk he had purchased back in Pittsburgh, he carried business letters from Ezekiel to General David Forman. He had folded Governor Gayoso's land grant for 800 choice acres, with William Dunbar's appended description and Spanish surveyor's certification, into a locked cubby in the trunk. And then he quite forgot about it. . . .

He arrived at the City of Brotherly Love in far better condition than his fur shipment, which seems to have become mildewed in the damp ship's hold during a weeks-long voyage marred by storms and heavy seas. Samuel S. failed to recover damages from the captain of the *Navarre*.

But the young man was no doubt pleased to reunite with family. Seeking to establish himself, he sought opportunities within the Formans' extended network. While in Natchez, Samuel S.'s favorite sister Eleanor married Philip Freneau, the "patriot poet" and Philadelphia publisher. With Thomas Jefferson's patronage, Freneau started the *National Gazette*, whose editorial policies were stridently partial to Washington's Secretary of State. In short order, Samuel S. hired on as an employee of Freneau's print shop, where a frequent visitor was his boss's Princeton College roommate, future president James Madison.

Samuel S. Forman was uninterested in the fine points of politics, publishing, or emerging political parties, even though his brother-in-law Freneau certainly was involved. Forman took scant notice of the implications stirred by the unstable affairs in the West. Aside from his attendance at the second inauguration of George Washington, where he stood, riveted, within six feet of the great man himself—something he recalled for the rest of his life that "made my blood run cold"—the young man grew impatient for something more.

His role at Freneau's print shop was not going anywhere. As politely as he could, he asked David Forman, still in Monmouth, for the 100 pounds payment promised for his work on the trek to Natchez. The general declared that he was short of cash and unable to pay just then. But he did employ Samuel S. to represent him as agent on some small business matters between New York City and Philadelphia.

There Samuel S. met Holland Land Company agent Theophilus Cazenove. Forman's experience of successfully transporting pioneer parties and trade goods along the western and southern frontiers, setting up viable commercial enterprises on arrival, and keeping meticulous financial accounts must have impressed the Dutch company. At twenty-seven, he signed on to assist in the development of a large wilderness property in Upstate New York.

The Holland Land Company was an unincorporated group of thirteen investors, resident in the Netherlands, who were excited by the profit potential of land-based speculations in the post-Revolution United States. By federal law in force at the time, Europeans could not own American land directly, but rather were required to act through American-citizen agents. Accordingly, Dutchman John Lincklaen had moved to Philadelphia and become a naturalized citizen in order to act on the company's behalf.

Prominent American financier Robert Morris sold the Dutchmen a large tract of wilderness in New York north of Fort Schuyler. The tract had been Iroquois land a few years before, passing first through speculative sale.

In early 1793, John Lincklaen and Samuel S. Forman departed Philadelphia for the undeveloped parcel, which they reached on May 8. Their assignment was to establish a settlement, land office, and store from which farm-sized parcels would be retailed to settlers. Lincklaen picked the site of the new town, which Samuel S. solicitously named Cazenovia. Holland Land Company investors expected a prompt turnover of their tract to settler buyers. From their comfortable offices in Amsterdam, the task must have seemed more trivial than it turned out to be.

Forman and Lincklaen would become close friends and business associates as they together supervised and personally "engaged in felling trees, and erecting the necessary houses in which to live and do business." The tasks and adventure were not unlike what Samuel S. had experienced when journeying to Natchez just three years before. But the frontier he ultimately chose was not to be dependent on African American enslaved labor. Eschewing the inducement to settle in Natchez in Spanish West Florida, he chose instead the challenges of the free-soil frontier in Upstate New York.

CHAPTER 15

Thriving in Natchez, 1791 to 1794

MEANWHILE, LIFE WENT ON IN NATCHEZ AND SPANISH WEST FLORIDA. Bursting with lush crops of tobacco, indigo, and Indian corn, existing plantations expanded and thrived. American arrivals coming downriver from Kentucky, Virginia, and Pennsylvania along with their slaves created new ones. Black hands, muscles, and backs performed most of the labor. Plantation owners imported additional enslaved laborers from the Caribbean and sometimes directly from Africa.

Tropical diseases—like yellow fever or the malaria that took Governor Gayoso's young wife—racked up their deadly toll. Death was never far away. Caucasians seemed particularly susceptible, an observation that contributed to the belief that Blacks were constitutionally better able to perform sustained hard labor in the semitropical climate.

Margaret Forman, who had been pregnant during the pioneer journey, gave birth to baby daughter Ann, who died within her first year. Ironically mother and unborn child had withstood the rigors of the frontier trek, but the little one could not survive Natchez's maladies. Mr. Bernard Lintot, a successful planter, also succumbed, as did Spanish official and expat American Stephen Minor's first two wives. The Formans' enslaved families, despite the back-breaking labor of clearing fields for tobacco, indigo, and corn, maintained their growing families largely intact.

Plagued as they were by infectious diseases, the plantation entrepreneurs were still able to rapidly amass property and extravagances. Ezekiel Forman, with Benajah Osman overseeing, reaped thousands of dollars in crop proceeds beginning with the 1791 harvest, chiefly in tobacco and indigo; and by the mid-1790s, increasingly in cotton. Indigo still fetched ready cash, but was harder on the land and natural irrigation than almost any other crop. Corn stayed on the plantation for the master's family, enslaved workers' core rations, and animal feed.

Ready to move up from his cabin of recycled boat timber, Ezekiel ordered the building of an elegant two-story grand house, christening it and the expansive surrounding fields Wilderness Plantation. In addition to crops in the field, a dairy barn, pig sty, smoke shop, and woodworking shop were all added to Wilderness. All were staffed by the Formans' enslaved laborers.

Ezekiel, Margaret, and their children enjoyed an increasing number of luxuries within the big house. They adorned the dining room with elegant imported china, silverware, and—the epitome of leisurely dining room comfort and elegance—a Dutch fan. Rigged on a ceiling hinge over the dining table, it rhythmically circulated air during meals via an ingenious pulley system hand propelled by a young slave.

Ostentatious luxuries were on display outside as well. Widowed Katherine Lintot, now remarried to Stephen Minor, developed a preference for all things golden, both the color and the metal. Her husband was happy to indulge her by dipping into his briskly accumulating fortune. Leap-frogging Ezekiel and Margaret Forman's enviable conveyance, Mrs. Minor assured that her coach was painted gold, the horses' manes were as near to golden as could be bought, and mixed-race enslaved people remarkable for their pale golden skin color were her liveried coachmen.

Other innovations invaded the region, but hid themselves among the nondescript wooden plantation work structures. Eli Whitney's cotton gin, or local reinventions of it, were constructed by planters keen on increasing their cotton production. Mechanization superseded the laborious and mind-numbing process of manually removing seeds from the dense cotton boll. William Dunbar recognized that short staple cotton, whose cultivation had been refined by Indians hundreds of years prior to the Spanish conquest of Mexico, was peculiarly suitable to cultivation in the Mississippi Delta. Where a slave working an entire day, sunup to dusk, could deseed only a few pounds of harvested cotton bolls by hand, the same slave using a new cotton engine fitted with a hand crank could now prepare fiftyfold more cotton in a day.

By 1795 some of the first Eli Whitney-style cotton gins were in operation in the Natchez District. Ezekiel Forman and Benajah Osman were early adopters on Wilderness Plantation. The machine would change the lives of everyone, Black and white, rich and poor. Planters could sell as much cotton as they could deliver to the hungry factors on the docks of Natchez and New Orleans for export to the early industrializing cities of England and the American Northeast. For the African Americans, this meant clearing more fields; more work planting, weeding, and picking cotton; and potentially more abusive treatment at the hands of slave drivers and overseers intent on feeding the insatiable gins.

Enslaved labor gangs could not be expanded fast enough. But unlike their Natchez District neighbors, who clamored to buy male slaves imported from the Caribbean, the Formans maintained their African American families who, seemingly less susceptible to the deadly seasonal fevers than their white owners, were fruitful and multiplied. Ezekiel Forman as a consequence did not need to purchase new slaves. That circumstance made the Forman plantations exceptional.

Other aspects of plantation life continued. Ezekiel came into a business understanding with an associate of General James Wilkinson to sell his Wilderness Plantation produce in New Orleans. Philip Nolan signed a note in favor of Ezekiel Forman for 332 Spanish silver dollars and 3 reales in August 1791, just as his young Forman cousin was likely settling into his new job in Philadelphia as a printer's assistant.

Even before the cotton gin made its debut in the territory, storms further afield blew ominous breezes toward West Florida's indistinct borders. Under the charismatic leadership of Toussaint L'Ouverture, restive slaves from the hellish sugar cane plantations of Saint-Domingue on the Caribbean Island of Hispaniola rose up against their French colonial masters. In so doing, they challenged the very existence of the Eurocentric colonial order.

Fleeing the bloody Haitian conflict, displaced Caribbean plantation owners from Saint-Domingue arrived in New Orleans in increasing numbers, many of them bringing their slaves along. Other such refugees sought safe haven and new lives in places like Savannah, Charleston, and Philadelphia. While fears of insurrection among the planter community turned out to be far worse than the reality, many slave owners were quick to mete out draconian punishments for any suspicion of incipient revolt.

Instability invited mischief as Citizen Genêt's effort to manipulate the United States into breaching its official neutrality between warring Britian and France had recently revealed. And there were other schemes. Closer to home, in 1793 a French General Collot, under the civilian guise of business, traveled the length of the Ohio and Mississippi Rivers, from Pittsburgh to New Orleans, carefully taking river soundings, mapping channels, towns and, especially, American and Spanish military installations. To this day it remains unclear exactly what Collot was up to. The territorial integrity of *Luisiana* and Spanish West Florida was surely not among his aims.

Meanwhile, with notable strategic insight, tact, and diplomatic skill, Governor Gayoso acted decisively to advance Spanish interests. Maintaining an island of calm at his West Florida seat of Natchez, he ventured further afield within the complex and potentially dangerous borderland to advance his agenda.

Gayoso oversaw the construction of several armed galleys to patrol the Mississippi River. He invited Choctaw, Chickasaw, Cherokee, and Creek Indians to a 1793 treaty conference to set aside inter-Indian differences under the promise of Spain's guaranteeing each nation's traditional territories against American encroachments. Stephen Minor distinguished himself by coordinating negotiations on behalf of the Spanish in what became known as the Treaty of Nogales.

Effective native leaders maintained their own agendas, but Gayoso helped to nudge their actions more toward the interests of stability among themselves and the checking of American expansion. Chief Alexander McGillivray and the Creeks were dissuaded from pursuing a war with the state of Georgia, which might well have drawn Spanish West Florida into open conflict with the United States. Instead, the Spanish drew McGillivray into their sphere by making him a principal in the Pensacola-based Indian trading firm of Panton & Leslie. Accepting this, McGillivray stepped back from warlike raids on the Choctaw and Chickasaw, born of the kind of rivalries that had resulted in the loss of so many lives at the Noxubee River ball game in 1790.

The Chickasaw had splintered into pro-Spanish and pro-American factions. Creek hostilities against American settlers in the Georgia backcountry, and westward expansion at the expense of the Choctaws and Chickasaws, diminished for a time with the unexpected death of McGillivray (possibly of then-rampant yellow fever) and Gayoso's diplomatic success brokering the regional Indian peace.

Not all the native tribes and nations in the region cooperated. Gayoso personally engaged with Wolf's Friend and his faction of the Chickasaw, who agreed to a new Spanish garrison in 1795 at Chickasaw Bluffs (modern Memphis, Tennessee). Gayoso grandly christened the new Spanish post encroaching on the US Southwest Territory as fort *San Fernando de la Barrancas*. Piomingo, longtime Chickasaw rival of Wolf's Friend, and one of the few Indian chiefs to have fought on the American side during St. Clair's defeat in 1791, complained bitterly of the Spanish presence at Chickasaw Bluffs. He remained firmly in the pro-American camp.

*

Ezekiel meanwhile acquired a new plantation a few miles away on Second Creek. He assigned African Americasn families to perform the arduous labor of clearing and preparing the fields and planting crops of corn and indigo. Prolific Nanny, her decade-younger second husband Toddy, and children Ben, Kate, and Henny were assigned to the new operation on Second Creek under a new overseer, Robert McComb. Toddy, only in his early twenties, would be most valued there. The African Americans moving on to this plantation were leaving familiar Benajah Osman and the many men and women with whom they had shared the odyssey to Natchez of a few years before.

The enslaved Forman families thrived in terms of births and in the face of endless sweaty and varied labor in fields, pig sty, milk house, stable, woodshop, weaving house, kitchen, and smokehouse. Since their arrival in the spring of 1790, twenty-seven children were born to eight couples and five single mothers within five years of settlement. There may have been others unrecorded and unnamed who died as infants.

Wilderness Plantation remained the seat of the Forman family. In addition to being the center of family life, it boasted a commercial retail store and a one-room school for the Forman children. The enslaved house servants stayed on in shacks along St. Catherine's Creek. Nanny's eldest son Wiring Jack remained at Wilderness Plantation. Like his stepfather, Jack was among the most highly valued slaves, all of them young men whose median age was twenty.

Ezekiel bought another tract of 2,000 acres, setting the work crews to clearing that new parcel for cultivation too. It seemed that the only limitations to the Formans' expanding empire were the ability to curry favor with Spanish officials for land grants, to muster enough credit to buy additional lands from previous grantees, and to encourage the multiplication of their enslaved African American workers.

CHAPTER 16

Fallen Timbers, 1794

AS GENERAL ANTHONY WAYNE'S FORCES STEELED THEMSELVES FOR combat in northwest Ohio and frontier disaffection over the new federal tax on distilled spirits threatened to turn into a full-scale Whiskey Rebellion, hostile Indians continued to range freely and pounced unexpectedly in the backcountry. The general was keenly aware of the turmoil but could do little about it. Direct communication was slow. It took weeks to get word down from Indian country to the Ohio River, then upriver to Pittsburgh, and overland 300 miles farther to the capital in Philadelphia. Meanwhile, the trans-Allegheny western frontier heated up.

On June 30, 1794, over 1,000 Ojibwa and Ottawa attacked an American Army baggage train, a guerrilla tactic they had pursued continuously since St. Clair's defeat. The beleaguered American soldiers retreated into Fort Recovery. This time the emboldened Indians attacked the fort itself, perhaps expecting the Americans to break before them in disorder. Instead, the Indians met disciplined and deadly accurate gunfire from shielded gunports and blockhouses. And unbeknownst to the attackers, American-allied Chickasaw scouts lurked behind them, picking off and scalping the unsuspecting Ojibwa and Ottawa.

The ensuing confusion was to the Americans' advantage. Encountering dead warriors on the retreat, the attackers falsely believed that their Shawnee Northwest Federation allies had betrayed them at the worst possible time—during the battle. While patently false, the assumption contributed to the collapse of the attack. Worse for the Federation's cause, the Ojibwa and Ottawa dropped out of the campaign completely, packing up and returning to their upper Great Lakes homes.

On August 20, 1794, at the Battle of the Fallen Timbers, General "Mad Anthony" Wayne's Legion of the United States decisively defeated the Northwest Indian Federation in a clearing where a recent storm had blown down trees. Engraving by R. F. Zogbaum for *Harper's Magazine*, 1896.

By July 1794, Whiskey Rebellion violence escalated in Western Pennsylvania. Armed protestors attacked inspector general of the new tax John Neville, one of the wealthiest citizens in Western Pennsylvania. When his home was besieged, several US Army soldiers and state militiamen defended it. A sharp gunfight ensued. Neville's slaves joined in to bravely defend his house against an alarmed militia numbering 500. One protest leader was shot dead while attempting to de-escalate matters. Neville himself barely escaped the mob.

On August 20, 1794, General Wayne led the main body of his Legion of the United States north toward the Indian towns along the Maumee River. The allied Indian force prepared for battle at the site of a recent tornado, a clearing in the wilderness formed by fallen trees. William Wells had by this time openly switched sides and headed a group of American scouts against his father-in-law's Federation warriors. Though Wells had been wounded a few days in advance of the impending battle, an

President George Washington reviews troops and prepares to confront the Whiskey Rebels, 1794. Resistance dissipated in the face of an overwhelming show of Federal force. Painting attributed to Kettlemeyer, courtesy of the Metropolitan Museum of Art.

American officer nonetheless later described him as "indispensable to our operation."

Buckongahelas of the Delawares wielded overall command at the center of their battle formation, a place of honor. The Indians attacked along a crescent-shaped front, similar to the one deployed with such devastating impact against General Arthur St. Clair's beleaguered army back in 1791. This time the American infantry held firm. They hit back from the Indians' assault with a bayonet charge. Instead of being lured too far forward by daring warriors, as St. Clair's unfortunate infantry had been, Wayne's troops maintained a disciplined formation while delivering deadly musket fire.

Meanwhile the American cavalry charged, rolling up both arms of the Indians' crescent formation. The action was brief and sharp, encompassing many instances of bravery and pathos. Dashing William Henry Harrison distinguished himself among the American cavalry officers. Tecumseh, a young Shawnee warrior, was forced to abandon his dead brother on the battlefield. But, years later, he would carry forth the spirit of resistance from the Federation war chiefs.

The Indian attack rapidly collapsed into a general rout. Indians retreated north along the Auglaize River rapids, expecting refuge a few miles from the battlefield with the British at their Fort Miami.

British forces from Upper Canada had audaciously built this fort on US soil earlier in the summer. Some Indian leaders had interpreted the move as concrete proof that the British would tip the balance of fighting, when required, to them. Little Turtle suspected otherwise, even in advance of the Battle of the Fallen Timbers. Just weeks before, his entreaty to the fort's commandant to supply strategically critical artillery had been politely but unequivocally rebuffed.

The British did supply the Indians with small arms, ammunition, and words to encourage resistance. They even permitted a company of white Canadian militiamen to fight alongside the Indians. Yet, a climactic scene left no mistake about the limits of British involvement. When defeated Northwest Federation warriors, closely pursued by Wayne's Legionnaires, arrived at Fort Miami, the British literally slammed the gates shut in their dejected faces. The English commander did not want to precipitate another American war on the spot. Indian hopes for an open British alliance were thus dramatically dashed.

General Wayne forbade a wholesale slaughter and butchering of the routed Indians, which could have been seen as revenge for St. Clair's army's fate. With rare exceptions, his subordinates maintained good order during and after the battle. Casualties were relatively low on both sides—33 Americans killed and about an equal number of dead on the Indian side along with 6 of their Caucasian Canadian allies. Considering the size of the opposing forces—3,000 US soldiers and militia versus 1,200 Indians and their allies, and the deadly arsenal both sides wielded, a truly grim toll had been avoided.

Unopposed, General Wayne marched his troops further into northwest Indiana, home ground of the Indian Federation. He ordered a new fortification, christened Fort Wayne, be built on the site of Kekiongo.

It was a proud day for the kind of American arms George Washington encouraged, and that was all too rare on the frontier—the achievement of

strategic goals with a minimal loss of life and almost no gratuitous mayhem. And Wayne's respect for the defeated Indian warriors, in adhering
to European-style rules of war, smoothed the way for negotiations. These
culminated in the Treaty of Greenville the following year. Wayne personally oversaw negotiations and met on multiple occasions with his recent
adversaries. William Wells served as a translator and cultural bridge. The
Americans got their land cessions and there would be peace in the Northwest Territory for almost two decades.

*

As news of Wayne's battlefield victory filtered east, the Whiskey Rebellion lost momentum. Questions lingered as to whether the Indians would
fully cease hostilities, and whether a treaty encompassing all of the hostile
tribes and nations could be negotiated and ratified by Congress. Yet the
underlying suspicion that the federal government had abandoned westerners to the Indian threat diminished markedly following the Battle of
the Fallen Timbers.

*

David Bradford, one of the Whiskey Rebellion's leaders, fled south. He
escaped on a coal barge departing from Pittsburgh, traveling all the way
to Bayou Sara in Spanish West Florida. Unlike Dr. Saugrain or the Forman pioneers, Bradford no longer had to contend en route with attacks
on the Ohio River by Little Turtle's, Buckongahelas's, and Blue Jacket's
Indian war parties. Manuel Gayoso welcomed Bradford as a new Spanish subject and provided the American fugitive with a generous 650-acre
land grant. Bradford promptly established The Myrtles, a grand slave-
based sugar plantation.

The combination of defeats in 1794 of the Northwest Indian Federation and of the Whiskey Rebels would have enduring repercussions
downriver, in Kentucky, Tennessee, Spanish Natchez and *Luisiana*, and
across the Atlantic Ocean among leaders in London, Madrid, and Paris.

CHAPTER 17

Master and Reaper, 1795

EZEKIEL ADAPTED COMFORTABLY TO LIFE AS AN ACTIVE AND ENERGETIC southern plantation owner. From the day he arrived in Natchez, he had ridden hard on horseback to select the finest lands available, pay calls on Spanish officials, and visit prospective neighbors. He had survived the cruel seasoning period for unacclimated immigrants, despite all the Formans except Samuel S. having suffered fevers in the course of their first year. Even after settling into the district, where he collected extra pounds and developed chronic gout, he roamed his properties from an equine perch for hours, even in the stifling heat and humidity.

But in the spring of 1795, almost exactly five years since arriving with his pioneers to settle at Natchez, Ezekiel's health gave out. It is not certain whether death resulted from yellow fever, malaria, or perhaps a complication of gout. Maybe some combination of seasonal fevers and intrinsic metabolic imbalances reduced Ezekiel from a usually vigorous country gentleman to a bedridden invalid unexpectedly on the verge of death.

In early May Ezekiel sensed his grip on the corporeal world slipping away. Always a no-nonsense individual, he systematically approached the legalistic tasks of the dying from the master bedroom of Wilderness, by now a showpiece plantation.

We imagine that he was attended closely by his spouse Margaret, whose sorrows at impending widowhood were rendered the more distressing by the knowledge that she was once again pregnant. Quite possibly, Ezekiel may have had conversations with the household servants with whom he had had the closest association over the years. They all had been pioneers in the early and intense years of creating two impressive plantations from a fertile, virgin land, wresting them from forests and dense canebrake. Perhaps such conversations included one with Phil the coachman, recalling how the Forman carriage was wrecked when crossing the Alleghenies and how creatively Philip refinished the carriage into an enviably stylish open chaise.

Ezekiel wrote out his last will and testament in a shaky hand. Educated in the law himself, he knew the proper format and phrasing needed to prove durable in any subsequent litigation. He expressed confidence in his "beloved wife Margaret" by appointing her executrix, with the assistance of "trusty & well beloved friends" William Dunbar, businessman Ebenezer Rees, and Benajah Osman.

"Weak in body, but of perfect mind," Ezekiel further directed an inventory be executed expeditiously by appraiser Joseph Barnard, bequeathing all his property and money left over after discharging the estate's obligations to Margaret. She faced widowhood supporting five surviving minor children, with yet another on the way.

Ezekiel made no mention in the will of his extensive obligations to younger brother General David Forman. Those binding agreements were, of course, among his "just debts" that the executors would assure be "regularly stated and discharged." He did not name any slaves in his will. Rather, he implicitly included them as chattel among "all my estate, real & personal."

The obligations Ezekiel had signed with brother David Forman, back in the fall of 1789, might leave the ownership of the slaves in question. It is unlikely that Dunbar and Osman knew the fine details of those documents, and Margaret may or may not have. In the course of Ezekiel's years in Natchez, the notion that the slaves and implements to establish and maintain the new plantations were not his property would have undermined his position in the community and his authority over the slaves. So, he may have confided that circumstance to very few people, or perhaps to no one at all. Now, with mortality intruding unexpectedly and urgently, Ezekiel may have decided to say nothing of the ownership matter in his will. If the executors missed those papers and their implications, Margaret and their children together would surely be far wealthier and more secure in the future.

In any case, he spelled out his wishes and identified a competent and well-connected group of executors "who have full powers" to settle his accounts "without having recourse to the [Spanish] Tribunal." As is the case today, complex estates seek to avoid unpredictable and prolonged deliberations that can lead to disputes among creditors and heirs. Ezekiel, though debilitated and nearing death, crafted a will sufficiently explicit to be settled directly. He ignored or minimized obligations to his brother David in favor of his "beloved wife." Ezekiel may have indeed convinced himself that he, his estate, and Margaret as survivor were the just owners of the Wilderness and Second Creek Plantations.

All family and marital relationships can be complicated, and so were those of the Forman brothers. After the passing of his first wife Augustina, Ezekiel had married Margaret twenty years before. Augustina was the half-sister of David Forman's wife Ann. Together, Ezekiel and Augustina had had a family, and those children were now adults who did not require or expect bequests. Any outcome that slighted Ezekiel's young second family while leaving the distant David Forman owner of all, or even the larger part of, the plantations could seem a supreme injustice to Ezekiel.

Gathering neighbors of means as his witnesses, Ezekiel signed his will. On May 29, 1795, within a month of signing the document, at age fifty-eight, he expired. These same witnesses probably consoled the newly widowed Margaret, calling at Wilderness Plantation to attend the funeral and interment.

*

Joseph Barnard duly inventoried Ezekiel's estate. This gentleman was adept at assigning and recording values within the Natchez District for items ranging from hogs and a demijohn of bear grease, to a bound printed set of Addison's *The Spectator* and human chattel. He convened the inventory at Wilderness Plantation on St. Catherine's Creek on June 24 in the company of overseer Benajah Osman, and continued at the Forman's satellite plantation on Second Creek two days later. George Fitzgerald and Gabriel Benoist served as appraisers at both locations. Stephen Minor's brother John and Robert McComb, Ezekiel's overseer at Second Creek plantation, joined the group as "assistant witnesses to the Inventory."

Margaret Forman likely had the support of Manuel Gayoso and influential friends who desired that she maintain her position in the community, regardless of the probate outcome of the estate. Margaret and her minor children were conferred a series of gratis land grants issued in their names. These grants would have been made on Gayoso's recommendation, surveyed by William Dunbar, and signed off on by various officials on behalf of the King of Spain. All together they involved hundreds of prime acres and were worth a small fortune. The new land grants were among the last issued to American settlers in Spanish West Florida.

Gayoso may have wanted to make a positive example of Spain's care for American expats while ameliorating Margaret's plight. The grants demonstrated, in the most concrete way area planters understood, that the Spanish administration would look after desirable immigrants, especially those like Ezekiel who actively supported the administration. Regardless of the probated outcome of Ezekiel's estate, Margaret and her children would have a land-based patrimony courtesy of the benevolent Spaniards.

*

We can only imagine the scene that played out as the slaves faced the piercing eyes of the appraisers. All were gathered in from their tasks, be they from the big house or from the fields, to be evaluated. Enslaved family groups and the few singles were paraded, each in turn, before the assembled whites. Benoist and Fitzgerald probably asked their names and ages, jotting down what they heard. They noted mixed-race people, by appearance, as mulattoes. As this was not an auction, there was no need to call out the assigned values loudly.

Four hundred and fifty Spanish silver dollars were assigned for a strapping young field hand; lesser amounts for older hands whose labor was behind them. There were lower amounts still for children whose escape from childhood diseases was not yet assured. The healthiest adult female slaves were assigned a value of $350 each in Spanish silver. The highest values among women were implicitly based both on their laboring abilities and anticipated fertility.

The most valuable single family was that of thirty-five-year-old Nanny and her younger consort Toddy who had earlier removed to

Second Creek. She clutched an as-yet unnamed eight-day-old babe to her chest, while her four other children, ranging from teens to toddlers, looked on. At seventeen, Nanny's strapping son Wiring Jack commanded the same highest value of 450 Spanish silver dollars as did his stepdad Toddy. The appraisers assigned a value of $350 to Nanny herself, which included her infant. Toddler Frank, having survived his first year but still vulnerable to foul Mississippi Delta "miasmas," commanded a value of $110. Collectively the nine members of this family were valued altogether at $2,660, or fully one-twelfth part of the entire value of this very rich estate. Their labors in the ensuing years would realize and exceed the plantation entrepreneurs' most sanguine aspirations to create wealth from this fertile wilderness.

But if there was ever any doubt about African Americans' place in this world they had wrought, the dehumanizing ritual of the inventory, done on the order of people they knew so well and served for so long—Margaret Forman, overseer Benajah Osman, and prominent white landowners from the area, acting in the name of the king of Spain—dramatized their limited horizons. The ritual reminded them that they were little more to the masters than the horses, cows, oxen, pigs, donkeys, and a lone bison of the Forman plantations.

By valuation comparisons, Ezekiel's two favorite riding and coach horses, Grey and Roan, were valued at $60 each; three teams of field-ready oxen at $105 for all; fifty-two head of horned cattle at $6 each, and fifty pigs at $2 each. Ezekiel's thoroughbred horse, Brunswick, was valued as "inestimable." Among the inanimate objects were a large cotton gin, likely one of the first in the entire Delta South, valued at $50, and the stylishly repaired four-wheeled coach at $150. All 3,910 acres of land, comprising the two plantations and several undeveloped properties, with crops in the ground, summed their value at $5,625 or 18 percent of the entire estate.

The entire estate was valued at $31,431 and 6 reales. Sixty-three percent ($19,800) comprised the value of the Formans' enslaved African Americans. A third of those ninety souls had been born since arrival of the group in Natchez five years before. As children of slaves, they were enslaved too, treated in Ezekiel's estate as chattel just like their elders.

All who were old enough would have shared in the collective anxiety concerning their fate when Ezekiel Forman's estate would be settled. Yet the appraisal was not quite as onerous as an auction would have been. Under those circumstances, African American families would be predictably and irrevocably torn apart. In being spared this, the Forman slaves could count themselves fortunate.

*

The most important documents among the estate papers were not assigned a value. "A box, which Mrs. Margaret Forman declares to contain all the valuable papers of the deceased" was opened and found to include several bundles of papers: "One Bundle containing old accounts & Agreements No29"; "one Bundle containing Letters from the United States No30"; and "[O]ne Parcel containing sundry old American papers No35." Surely included somewhere among those packets was an October 1789 agreement between General David Forman and his older brother Ezekiel.

These papers do not survive, but we know of their contents from subsequent litigation. No one called attention to them during the making of the inventory, an official record memorialized for the Spanish Natchez District court.

Benajah Osman, employee "and dear friend" to Ezekiel, and former employee, Masonic brother, and military subordinate of General David Forman, was still in the employ of the estate. His role and future at the Wilderness and Second Creek Plantations was probably uncertain. During the journey, like Samuel S. Forman, he had taken orders from Ezekiel but was to be paid either by the general, or by Ezekiel. As long as Ezekiel was alive, any imprecision of the employment relationship was glossed over. Now that Ezekiel had died as a Spanish citizen, with David Forman a citizen and resident of a foreign country thousands of miles away, the international nature of the family ties and ownership made for an unprecedented state of affairs.

Benajah Osman was likely the first to notify General David Forman of his brother Ezekiel's demise. He may have also informed the general that Ezekiel's widow had not fully represented the general's ownership interests in the operation and the benefits accruing from the two plantations.

It would have taken as long as several months to get word from Natchez to Maryland, where the general had relocated from Monmouth County to his wife's Maryland property early in 1794. Osman might not even have known that. Had he sent a letter to Monmouth first, there would have been additional delay in forwarding the sad news to David Forman in Maryland. One way or another, he learned of his brother Ezekiel's death by March 1796.

General Forman was also aware, from all the newspapers of the time, of the Treaty of San Lorenzo, requiring, among other provisions, for a joint American and Spanish commission to set the boundary between the American Mississippi Territory and the remainder of Spanish West Florida. Natchez would most likely fall within American territory, but that would not be certain until the border could be surveyed with precision.

The general humbly approached George Washington seeking appointment to lead the upcoming joint commission to induce the Spanish to cede Natchez, and coincidentally to assert his interests in his brother's estate. He outlined his having sent "a considerable number of Negro slaves and other property [to the] value of ten thousand pounds currency to the then-held as Spanish country of Louisiana" in the care of his brother. Now his brother was deceased and:

> *His widow and six children [were] returned to my protection . . . leaving behind them of my property and in the hands of the Spaniards, near ninety Negro slaves, stock &c. to the value of between twelve and fifteen thousand pounds. For the recovery of which, I propose this Spring to go to that Country.*

The general heard that an American commissioner was required by the Treaty of San Lorenzo to fix the border. He felt Washington should designate him for the role on the basis of past services in delicate matters.

George Washington never responded. Perhaps he remembered how Forman had fanned the flames of an international incident involving the young British Lieutenant Asgill while the aristocrat was a prisoner of war under Forman's custody during the Revolution. Perhaps President

Washington recognized that Forman lacked the requisite surveying skills, or he was just distracted with other matters of state.

Forman decided to proceed south nonetheless. He put his northern affairs in order, made out a will, and embarked on the strenuous trip west and south on September 10, 1796. Unlike his brother Ezekiel, who had traveled six years earlier, the general did not need to anticipate Indian attacks en route along the Ohio River. General Wayne's defeat of the Northwest Indian Federation and the subsequent Treaty of Greenville restored peaceful navigation along the river and defused native resistance in the Northwest Territory for a generation. Thus, General David Forman could march and sail unopposed, as an army of one, all the way from the East Coast to Natchez. He would arrive in person for his first and only extended visit from the North to settle Ezekiel's estate in his own favor.

CHAPTER 18

Family Feud

STEPHEN MINOR ASCENDED THE BRICK STEPS TO GOVERNMENT House, overwhelmed by the scent of azaleas and luxuriant spring flowers, and the commanding view of the Mississippi River. Whitewashed walls and pillared porches made the seat of Spanish government in the Natchez District one of the noteworthy structures of the growing upper town, whose avenues Manuel Gayoso had laid out during his first year of residence.

Government House served multiple functions, although it had originally been built as an inn. Chief among them, the conduct of public government business. From Minor's and Gayoso's perch, weekly court convened in the first-floor common room.

Minor probably wore his colorful official Spanish military uniform to the proceedings. Its crimson color and gold facings set off his height and barrel chest to good effect. He followed Gayoso's example, personifying the dignity and pomp of Spanish authority, while projecting an engaging personality.

Minor had come a long way both literally and figuratively since floating down the Ohio and Mississippi Rivers from his native Western Pennsylvania in 1779. He had arrived in Spanish New Orleans just a year after a disastrous American raid on the then British-controlled Natchez. Minor was readily accepted as a soldier among the Spanish. There were simply too few Iberians and Spanish Creoles there to bear arms on behalf of His Most Catholic Majesty despite the governor's efforts to entice small groups of European immigrants, including Germans and Canary Islanders. More recently, Americans like Ezekiel Forman's group were invited to immigrate. The promise of generous land grants made the difference and drew adaptable and adventurous American planters and merchants in droves.

Now that West Florida had been formalized as Spanish following the Peace of Paris, Spanish governors worked creatively to blunt the expansionism of their one-time American allies by the requirement of Spanish allegiance. It was under this new policy that David Forman had obtained the Spanish land grant from the Spanish envoy in New York. That grant enabled Forman's entire pioneering endeavor to Natchez.

For the new residents, international disputes among the colonial powers within the immediate district played out in a benign manner that could be easily mistaken for comic opera. There were many potentially serious and sometimes byzantine plots, but somehow the Spanish, French Creole, Anglo-American, and Anglo-British residents found ways to get along without fatal consequences. Serious bloodshed occupied the Americans far away in the Northwest Indian War and among the Native American tribes in the West Florida backcountry. Chief Alexander McGillivray of the Creeks fomented much of the unrest. Rather than helping stoke conflict, Spain's regional Governor Gayoso had successfully brokered peace among them.

As for any rebellious enslaved African Americans, the result was death, as occurred twice in slave rebellions on the sugar plantations at Point Coupee in 1794 and again a few years later. Those were the exceptions in Spanish West Florida. The vast majority of Blacks remained in bondage, their labor and lives too valuable for their owners to fatally abuse.

For those pragmatic colonial leaders, wayward residents such as the sly Anthony Hutchins—who took a leading part in an unsuccessful uprising against Spanish dominion in Pensacola in 1781—could return eventually to their good graces. Their policy was to increase the population in the region, make it economically sound, and cement it into Spanish *Luisiana*—whatever it took to advance their larger colonial empire. Hutchins had over his long tenure in the area advanced Spanish economic ambitions so well that they were willing to overlook his shortcomings as a loyal subject. To them he was a successful planter who had dedicated himself to expanding the Natchez plantation economy.

*

Through 1796 and some months into 1797, it was business as usual in Natchez commercial and court transactions. When General David Forman at last arrived in Natchez, it was from Gayoso's Spanish tribunal that he sought to assert ownership over brother Ezekiel's estate, rather than from the newly arrived American border delegation. This was the same entity he had sought to lead and, being American, might be presumed to be friendlier to his appeal. For his part, Gayoso may have been pleased that the former Revolutionary War general openly preferred the Spanish tribunal to adjudicate his concerns.

However, Gayoso and his small staff, including Carlos Grand Pré and Stephen Minor, had more immediate concerns than the pending litigation within the Forman family. A small American border commission, dispatched to the region by Thomas Jefferson, was headed by Andrew Ellicott. He was there to meet with Spanish counterparts to mark the new southern border with the United States along the thirty-first parallel of latitude, thereby executing the December 1795 Treaty of San Lorenzo.

Following delays in his appointment, outfitting, and seasonal travel down the Ohio and Mississippi Rivers, Ellicott and an escort of several dozen American soldiers reached Memphis, in territory disputed with Spain, early in 1797.

Governor Gayoso dispatched Stephen Minor to meet Commissioner Ellicott and convince the delegation to camp out fifty miles north of Natchez at Vicksburg. Minor offered that it was a safe enough distance to avoid needless friction between the American contingent and an aroused Spanish garrison. Although Elliott complied for a couple of weeks, his patience wore thin, and he insisted on proceeding downriver to Natchez. Arriving February 24, 1797, he selected a campsite on the upper town ridge on James Moore's property. He promptly commenced pestering Gayoso, and *Luisiana*'s Governor Baron de Carondelet in New Orleans, almost daily with missives to get on with the survey.

Unlike the presumptuous David Forman, Ellicott was eminently suited for technical aspects of his role, having supervised surveys extending over several states' boundaries and leading the boundary surveys for the new capital city of Washington, DC. He distinguished his work by conducting surveys on the basis of celestial coordinates, a more accurate method than the conventional reliance on mutable landmarks like rocks, streams, and big trees. But Ellicott's inexperience with the ways of politics and diplomacy would stretch his tact and have disruptive international implications.

Unpacking his instruments, Ellicott quickly determined that Natchez was about thirty miles north of the thirty-first parallel. The conclusion was obvious to him: Natchez, the largest and most important district in all of West Florida, was within US jurisdiction! He ordered the American flag raised above the camp, flying defiantly within rifle shot of the Spanish fort topped by the white flag of Bourbon Spain. His barrage of letters to Gayoso demanded that the governor hand over the Natchez District to him. These requests, which would have been run by courier, were constantly met by polite excuses and obfuscations. They might have assumed a comical air if something other than ownership of an entire region had been at stake.

Matters were more complex than simply compelling everyone to dance to the tune of Ellicott's measure of latitude. His mission was jointly to survey, cut a path through the canebrake and forests, and mark the border, in concert with Spanish representatives all the way from the Mississippi River hundreds of miles east, across Seminole lands, to the Apalachicola River in Spanish East Florida. By seeking to take possession of Natchez for the United States immediately, he had exceeded his mandate. The Spanish remained unwilling to concede the prize to the Americans, and a stalemate persisted. Two flags flew over Natchez, representing two armed camps, warily eyeing one another. It was a tense, volatile situation.

*

Meanwhile, David Forman was about to plead his suit before the tribunal. As the Formans represented the largest single group of Americans settling in Spanish West Florida under the liberal land-grant policy, any action regarding such a significant family was sure to gain notoriety among the tightly knit Natchez plantation society.

Minor, Gayoso, and Grand Pré were compelled to handle this case with care. If widow Margaret Forman, now a Spanish subject, were perceived by other area expats in Natchez to be ill-used concerning a fair share of her husband's considerable fortune, it could estrange other American expat settlers from the Spanish regime. Yet, if Gayoso and the Spanish leaders of Natchez were perceived by David Forman as negligent of *his* interests in the estate, the general might throw in his lot with Ellicott, who was fomenting a prompt takeover of the region by the Americans. The general was not vested in the Spanish dominion, aside from the original land grant, while Margaret had become an integral part of that community. We can only speculate what Minor, himself an expat, was thinking.

Court day on that second Saturday of 1797 provided a forum for Governor Gayoso to negotiate among the diverse interests involved, and to demonstrate the practical advantages of Spanish dominion. In deference to the majority of his subjects, proceedings were typically conducted and recorded in English. While acknowledging Spanish legal codes and procedures, the actual conduct of cases owed much to English common law as adapted from the previous English dominion in West Florida.

In preparing his old boss the general for the proceedings, Benajah Osman, who after six years in Natchez was now respected in the community of planters as an effective and experienced overseer, may have coached him to take a conciliatory tone. Perhaps Stephen Minor also tried as well. But David Forman would have none of it.

The general possessed absolute confidence in his own judgment. His decision to challenge the estate of his brother in Spanish court, instead of casting his lot with the American contingent, may have been based in part on his disdain for Washington's selection of a scientific technocrat over him. In any case, the situation freed Forman to focus single-mindedly on his own affairs. Let Andrew Ellicott deal with the southern border and the Spanish, who were in no hurry to depart!

David Forman had been looking forward to this moment ever since hearing of his brother Ezekiel's unexpected demise eighteen months earlier. The settling of affairs up north, his appeal to President Washington, the departure from his family in Maryland, the long trip downriver, and indeed, his initiation of the Natchez settlement enterprise back in 1789, were all prologue to this moment. For the general, now was the time to reap the benefits of his vision: without trifling, without mincing Spanish courtly dissembling, and without giving away any of it to his sister-in-law Margaret. Ezekiel's fellow planters and coexecutors Dunbar and Rees looked on from the audience.

General Forman held forth, firing a volley of words: "It being notorious that the whole property and effects enumerated in the inventory of the estate of Ezekiel Forman" legally belonged to him as "his true and absolute property and right." Lest there be any confusion as to what property, it was "all and singular," "[p]roperty and effects of every kind, whether lands, slaves, stock, and all other objects enumerated." There was no need to consider Margaret Forman and her children because "as appears by authentic documents," he asserted, there was "an instrument by which Margaret Forman, Widow of said Ezekiel Forman, renounces all claim of dower on said Estate."

William Dunbar and Benajah Osman, coexecutors of Ezekiel's will, were signatories to that official inventory that had been for so long concealed among the deceased's box of papers and were present in the courtroom now. In David Forman's mind there could be no doubt of his ownership. He concluded, nay demanded: "Your Excellency will be pleased to confirm the surrender now . . . of all the property and slaves by the estate's executors. . . ." There was no need for delay.

We do not know precisely how Manuel Gayoso, Stephen Minor, and William Dunbar reacted. They might have wondered: Had the general forgotten himself? This was Natchez in Spanish West Florida. True, the Treaty of San Lorenzo and Andrew Ellicott's recently arrived American delegation put the region's future into question, but that was far from resolved. One simply did not address this court in such a peremptory tone.

We can imagine an uncomfortable pause following Forman's declaration, accompanied by puzzled expressions among Gayoso, Minor, Dunbar, and Osman. Perhaps at least one of them rolled his eyes. Osman was likely deeply embarrassed by the general's tirade.

But how to resolve the dispute? Quite aside from the dissonant tone, the proceeding would seal the fate of long-standing residents, and an affectionately held part of the Natchez District's social scene, namely Margaret Forman and her children. She was not present for General Forman's initial audience; women apparently rarely made their cases personally before the Natchez Spanish court. Her allegedly definitively renouncing all estate ownership interests in favor of her brother-in-law, as unequivocally pronounced by the general, however, begged for confirmation, further scrutiny, and consideration.

Manuel Gayoso deferred further discussion to a future session. It was the diplomatic thing to do, and Gayoso was especially adept at the judicious application of delay.

CHAPTER 19

Peripety, Another Planter's Demise, 1797

A week after his dramatic appearance at court, likely back at Wilderness Plantation, David Forman collapsed. As marked by bells summoning the Catholics to Sunday Mass in town, it was the 19th of March.

Protestant services could proceed at private homes, but nothing suggests that the Formans held or attended any. The otherwise tolerant Spanish in West Florida remained adamant that Roman Catholicism be the official and publicly observed religion. People could worship as they wished in private. But David Forman, desperately ill and unconscious, was in need of divine intervention in order to survive, regardless of Jesus in any particular Christian denomination.

Ginnie and the other plantation slaves may have felt justifiable concern. If Ezekiel's estate settlement did not pass to Margaret Forman or to David Forman, who himself appeared to be at the cusp of eternity, then the Black people's fear of the dehumanizing public auction block and heartrending family separations could be imminent. David Forman had gone out of his way to keep enslaved families intact for the migration to Natchez. His recent arrival there, either to run the plantations himself or to assign them within his immediate family, may have allayed their festering uncertainty. But if General Forman should die too, prospects dimmed for the enslaved families to remain together at either plantation.

After three days in a coma, the general miraculously regained consciousness. Having narrowly evaded death, he was, however, paralyzed on his entire left side, mouth drooping and drooling, speech garbled, and entirely dependent. "In this situation he continued till August."

By April Ezekiel Forman's creditors grew anxious that, if ailing David Forman inherited all of Ezekiel's estate, the general might not honor his brother's obligations. They came before Stephen Minor first thing on a Monday, a month after the general's initial pleading, to complain that having privately pressed Osman on the matter, they found his reply less than reassuring. The creditors therefore beseeched the Spanish court for "your Excellency to suspend the transfer" of their claims to the estate. Stephen Minor must have already concluded that the entire Forman clan, their retainers, and friends generated controversy at every turn.

Governor Gayoso himself replied, reassuring the creditors that the Spanish government would guarantee that the fair and valid payment of their debts by Ezekiel Forman's estate took precedence over General Forman's claims.

This court drama transpired as Ellicott's little camp defiantly flew the American flag nearby. Yet transfer of sovereignty to America remained in the hazy future. There were neither American institutions of government in place, nor a firm schedule to implement them. Gayoso's reassurance to Ezekiel's creditors also implicitly asserted that Spain would uphold their land grants and defend the wealth flowing from them: "[D]ebts so contracted by Ezekiel Forman, Esquire, or his Executors, are to be considered privileged and settled before the said property is disposed of otherwise." The message was clear to all parties: Governor Gayoso and the Spanish were still very much in charge.

Gayoso had already tipped his hand long before David Forman's arrival when he recommended to *Luisiana* Governor Carondelet the granting of several hundred acres of land to Margaret and her underage children—a gesture that would go a long way toward assuring their future and continued residence in Natchez. Margaret could remain among the planter elite, even if it turned out that she ultimately gained little from her husband's estate.

The knowledge that Gayoso had shown such favor to David Forman's sister-in-law, and now his own brush with mortality, conspired to soften the general's demands against Margaret's interests. There was much to be said for compromise and a final settlement.

Meanwhile, another spectacular growing season progressed on the sweat of Black plantation labor gangs. Soon, the new sown crops and warming days gave way to the sweltering Delta sun, over sweeping, orderly fields of tobacco, indigo, corn, and increasingly, cotton.

David Forman gathered his strength during this season of rebirth and growth. The presence of his trusted Benajah Osman and the same enslaved dark faces that had populated his farm in Monmouth must have provided some comfort.

The general could also hope to see his beloved daughter Sarah once again back North if he rallied. He must finish the estate business before the Spanish tribunal, even if that meant compromising his initial position of denying anything to sister-in-law Margaret and her brood.

We imagine Osman reporting daily and with military bearing to the ailing, initially bedridden general on all activities on Wilderness and Second Creek Plantations. The enslaved denizens of Wilderness and Second Creek were succeeding in building a lucrative enterprise. They were adapting their rich African agricultural traditions, their years of experience working together in New Jersey, and the newfangled rhythms of harmonizing the plantation tasks to the recently imported cotton gin. Natchez's diversified plantations were proving to be engines for rapidly generating agricultural wealth for their owners, exceeding by far anything yet seen in the European settlement of North America.

As the general's plantations prospered, he came to appreciate the Spanish for their land grants and indulgence toward the resident landowners' interests. That support extended to him, even if he did detect more sympathy for Margaret's position than he would have liked. The more established planters, regardless of their English Loyalist, Spanish colonial, and sometimes old French origins, almost all reached out to him with hands of friendship and common business interests.

Returning to court months later, General Forman had in the interim acquiesced in asserting his ownership of most but not all of Ezekiel's estate. He knew his brother's creditors would have to be satisfied before he could claim his due. Meanwhile, the residual paralysis afflicting the general seems to have softened his demands. Better now, he was more focused on gaining his strength for a return to his home in the North.

*

We do not know if Margaret herself led the negotiations involving her interests or if she deputized others to represent her. Regardless, she proposed retaining ownership of several slaves, who may have been her house servants. And she raised the possibility of a cash annuity to compensate her in exchange for surrendering her dower rights on the estate.

By the end of June 1797, when the general weakened and pressed to conclude a deal, the parties came to a definitive understanding. The final arrangement was in fact quite favorable to him. Wilderness and Second Creek Plantations and the bulk of Ezekiel's wealth and slaves would all come to him. Margaret would retain ownership of two enslaved families and receive an annuity from David Forman of $100 every year for her lifetime. She achieved these concessions despite papers her late husband and she had signed seemingly assigning *all* ownership rights over the enslaved, lands, crops, dwellings, and tangibles away. As for the general, just as he had dreamed when planning the enterprise, he was about to be confirmed as a very rich man in the land of Spanish silver.

He also formally acknowledged receiving ownership from executors William Dunbar, Ebenezer Rees, and Benajah Osman of "a certain number of Negro slaves, which were in the care and possession of the said Ezekiel Forman" appraised at $12,720, a half share in the proceeds of the 1790 through 1795 harvests, and household furnishings and contents. Ezekiel's Natchez creditors were paid off prior to David Forman's settlement. The agreement accounted for the notes and letters of credit he had extended to Ezekiel. The enslaved African Americans accounted for 40 percent of the entire estate's value, far surpassing the value of the extensive acreage, plantation houses, livestock, or any other type of valuable.

"Don Estavan" Minor made the final decree on August 11, 1797. Manuel Gayoso by then had already departed Natchez for New Orleans as the recently promoted governor of all of Spanish *Luisiana*. For all the time that the Forman estate drama proceeded in Spanish colonial court, the Spanish and American flags continued to fly atop their respective military camps in Natchez. One standoff had ended, while the other persisted throughout the entire estate litigation and well beyond it.

*

The following day, the general limped aboard a New Orleans-bound riverboat. He would never again see his relations, employees, enslaved African Americans, or the voluptuous fields of Wilderness and Second Creek Plantations. There were no effusions of tears, like those that accompanied Samuel S.'s departure six years before. In spite of the sweltering summer heat, David Forman was anxious to embark on the journey home. Once successfully downriver, he signed on as passenger on the first available merchantman bound for New York, departing New Orleans on August 20, 1797.

Entering the Caribbean, the merchantman was quickly overtaken by an English privateer. Capitalizing on international tensions between England and France and her nominal ally Spain, such privateers had their governments' permission to prey on their rivals' commercial shipping. The captain of the American-flagged merchantman, as a declared neutral, had little to fear of deadly attack or sinking. However, his cargo originating in New Orleans was Spanish, and therefore fair game for the profit-minded marauders.

The privateer seized control of Forman's ship and set sail for British Bermuda. There, the American captain could expect that the Spanish cargo would be taken and auctioned off. Unlike the flamboyant Caribbean buccaneers preying on the Spanish Main almost a century before, these high seas seizures were more the business of entrepreneurial privateers and admiralty lawyers. Disrupting their enemies' commerce, privateers were doing the dirty work of the English king while enriching themselves with prize cargoes. There were none of the ransoms, plank walking, and random mayhem of early eighteenth-century fact and legend. This was legal piracy: Privateers were big business on Bermuda.

The American ship's captain could expect the financial embarrassment of not delivering the seized cargo as contracted. But his ship and passengers would be released. And if the captain could prove that some of the cargo was American-owned and of American origin, he might hope to save that portion from seizure. That would absolve him of personal and business responsibility for the loss back home.

Many of the British Bermudians were displaced American Loyalists. Most notable among them was Lord Dunmore, who endured the infamy of being among the last British Crown-appointed governors ousted by American Patriots. He was notorious among Americans for the freedom he promised to escaped Virginia-based Black slaves in exchange for British military service. General David Forman would have known of that decree, and may have had reason to fear a darker experience.

The prospect of being detained in Bermuda in his weakened state, in the custody of Lord Dunmore's displaced Loyalist associates, would have been David Forman's worst nightmare. Surely the Loyalists would recall the general's fearsome reputation as the persecutor of Anglo-American subjects in Monmouth County. Would his jailers treat him as his men had treated the British captive Lieutenant Asgill, an object of curiosity and torment? And unlike the well-connected Asgill, whose plight generated an international incident when his mother interceded with the Queen of France, there was no one who would know that David Forman currently languished in a Bermuda prison, much less care to intervene on his behalf.

Family tradition—related perhaps by his fellow passengers—describes the general as becoming acutely demoralized at the prospect of this most unwelcome interruption of his voyage. General David Forman died at age fifty-two at sea on September 12th, 1797, even before the ship reached Bermuda.

The captain, employing materials readily at hand, preserved the general's mortal remains, likely pickled in a barrel of rum. Throughout his adult life General Forman had participated in and benefited from various aspects of the triangular trans-Atlantic trade—exchanging enslaved Black captives, commodities, and manufactured trade goods among North America, the Caribbean, and Africa. On his final homeward journey "Black David" Forman experienced a portion of that seagoing route, while immersed in its most characteristic product.

*

A consolation was that he had prepared his will almost a year before, prior to departing for Natchez. Following bequests to his wife and children, his sister-in-law Margaret would receive a one-time payment of 100 pounds, an amount far below what she negotiated when settling Ezekiel's estate. The general's favorite eldest daughter Sarah, and her husband and cousin William Gordon Forman, stood to inherit both Natchez plantations. Forman likely would have asked Benajah Osman to stay on as overseer until his grown children could arrive.

On reaching their northeast destination, the ship's captain assured that the general's remains were returned to the family. Sarah and William probably oversaw the funeral arrangements, interring David in the cemetery of Old Tennent Church. It was the same Monmouth County churchyard in which Samuel S. had once played schoolyard games.

The general's passing was noted in an obituary. In spite of his wealth and prominence, his military career and success as a New Jersey planter, there were no broad lamentations. The New Jersey chapter of the Society of the Cincinnati, whose full hereditary membership he had lobbied for, did not so much as mention David Forman's passing in their minutes. Passings during the 1790s of other, more significant Revolutionary War figures of cultural, political, regional, and military importance—like Benjamin Franklin, John Hancock, General Anthony Wayne, and George Washington—generated far more attention and sympathy.

CHAPTER 20

Stars and Stripes

WINDS OF CHANGE BLEW IN FROM FAR AFIELD, FOREVER TRANSFORMING life in what Americans were coming to call the Mississippi Territory. Plantation settlers wore their allegiances and citizenship as lightly as cotton smocks in summer, shifting their positions to those most expedient in the sultry and shifting Delta breezes.

By late 1795 the Treaty of San Lorenzo, from which Andrew Ellicott's stalled mission proceeded, agreed to set the southern border between Spanish West Florida and the American Mississippi Territory at the thirty-first parallel. This was the same border that had been asserted by the former British colonials, ousted just fifteen years before by the Spanish under Bernardo de Gálvez. Still, no one had yet marked the border on anything other than paper maps, while Spain claimed far more territory by right of conquest during the Revolutionary War—West Florida territories and beyond into Tennessee and Kentucky. Manuel Gayoso attempted to back up these declarations, establishing Spanish forts at Vicksburg in 1793 and the Chickasaw Bluffs at Memphis in 1795.

The Washington administration in those years was spread too thinly to confront the Spanish claims aggressively. Americans had their hands full with the Northwest Indian Federation and the Whiskey Rebels. The indistinct southern border was an annoyance American leaders deferred acting on. Meanwhile, self-aggrandizing schemers like General James Wilkinson thrived on borderland vagaries.

Now the United States and Spain pledged to clarify ownership of growing settlements along the eastern side of the Mississippi River, and American commerce downriver to New Orleans. The pact did not deal with Spanish ownership of vast *Luisiana* on the far side of the Mississippi River, the thriving City of New Orleans, or interactions with southeast Indian nations. Conditions in Europe, quite disconnected from Manuel Gayoso and Baron de Carondelet's generally successful regional initiatives, preoccupied overseas Spanish royal leaders.

Strategies that for years had been so ably carried out in West Florida and Spanish *Luisiana* suffered by the neglect of the imperial metropole. Spain, seeking to reduce friction with the Americans, agreed to open the Mississippi River to American commerce duty free for three years, and on reasonable terms thereafter.

The Americans were realizing the benefits of having vanquished the Northwest Indian Federation at the Battle of the Fallen Timbers. By Jay's Treaty, the British relinquished Fort Miami, where defeated Indians had been refused protection after that pivotal campaign, along with other forts on the upper Great Lakes. The Americans cemented the peace and northwest territorial Indian concessions by the Treaty of Greenville in late 1795.

George Washington and his second administration initiated measures to preclude Native Americans from ever again seriously challenging the sovereignty of the United States. In addition to establishing a standing army to remain in the place of Wayne's victorious Legion of the United States, Congress authorized a new military academy at West Point to groom elite army leaders. New industrial arsenals would assure a reliable domestic supply of armaments.

Also consolidating the federal position, import tariffs joined Alexander Hamilton's arsenal of revenue measures, and rapidly exceeded the distilled liquor excise and land sale schemes as income generators. Newly commissioned revenue cutters, the forerunner of the US Coast Guard, enforced the tariffs. The treasury secretary also got his Bank of the United States to assume all the states' Revolutionary War debts and to manage centrally federal debt issues and payments.

American military leaders still managed to chafe one another. Following the now-concluded Indian war, General Anthony Wayne became convinced that his second-in-command James Wilkinson had tried to undermine him during the recent campaign. He contemplated reprimanding or court martialing his scheming subordinate. "Mad Anthony" was also upset at Winthrop Sargent for extending the Northwest Territory's civil government to Detroit after the British evacuation. Wayne groused that it undermined his and the army's authority.

Fortunately for Wilkinson, he not only escaped the consequences of his mischief yet again when Wayne died unexpectedly, but he also ascended to replace General Wayne as the ranking general in the US Army.

*

Manuel Gayoso continued to nurture Spanish influence in West Florida as best he could. From his standpoint, peace in the American Northwest Territory brought the unfortunate prospect that British adventurism from Upper Canada might now be directed toward Spanish *Luisiana* and its former possession West Florida, rather than against the Americans. With the Spanish monarchy allied with France from 1796, the European situation potentially opened a flashpoint between the English in Canada and the Spanish in the Mississippi Valley.

Gayoso schemed with *Luisiana* governor Carondelet to delay the surrender of Spanish posts in West Florida to the Americans. Any sea captain with a sextant could see that the thirty-first parallel of latitude, on which the Treaty of San Lorenzo hinged, fell within the vicinity of Baton Rouge. Spanish posts to the north along the Mississippi River at Natchez, Vicksburg, and Memphis' Chickasaw Bluffs were certain to be within the boundaries of the treaty-defined United States.

Gayoso maintained clear communication, reinforced by his armed Spanish river galleys, among New Orleans, the Mississippi Delta, and Spanish St. Louis on the Upper Mississippi. Not at issue, thankfully for Spanish interests, were the frontier settlements of New Madrid, at the confluence of the Ohio and Mississippi Rivers, and St. Louis, on the western or far shore of the Mississippi River. Only at stake were ownership of Spanish West Florida, which was east of the Mississippi River, and American rights to navigate that river.

So Gayoso played for time. He asserted that the location of the thirty-first parallel border was in doubt until a mutually verifiable survey was conducted by a joint border commission, adhering strictly to the treaty provisions. Rather than surrender Natchez and his forts along the Mississippi, he reinforced them. Perhaps Gayoso hoped the Americans lacked sufficient resources and resolve to enforce the treaty. Perhaps he hoped that the Anglo and American immigrants, many of whom he knew personally, would prefer the generous Spanish land grants and his *laissez-faire* administration to an uncertain future with the United States. With nascent cotton production in the region promising to be more lucrative than tobacco and indigo had ever been, why speed along cession and forever lose the region for Spain?

*

Much to Andrew Ellicott's chagrin, Gayoso thus prolonged the evacuation for well over a year. The Spanish did dismantle their fort at Memphis in April 1797, but despite Ellicott's armed camp, the Spanish stayed put in Natchez. Fort Panmure, Spanish Government House, and the Spanish civil administration continued operations without pause or diminution.

Meanwhile, Gayoso counted on the social capital he had amassed over the years with the expat community to keep them loyal to their Spanish leaders. He had reason to expect such support, since he socialized with so many of them, even twice marrying the daughters of an American plantation owner. In an effort to strengthen that affinity, he declared a moratorium on debt collection that disproportionately benefited this same influential group.

In Andrew Ellicott's corner were some locals, whose pro-American Committee of Safety had come to be known as the Natchez Revolt. He characterized some of these partisans as ne'er-do-wells who expected an American administration to relieve them of any debts they owed, were Spanish West Florida to go out of existence. Other Committee of Safety supporters, like Peter Bruin, were substantial plantation owners who may have felt slighted that the Spanish had not granted them even more free land. And there were others, like the seventy-two-year-old curmudgeon Anthony Hutchins, who in earlier years had schemed to oust the Spanish by force in favor of the British. Most but not all of these disparate characters agreed with Ellicott, who wanted an immediate but orderly and peaceful transfer of sovereignty.

Though he was his nemesis with respect to the pace of the border commission's work and timing of transfer to the United States, the commissioner came to respect Manuel Gayoso's personal qualities. Gayoso met personally with the Committee of Safety's representatives, at some risk to his reputation and person. By force of charm and reason, he acceded to some of their demands to act as an advisory council, yet maintain the Spanish administration and dominion for the near term.

During the summer of 1797, after Baron de Carondelet assumed the more prestigious Spanish governorship in Quito, South America, and Gayoso relocated to New Orleans as governor of all of *Luisiana*, Stephen Minor, his loyal protégé and Pennsylvania expat, got the role as last Spanish governor of the Natchez District.

Minor stayed in close contact with Gayoso by letter, informing his mentor of the many challenges he faced in Natchez and how he resolved them in favor of continued Spanish administration. Minor negotiated among the parties and was able to defuse the more bellicose American voices. He was able to continue Spanish ownership and administration of the region for nine more months.

*

On the evening of March 30, 1798, the Spanish finally acquiesced to the inevitable. Running out of excuses and bowing to the direction of their ministry finally to comply with the San Lorenzo Treaty terms, the Spanish garrison packed up and withdrew their Natchez garrison at Fort Panmure, pushing off downriver toward New Orleans. Now only one flag flew over Natchez, the fifteen stars and fifteen bars of the United States.

Yankee New Englander Winthrop Sargent, far from his roots in the Ohio Land Company, controversial stint as secretary of the Northwest Territory, and his harrowing war experiences at the hands of Little Turtle's warriors, arrived in Natchez as newly appointed governor.

The date April 7, 1798, marks the founding of the United States's Mississippi Territory. Natchez was its first capital, and for years afterward, surrounding Adams County was its most populous area.

On arrival Sargent perceived that "a refractory and turbulent spirit prevailed . . . with parties headed by men of perverseness and cunning."

Such were the leading citizens he had to deal with, people who "have run wild in the recesses of government."

He unilaterally decreed a criminal code for the territory, reflecting his strict Puritan morality and sternness. It was as unwelcome among plantation grandees and ordinary white citizens of the Delta South as a similar document had been among frontiersmen and settlers in the Northwest Territory. The region's enslaved population realized scant difference in their lives between the Spanish and American regimes. In any case, they were not consulted.

*

With Sargent's arrival and Gayoso's departure from Natchez, the real work of cutting the path and marking the southern US border began in earnest. William Dunbar led the Spanish delegation; Andrew Ellicott acted on behalf of the Americans. Dunbar, an engaging fellow, apparently got along well with Ellicott, united as they were in scientific interests and pursuits. While on the expedition, which extended from 1798 through 1799, Dunbar supplemented his surveying with descriptions of newly encountered plants, trees, and shrubs.

Dozens of hired woodsmen hacked a path dozens of yards wide through forest and canebrake on a path mutually agreed upon by the surveyors. Ellicott and Dunbar ordered stones set at mile intervals to mark the division between the United States and Spain, traversing traditional Creek and Seminole lands.

One band of Seminoles attacked, resulting in lost pack animals, stolen supplies, and long delays. Indians were rightly concerned that the survey marking the border would inevitably lead to settler incursions, even into mosquito-infested swamps. During the expedition Dunbar sickened with fever. Though he later recovered, Stephen Minor, who had to learn about celestial-based surveying from Ellicott on the job, completed the survey as the Spanish representative.

*

Following their work on the southern border survey both Dunbar and Minor became US citizens and remained in Natchez. Over the years, as their enslaved African Americans labored on greatly expanded cotton acreage, both magnified their wealth.

Dunbar's scientific writings gained Thomas Jefferson's attention and the two corresponded. Minor purchased Manuel Gayoso's magnificent Concord Plantation under favorable terms, where he continued in his mentor's stead during the last months of Spanish dominion.

Minor secretly remained on the Spanish payroll until at least 1809, although he repatriated as an American citizen. He was a founder of the Bank of Mississippi and a major shareholder throughout his life. When Thomas Jefferson asked Dunbar to undertake a southern equivalent to the Lewis and Clark Expedition, Minor convinced Dunbar to embark on a more limited venture. Not coincidentally, Spain did not favor an American Corps of Discovery ranging so close to their far southwestern holdings.

Now, men like David Bradford, former Whiskey Rebellion leader, escaped American fugitive, and prosperous four-year Natchez area resident, as well as the irascible Anthony Hutchins, who formerly disagreed with federal authority, renounced their prior transgressions. Bradford even received a presidential pardon. As the Americans were ever practical and sensed what card to play, the result was that they henceforth collectively helped cement American sovereignty in the region.

In addition to his own strict laws issued by fiat for the territory, the always skeptical Governor Winthrop Sargent was keen to enforce President John Adams's Alien and Sedition Act against opponents in the new American territory. In response, Hutchins and like thinkers, energized at the prospect of ousting the unpopular territorial governor, won the day. They succeeded in limiting Sargent's near-dictatorial powers by accelerating the next stage in territorial governance—an elected legislature for the Mississippi Territory. Despite his direct appeal to President Jefferson, Sargent, a Whig appointed by John Adams, lost the governorship in 1801.

*

Manuel Gayoso, now residing in New Orleans as governor of Spanish *Luisiana* and the greatly reduced remainder of Spanish West Florida, contracted yellow fever and succumbed on July 18, 1799, at age fifty-two.

Surprisingly, the sociable and appealing gentleman who had so wisely guided the Natchez District through a maelstrom of competing factions, died bankrupt. Gayoso's extensive and well-used personal library attested obliquely to the fact that he was a well-informed leader who did not abuse his office for personal gain.

Gayoso's only consolation in death was that he did not live to see the systematic unraveling of his efforts to make West Florida and *Luisiana* viable and prosperous provinces of New Spain. Nor did he witness Spain, driven by Napoleonic politics and preoccupations in Europe, secretly cede all of *Luisiana* to France in 1800. Nor how, in turn, the abject failure of a French expeditionary force to reclaim sugar-rich Saint-Domingue in 1800 from rebellious Black slaves led by Toussaint L'Ouverture would permanently sour Napoleon's dream for a renewed French empire in North America.

*

In parallel with shifting French imperial ambitions, President Jefferson, seeking a way to permanently open the Mississippi to American river traffic, sent a diplomatic delegation to Europe to purchase the city of New Orleans. Though generating constitutional issues and challenging his conception of limited government, Jefferson and Congress jumped at the proffered opportunity to purchase not only New Orleans, but the entirety of now-French *Louisiana*, much of it still unexplored by Europeans or Americans. In 1803 Napoleon sold the city and extensive territory to the United States for $15,000,000, just a third more than Jefferson was willing to pay for New Orleans alone. At one stroke the Louisiana Purchase more than doubled the area of the United States.

Spanish cession of the area to France had been kept secret until just three weeks prior to the formal transfer of sovereignty in New Orleans to the Americans. US Mississippi Territory governor William C. Claiborne, Winthrop Sargent's successor, and General James Wilkinson, representing the US Army and the federal government, came downriver from Natchez to attend. On December 20, 1803, the standard of the First French Republic was ceremoniously lowered and replaced by the American flag.

At St. Louis town, the regional capital of Upper *Luisiana*, the transfer of sovereignty occurred on successive days, March 9th and 10th, 1804. Lately of Gallipolis, Ohio, Dr. Antoine François Saugrain and his family, now residents of St. Louis, were likely among the crowd of onlookers. Saugrain helped with the final outfitting of Lewis and Clark's Corps of Discovery, which departed for the Pacific Northwest immediately after formal cession of the territory. Appointed physician to the newly established US Army garrison, Saugrain served for many years as the only physician in the frontier town and region.

*

Benajah Osman made the transition from overseer to self-made planter by the early 1800s. Following David Forman's departure from Natchez in August 1797, where he had lingered just long enough to complete the transfer of Ezekiel's estate assets to himself, Osman probably continued for a time at Wilderness Plantation. Then, soon after hearing of the general's demise, Osman appealed directly to President John Adams to be appointed a marshal in an anticipated American territorial administration.

> *Eight [years] Absence from the actual Jurisdiction of the united States has Nither lessend my Attachment for there welfare not my Reverence for there Laws . . . Great indead will be my Satisfaction in finding a Steady and Compleat Assumption of the American Government in this Cuntry. . . .*

Osman did not win a federal appointment. So he struck out on his own, establishing what became a substantial planation for himself at Windy Hill. He became a US Mississippi Territory militia colonel, with rank and honor far exceeding any he could have realized had he remained in New Jersey. Aaron Burr visited his Windy Hill Planation mansion in 1807, at which time the visitor courted teenaged neighboring beauty Madeline Price prior to his arrest for treason. It is unclear if Osman played any role in the former vice-president's quest to establish an independent country in the American Southwest or to seize territory in Mexico for the same purpose. The fact that Osman joined others to post Burr's $10,000 bail suggests he had more than a passing interest in Burr's scheme.

While Osman was always considered an upstanding resident of Natchez and Adams County, he did raise a few eyebrows posthumously with his desire to manumit Jerry, a provision made public on the probate of his will in 1815. Jerry was just one of the many enslaved at Windy Hill and the only one Osman wished to free. Since Osman never married and had no acknowledged offspring, a modern observer might wonder just why Jerry earned his freedom. However, the manumission was contested before the Mississippi Legislature, as the ascendency of King Cotton in the antebellum period closed any path to freedom. Unfortunately, we do not know anything else about Jerry, including whether he was ever emancipated.

*

William Gordon Forman, husband of David Forman's daughter Sarah, had worked to put the general's estate affairs in order in the East and to emigrate to Natchez. He intended to arrive with Sarah to assume residence and management of the general's plantations. Unusual for a woman at the time, Sarah actively took part in her father's estate as coadministrator alongside husband William, liquidating both the general's New Jersey and Maryland assets.

On September 9, 1798, just one year after the general's death, his widow Anne Marsh Forman died at age forty-six. She was laid to rest beside her imperious husband at Old Tennent Church Cemetery in Monmouth.

Daughter Sarah enjoyed the role of wealthy heiress but briefly, dying at age twenty-six, possibly in childbirth, on January 18, 1799. She was buried in the same churchyard as her parents. She too had fallen prey to the adverse fates afflicting the general, his brother Ezekiel, and her own mother. Many of the Formans' lives were cut short, while their wealth long outlived them.

William Gordon Forman, now the beneficiary of Sarah's portion as well as his mother-in-law's portion, and executor of the entire David Forman estate, relocated to Natchez by 1800. There, he took up residence at Wilderness Plantation. Unlike the original Forman family members, William would not have shared the prior history and intimacy with the general's slaves that his elders had enjoyed. Over the course of years in administering General Forman's estate, he sold off the slaves in groups. It is unclear whether or not he kept family units intact.

William G.'s protracted challenge in administering David Forman's estate was to convert riches denominated in land and slaves into cash to settle the estate shares of the general's three surviving daughters and fuel his own acquisitive business interests.

One of William G.'s first actions as a new resident in Natchez was to convince his brother Joseph to join him from New Jersey, sell Wilderness Plantation to him at a low price, and buy it back at the same price several months later. It is unclear to what purpose the circular, brother-to-brother transaction was intended, although the effect of the sale was to reset the value of Wilderness Plantation at an artificially low price. The low valuation would also reduce the cash amount due his wife's sisters—Rivine Forman Neilson, Malvina Forman, and Emma Forman Cummings—as their share of the estate.

Later, William G. went into partnership with Abijah Hunt for other plantation ownership and trading enterprises. He became prominent in Mississippi society as speaker of the Territorial House of Representatives. Feeling lonely and perhaps nostalgic, however, he returned a few years later to New Jersey and courted Reverend John Woodhull's only daughter. Sarah Woodhull's dowry of $80,000 was enough to qualify her as one of the richest women in America. Her fortune was still entrusted to her father, pastor of Old Tennent Church, who also appears to have been an astute investor and businessman.

She accepted William G.'s marriage proposal and they married in her father's church. The couple traveled to Natchez to join the *nouveau riche* plantation society there. Sarah bore a daughter, Ann Augusta, early in 1808, but did not "season" well in the fever-ridden Delta climate. She was dead and buried in Natchez within a few years, leaving William Gordon Forman twice widowed and now the single parent of a young child.

The general's surviving daughters grew weary of being repeatedly put off in their requests to William G. for the cash distributions due them as estate beneficiaries. Even Samuel S. still awaited payment of General David's old debt to him: "I have been of great service in effecting their plans; not a little did Osman and I suffer with the Blacks between Monmouth and Pittsburgh." Samuel S. tried without success to induce the estate to pay the $100 with interest, as he was entitled and promised by the general. Eventually Samuel S. gave up his quest but the general's daughters pursued their former brother-in-law with vigor and persistence.

William G. was also depriving Ezekiel's widow Margaret of the annual $100 stipend that had motivated her to relinquish larger claims on her husband Ezekiel's estate. It now came to the general's estate and executor to pay the yearly amount due during her lifetime.

In early 1812 the three daughters determined to wait no more. The two married sisters dispatched their husbands to Natchez to obtain their estate shares. Arriving that February, the men found William G. debilitated from illness, but promising to pay as soon as he was recovered and could raise cash from the general's remaining assets.

Gathering his strength, William G. and his four-year-old daughter Ann Augusta set off for New Jersey overland on the arduous Natchez Trace. He intended to return the girl to New Jersey to be looked after by her grandfather and, perhaps, access his deceased wife's dowry, which evidently had not been disbursed.

Fate planned otherwise. He died when passing through Lexington on October 3, 1812, leaving little Ann Augusta to the kindness of strangers. The local newspaper documented that William G. had died of natural causes, having long been in "a bad state of health." The paper reported that the funeral was attended by "a numerous concourse of our fellow citizens, who all felt for the death of a stranger, that had no old friend about him to close his eyes." His burial place is unmarked and unknown, possibly in some potter's field in use at the time.

Unlike William G., the remaining enslaved African Americans still resident on Wilderness and Second Creek Plantations, where one by one, they died over the years of old age, overwork, disease, or perhaps trauma, were at least able to depart life among friends and neighbors in a tight community. Their experiences were ones of a remote, shared African heritage, New Jersey origins, their epic trek across the frontier, and lifetimes of hard labor. Both master and servants came to rest without monuments in the bountiful southern soil.

Estate litigation dragged on into the 1830s, exposing the complicated and insolvent dealings of William G. Forman and pitting his executors against General David Forman's surviving daughters and their husbands. Eventually the women did receive a portion of the $200,000 they felt the estate owed them, from William G.'s father's estate in Delaware.

Several very old and very young African American slaves, resident in Natchez, were part of the final estate closure in 1834. They evidently were not part of prior estate property sales of the original sixty Black emigrants from General David Forman's Monmouth, New Jersey, farm to Natchez in 1790, and their enslaved descendants.

*

Back in the Northwest Territory, Chief Little Turtle took up residence, along with his son-in-law William Wells, daughter Sweet Breeze "Wanagapeth," four grandchildren through Wells, and some of the Miami nation, in the vicinity of Fort Wayne. The area was familiar to him as Kekiongo, the principal town of his vanquished Northwest Indian Federation.

Little Turtle became an advocate for Indian adaptation and adoption of American and European ways that he judged helpful to his people. He lived comfortably on a modest US Government stipend. William Wells landed a desirable federal appointment as Indian agent, managing the distribution and business aspects of government-mediated trading with Indians in the region. Wells accompanied Little Turtle on visits to American presidents, where Indian delegations were respectfully received.

Nativists were concerned that Little Turtle had grown too close to federal authorities and settlers, to the detriment of traditional ways. Tecumseh and his brother Tenskwatawa spearheaded multitribal opposition to accommodation and assimilation, advocating nothing short of the reconquest of previously ceded Indian lands.

Wells ultimately departed life in a poignant tableau of complex identities, conflict, and accommodation in the trans-Allegheny borderlands. As an American Army officer during the War of 1812, his forces greatly outnumbered by hostile Potawatomi warriors, he attempted to evacuate Fort Chicago under a negotiated flag of truce. Anticipating that hostile

Indians would descend on the civilian column he led, Wells applied black face paint—the hue denoting bravery and death in Indian traditions he knew his opponents would understand—to complement his American Army officer's uniform, as he led from the front. A rifle shot took his life. It is said that his triumphant enemies, although vehemently opposing the assimilationist path he embodied, cut out and ate his heart in deference to his bravery and to gain his strength.

CHAPTER 21

North and South

FOR THE REST OF HIS LIFE SAMUEL S. FORMAN WOULD RECALL FONDLY the first few years in Cazenovia, New York, as a pioneer adventure: cutting a new wagon road from Utica, naming new settlements, and welcoming eager settler farming families. Arriving with his employer John Lincklaen on May 8, 1793, the two young men were busily involved in the initial years with parceling out their Holland Land Company grant to create its first settlement. Samuel S. took charge of the company store, shipping in farm implements, retailing them, then acquiring and aggregating harvests for sale to more distant markets.

Samuel S. convinced his older brother Jonathan to leave New Jersey and join him in Upstate New York. Jonathan warmed to the idea, arriving in Cazenovia with his wife and child in 1796. The brothers joined in partnership to manage the Holland Land Company's store.

In the first few years Samuel S. lived in a log cabin adjacent to his brother. Jonathan's old tent, which had seen service through the Revolutionary War, "was pitched between the house and the lake during the warm weather, doing duty as a summer house." There the family and their employer enjoyed refreshing breezes off Lake Cazenovia and alfresco dinners of fresh-caught perch. The brothers and the company thrived.

Though the new settlers fenced fields and sowed crops, the area was still quite wild just outside the clearings. For years after, Samuel S. shared tales of hunting bears and serving up their meat for dinner.

John Lincklaen married Helen Ledyard, a niece of the Forman brothers from New London, Connecticut. As a teenager Helen had been a nurse who "went over her shoe tops in blood" in caring for those wounded in traitor Benedict Arnold's 1781 amphibious assault on Fort Griswold, her hometown. Her uncle William Ledyard, a colonel in the Connecticut militia, was summarily executed in an outrageous war crime by Arnold's troops following the American surrender in that episode. Samuel S. delighted in adding these Revolutionary War exploits to his considerable repertoire of stories.

John Lincklaen prospered in Cazenovia. He built a stately brick Federal mansion in October 1808 that easily became the most impressive habitation in the rapidly developing region. But the Lincklaens remained childless, evidently a disappointment to both John and Helen. Before he died in 1822, John adopted Helen's youngest brother Jonathan and made him the couple's heir. John assured that his adopted son was accepted by the Holland Land Company proprietors, succeeding him as their regional agent.

A few years into the nineteenth century Samuel S. faced a personal loss when his brother and partner Jonathan died at age fifty-four on May 25, 1809. Quite possibly that loss set him to thinking about fresh opportunities. Economic disruption, brought about by President Jefferson's international trade embargo, was being felt even in frontier Upstate New York. Both circumstances perhaps caused Samuel S. to consider returning to Natchez to claim the 1791 Spanish land grant of 800 choice acres made him by then-Governor Gayoso.

Asserting ownership at that late date would have been a speculative but conceivable quest. At one stroke it would have vaulted Samuel S. into the realm of wealthy, slave-owning planters at the center of the burgeoning Cotton Kingdom. Though residence and active cultivation of the land constituted the strongest argument for upholding the Spanish grants, he could have retained an aggressive Natchez lawyer to make his case. Samuel S. Forman's relatives, now leading citizens and planters in the area, might also become advocates and corroborating witnesses for upholding the old claim, a decided plus in his calculations. Certainly other absent grantees had prevailed with such claims. Why not try?

Samuel S. could also have elicited the intercession of William Gordon Forman, at that moment an eminent Mississippi businessman and politician. As ongoing executor of General David Forman's estate, this cousin surely owed him a favor to atone for nonpayment of principal and interest still due Samuel S. from his services during the epic 1789–90 trek to Natchez. Samuel S. perhaps understood as he never had before, the debt owed him for holding the immigrant train together at its most tenuous juncture, when traveling across Pennsylvania. Had the enterprise collapsed, neither the general nor William G. would have realized their plantation riches.

Samuel S. could have expected additional influential allies as well. Stephen Minor, who had been solicitous of the Forman arrivals' welfare under the Spanish regime, was now a substantial repatriated American citizen in the Mississippi Territory. William Dunbar, the very same Spanish official who had surveyed Samuel S.'s land grant, had now earned the trust and confidence of President Jefferson. Benajah Osman, with whom Samuel S. had shared the rigors of the epic pioneer journey, was a rich and respected proprietor. All could be expected to vouch for the claim and for Samuel S. personally, although he hadn't seen any of them in eighteen years.

By Samuel S.'s recollection, he was ready to depart Cazenovia for the trip south, when he was appalled to discover that the pivotal Spanish land grant was missing. He offered no plausible explanation for the disappearance of this potentially valuable document, only that be believed it had remained locked away in the custom cherrywood chest he had borne across his frontier travels. He vaguely intimated that he perhaps was victimized by some supernatural force or spirit, cast in his own version of a headless horseman tale so popularized at the time by Washington Irving, grist indeed for an inveterate storyteller like Samuel S. He would concede: "So vanished my eight hundred acres of valuable land in the promising Mississippi country."

So he remained in Upstate New York, where his business interests rapidly stabilized and then thrived. He had married eighteen-year-old Sarah McCarty on March 21, 1808, moved to nearby Syracuse instead of Natchez, and went on to build a mansion to house his new family. The couple's first child, a boy, died in infancy, followed a few years later by Samuel's young wife. He did not remarry. But their second child, Mary Euphonia, grew to a healthy adulthood and married. Samuel S. lived as an esteemed member in her household for the rest of his very long life.

He continued to manage the Holland Land Company store as an independent businessman. In addition to his retail operations, he sponsored cattle drives to Philadelphia and markets on Long Island. For many years, he served on the board of a canal company and a turnpike. In the course of running his businesses, he took on a number of clerks and assistants. The young men looked upon their time working under Samuel S. Forman as one of the more gratifying experiences in their lives. Not having sons of his own, Samuel S. was an uncommonly involved and encouraging mentor.

The man who had so much admired the military since boyhood was himself appointed colonel in the New York militia. During the war of 1812 Samuel S. provided important organizational leadership skills to the state militia. Perhaps his skills in supply and support functions were ultimately more valued and appropriate to the times than leading combat troops. From that point onward, he acquired the honorific Colonel Forman.

All of which gave the genial Samuel S. a forum to tell his own anecdotes, and those of his extended family, along with those other stories born of his pioneering adventures of a lifetime. He was frequently called upon to deliver keynote speeches at patriotic events in the area. Less formally, he would delight generations of children with his tales of the old West and South and of the Revolutionary War.

*

At age ninety-seven, in 1862, Samuel S. Forman had outlived almost all of his family as well as his Revolutionary War–era contemporaries—white, Black, red, and brown. He recalled holding his own father's hand until he felt the old gentleman's last pulse. Perhaps as Samuel S. entered his own decline, his memory flickered with faces and personalities "never to be seen again." These included people like Washington and Madison, whose roles in the enlarged United States would become noteworthy. And others who would have their moment on the historical stage of the new American nation, only to have their life's work cast off, like the capricious Mississippi currents, lost in tangled eddies and sleepy bayous. He would soon join them all in the grave.

As he reviewed his life and prepared, as he would have believed, to come to account before his Maker and be judged by his character and actions, one wonders how he would regard that road not taken. Did he think how close he had come to living a far different life, had he remained in Natchez as a Mississippi plantation owner, or returned there? For then he would be today observing gray-clad young men, the grandsons of his relatives and neighbors, marching off to war on behalf of the Confederacy.

It would be so like what he could view now in the serried ranks of Syracuse's and Onondaga County's Union volunteers, marching past his window, their Springfield rifles barrels glinting like organ pipes in the sunlight. As a veteran of an era that had known conflict that had birthed a nation—the clash of Patriot and Loyalist soldiers, of Indian warriors, of enslaved people and imperial powers, Samuel S. would know that soon "loud lament and dismal misery will mingle with their awful symphonies." Could he have realized that the deeds of his generation—and some even done by his own hands—had now come to account for others to pay?

General David Forman had never compensated Samuel S. for his services in relocating Ginnie, her husband Jess, the "two disaffected fellows," and the other enslaved African American families, to become the engine of the Formans' wealth in the Mississippi Delta Cotton Kingdom. Over the decades, that liability had seemingly morphed in ominous and divergent ways: into a challenge to the institution of slavery, the assertion of states' rights within a federal republic, and the threatened imminent disintegration of the United States of America.

Installments on those debts would be made in blood on battlefields and in geographies Samuel S. would recognize, although some of the names had changed from those of his youth: Fort Sumter, Donelson and Pillow, Island Number Ten, Shiloh, Chickamauga, and Vicksburg. Distant Forman relatives, branches of the family with whom he had long lost touch, had become leading Confederates and citizens of secessionist Southern states.

A visitor was struck to the degree that the nonagenarian "though feeble and ill [. . .] retains all his mental faculties," but noted that Samuel S.'s "closing years were embittered over the distracted condition of his country, embroiled in fratricidal war. . . ."

His family recorded that his earnest prayer was that a proud American flag might again wave its ample folds over a firmly united American nation. Having contemplated the precipice, Samuel S. knew that there was work yet to be done to achieve the Founders' aspirational vision of "a more perfect Union" characterized by "one flag, one land, one heart, one hand...."

Samuel S. Forman died quietly in his daughter's house on August 16, 1862, and was buried at Oakwood Cemetery. His passing went unnoticed by Syracuse and Upstate New York citizens, as incoming casualty reports from the Seven Days Battles around Richmond arrived to grim anticipation and dread.

Acknowledgments

RESEARCH TOOK ME TO TEN STATES, THE DISTRICT OF COLUMBIA, AND more than three dozen libraries and historic sites. Their staffs were unfailingly helpful, knowledgeable, and welcoming. I acknowledge their support here:

In New England, I wish to recognize Peter Drummey of the Massachusetts Historical Society; Don Friary of the Colonial Society of Massachusetts; the staff of the New England Historical and Genealogical Society; J. Archer O'Reilly III of the Massachusetts Society of the Cincinnati; Jeffrey Croteau of Scottish Rite Masonic Museum's Library and Archives; Deborah Barlow Smedstad of the Boston Museum of Fine Arts Library; Meghan Sullivan-Silva at the John Carter Brown Library of Brown University; and Ed Surato of the Whitney Library of the New Haven Historical Society. Harvard's Peabody Museum of Archeology and Ethnography displays artifacts and modern interpretations of relevance to the Native American experience in the Old Northwest and preremoval Southeast. A Choctaw horsehair athlete's collar became part inspiration for chapter 12's description of the 1790 Noxubee River ball game.

I thank for invaluable assistance Tammy Kiter at the New York Historical Society; John Cordovez, Tal Nadan, and Meredith Mann at the New York Public Library's Manuscripts and Archives Division; Elisha Davies at the Cazenovia Public Library; Sharon Clooney and Jackie Roshia at Lorenzo State Historic Site in Cazenovia; and the staff of the New York State Archives in Albany. At the National Museum of the American Indian in Manhattan I was inspired by visually arresting artifacts and interpretation capturing a broad range of North American Indian nations.

In New Jersey I benefited from the assistance of Joe Zemla of the Monmouth County Historical Association and John McC. Shannon, Secretary of the New Jersey Society of the Cincinnati.

In Pennsylvania I acknowledge Linda August, Sarah Weatherwax, Connie King, and Krystal Appiah at the Library Company of Philadelphia; the staff of the Historical Society of Pennsylvania; Roy E. Goldman at the American Philosophical Society in Philadelphia; Katherine A. Ludwig and Meg McSweeney of the David Library of the American Revolution (since integrated into APS); the staff of the Lancaster County Historical Society; Shannon Schwaller, Tom Buffenbarger, and Rodney Foytik of the US Army War College Library and US Army Heritage and Education Center in Carlisle; Anita Zanke of the Westmoreland County Historical Society; and Jon Klosinski and chief librarian Mary E. Jones of the Detre Library at the John Heinz Regional History Center in Pittsburgh. Karie Diethorn and Courtney Christner of the Independence National Historical Park in Philadelphia lent expertise on a number of portraits.

In Washington, DC, I gratefully acknowledge Ellen McAllister Clark, Library Director, and Michele Lee Silverman of the American Revolution Institute at the Society of the Cincinnati's Anderson House and staff of the DC location of the National Archives and Records Administration. Paul Gardullo of the Smithsonian's National Museum of African American History and Culture was enormously helpful for access to collections and introductions to relevant works. The National Museum of the American Indian on the National Mall offers historical and contemporary displays surveying a broad range of North American Indian nations.

In Ohio I acknowledge Mr. Westmoreland, senior historian at the National Underground Railroad Freedom Center, and the museum's endeavors to educate modern Americans in creative ways about antebellum stories difficult to tell, and doing so as a basis for uniting all Americans. Their 1830 slave pen is a unique immersive exhibit of a commercial jail where African American slaves were aggregated and housed in advance of being driven in coffles 800 miles south along the Natchez Trace for sale in the slave markets at Natchez. We sat in silence on austere benches illuminated by tiny claustrophobia-inducing barred windows, among iron rings still protruding from rough timber walls. To paraphrase historian Edward Baptist, "The half has never been told." I also appreciate introductions within the museum and to its mission by John Pepper, the former CEO and board chairman of Procter & Gamble and a consistent supporter of the creation and functioning of the museum. Others in the state facilitating my research were Katy Scullin and Linda Schowalter of Marietta College Legacy Library's Special Collections; Anne B. Shepherd, Clasire Smittle, and M'Lissa Y. Kesterman of the Cincinnati Historical Society Library; and staff of the Cincinnati Public Library.

I enjoyed insightful correspondence with Jennie Cole at the Filson Historical Society in Louisville, Kentucky, and with naturalist Paul Oligies of the Falls of the Ohio Interpretive Center and State Park in Clarksville, Indiana. Unfortunately, I did not have the pleasure of visiting these Ohio River destinations in person.

Lori Bessler, Tom Farrell, and Lee Grady at the Wisconsin Historical Society answered my free-ranging inquiries about Lyman C. Draper, their founding figure and editor of Samuel S. Forman's published travel accounts, and his collections.

I want to thank Dennis Northcott at the Missouri History Museum, Library and Research Center in St. Louis.

In Mississippi I benefited from the advice of Mary (Mimi) Miller of the Historic Natchez Foundation; Willie Hutchins and Hayden Kaiser Jr. at the Adams County Courthouse Chancery Archive; interpretive rangers Barney Schoby Jr. and Kathleen Bond of the National Park Service's Melrose Plantation in Natchez; and Jim Woodrick of the Mississippi Department of Archives and History in Jackson. Dr. David Conwill joined me on his home turf for deep dives at the Mississippi State Archives, and subsequently located copies of key long misplaced Spanish colonial estate records.

I am grateful to the many genealogists who preserved and made accessible the Forman family histories and source documents—Helen Lincklaen Fairchild (d. 1931) and Lyman C. Draper (d. 1891). Among the vibrant living, Winn Forman has been my go-to genealogist for his encyclopedic and discerning knowledge of the historic Formans.

Professor David Hackett Fischer made a number of suggestions on historiographic issues, and provided advice on the nature and significance of internal slave migrations in the Early Republic and the impact of infectious diseases on the colonization of the Delta South. He generously allowed me to review relevant chapters of his work-in-progress, *Africa's Gifts*, exploring distinct African folkways carried over into the American experience.

Nathaniel Philbrick shared his insights into engagingly presenting popular history while maintaining a rigorous scholarly foundation. The thoughts he shared, based on his *Mayflower* and *The Last Stand*, increased my understanding of incorporating Native American sources and scholarship into accounts of colonial settler conflict on the frontiers.

Charlene Smith, South African expat and authorized biographer of Nelson Mandela, provided her views on preparing effective and affecting written descriptions of violence in nonfiction and history. I enjoyed conversing with her on topics as diverse as the Afrikaners Great Trek across the Transvaal and the postapartheid Truth and Reconciliation Commission.

Charles Weeks kindly offered advice along with pertinent draft chapters from his new book (with Christian Pinnen) about colonial Mississippi. Historian Michael Adelberg shared his knowledge of Revolutionary War-era Monmouth County and General David Forman.

David McCullough, author of *Pioneers*, has brought renewed attention and a broad audience to compelling sagas arising from the trans-Allegheny West of the Early Republic.

I reference several authors' works frequently, and depend on them heavily, for important events occurring "offstage" of the Forman pioneers' saga. I am grateful for secondary sources and the fruits of recent decades of scholarship on these topics, in addition to numerous works found in *Ill-Fated Frontier*'s bibliography and endnotes (the latter appearing on the author's website, www.ill-fatedfrontier.com). Collin Calloway's *The Victory with No Name* and his *Indian World of George Washington* combine authority, frequent quotations from primary sources, and riveting storytelling. He is more sympathetic to Indian points of view than previous accounts.

Other books in this spirit include Robbin Ethridge's *From Chicaza to Chickasaw*; Kathleen DuVal's *Independence Lost*; Claudio Saunt's *West of the Revolution* and *New Order of Things*; Richard White's *The Middle Ground*; Frederick Hoxie's *Oxford Handbook of American Indian History*; and William Hogeland's *Whiskey Rebellion*.

I call appreciative attention to Tiya Miles's *The House on Diamond Hill* and Erica Armstrong Dunbar's *Never Caught* for leading the way in telling rigorous African American histories in the face of scanty primary sources.

Children Luba, Alex, and Gabriel shared with their father his pursuit of the stories of long-dead Forman non-ancestors. Sister Elizabeth Y. Forman critiqued and edited the entire manuscript. Debbie Banda encouraged the book's progress and provided important introductions.

Agent Jeanne Fredericks has encouraged this title from its inception.

Bibliography

Archives, Manuscript Collections, and Dissertations

Multiple versions of the Forman autobiographical and travel accounts exist, both published and unpublished. I have amalgamated details found in one or another of them to provide the fullest possible entirely nonfiction account.

Lyman C. Draper came across a version of Samuel S. Forman's (1765–1862) autobiographical writings in the 1880s. They were originally written by Forman almost fifty years after the memorialized events. Draper recognized the writings as a rare firsthand account of trans-Allegheny westward and southern pioneering. Draper was able to verify Forman's recollections of the vast majority of people and places named in the autobiographical narrative, a situation lending credence to those details for which Forman remains the only source. He saw to its publication in 1888 accompanied by his own commentary.

I tracked down and drew upon several unpublished versions in archives of Samuel S. Forman's writings. Two were published prior to 1870 in periodicals and unknown to Draper. I personally acquired a handwritten manuscript apparently circulating with family descendants prior to Draper's publication. Slight variants and additional details appearing in one or another of the unpublished manuscripts enabled me to flesh out the tale. Enslaved Formans' names appear inconsistently among manuscript sources, and not at all in Draper's published book version.

In Natchez I discovered transcripts of Spanish probate legal proceedings and an extensive estate inventory that shed further light on the white and Black pioneer immigrants of 1789–90 and elucidated their experiences during the first few years of settlement. The circumstances of the

1795 slave inventory (extracted on Ill-FatedFrontier.com) render it a possibly unique, comprehensive census of a large single group of enslaved Black northern pioneer immigrants embarking on the Final Passage. Not comingled with others and most traveling as intact families, the Black emigrants from New Jersey are identifiable by name, family, and other attributes, and were destined to become unwitting cofounders of the Mississippi Delta Cotton Kingdom.

New York Public Library, New York City
    Fairchild Collection, Forman Papers
New York Historical Society, New York City
    Fairchild Collection, Forman Papers
Monmouth County Historical Association, Monmouth, New Jersey
    Forman Papers
Special Collections Research Center, Syracuse University, Syracuse, New York
    Lorenzo Collection, Forman Papers
Adams County Courthouse, Chancery Archive, Natchez, Mississippi
    Spanish Colonial Natchez District Administration Records 1778–1798

Outside of the many relevant primary source documents in Forman-named collections and at the Adams County Courthouse in Natchez, additional archival sources, electronic databases, and doctoral dissertations each offer few but important manuscript materials drawn upon for this history. I have posted the full citations along with the relevant endnotes on Ill-FatedFrontier.com.

BOOKS

Anon. *African-Americans in Monmouth County during the Age of the American Revolution*. Lincroft: Monmouth County Park System, 1990.
Anon. *New Jersey and the Negro: A Bibliography, 1715–1967*. Trenton: New Jersey Library Association, 1967.
Anon. *New Jersey Road Maps of the 18th Century*. Princeton: Princeton University Library, 1964.

Anon. *The Oldest Abolition Society, being a short story of the labors of the Pennsylvania Society for Promoting the Abolition of Slavery*. . . . Philadelphia: Pennsylvania Abolition Society, 1911.

———. *Proceedings of a General Court Marshall . . . of Major-General Charles Lee*. New York: J. M. Bradstreet & Son, 1864.

Abbott, Carl. *Imagined Frontiers: Contemporary America and Beyond*. Norman: University of Oklahoma Press, 2015.

Abernathy, Thomas Perkins. *Western Lands and the American Revolution*. New York: Russell & Russell, Inc., 1959.

Ackerknecht, Erwin Heinz. *Malaria in the Upper Mississippi Valley, 1760–1900*. New York: Arno Press, 1977.

Adair, James. *The History of the American Indians*. London: Edward & Charles Dilly, 1775.

Adams, Richard C. *Brief History of the Delaware Indians*. Washington, DC: US Government Printing Office, 1906.

Adelberg, Michael. *The American Revolution in Monmouth County: The Theater of Spoil and Destruction*. Charleston: The History Press, 2010.

———. *Roster of the People of the Revolutionary Monmouth County [New Jersey]*. Baltimore: Clearfield Co., 2009.

Adler, Jonathan, and Larry L. Nelson, eds. *A History of Jonathan Alder: His Captivity and Life with the Indians*. Akron: University of Arkon Press, 2002.

Agnew, Jeremy. *Spanish Influence on the Old Southwest: A Collision of Cultures*. Jefferson: McFarland and Company, 2016.

Albert, George Dallas. *History of the County of Westmoreland, Pennsylvania, with Biographical Sketches*. Philadelphia: L. H. Everts & Co., 1882.

Allen, Michael. *Western Rivermen, 1763–1861: Ohio and Mississippi Boatmen and the Myth of the Alligator*. Baton Rouge: Louisiana State University Press, 1990.

Alton, James. *Oliver Pollock: The Life and Times of an Unknown Patriot*. New York: Appleton-Century Company, 1937.

Ambler, Charles H. *George Washington and the West*. New York: Russell and Russell, 1936.

Ambrose, Stephen. *Undaunted Courage: Meriwether Lewis, Thomas Jefferson, and the Opening of the American West*. New York: Simon & Schuster, 1997.

Anderson, Gary Clayton. *Ethnic Cleansing and the Indian: The Crime That Should Haunt America*. Norman: University of Oklahoma Press, 2014.

Andrews, Johnnie Jr. *Natchez Colonials: A Compendium of the Colonial Families of Southwest Mississippi, 1716–1800*: Bienville Historical Society, 1986.

Andrews, William L., Minrose C. Gwin, Trudier Harris, and Fred Hobson, eds. *The Literature of the American South*. New York: W.W. Norton & Co., 1998.

Apel, Thomas. *Feverish Bodies, Enlightened Minds: Science and the Yellow Fever Controversy in the Early American Republic*. Redwood City: Stanford University Press, 2016.

Aptheker, Herbert. *American Negro Slave Revolts*. New York: Columbia University Press, 1943.

———. *The Negro in the American Revolution*. New York: International Publishers, 1940.

Aron, S. *How the West Was Lost: The Transformation of Kentucky from Daniel Boone to Henry Clay*. Baltimore: Johns Hopkins University Press, 1999.

Axelrad, Jacob. *Philip Freneau, Champion of Democracy*. Austin: University of Texas, 1967.

Axtell, James. *The Indians' New South—Cultural Change in the Colonial Southeast*. Baton Rouge: Louisiana State University Press, 1997.

Ayers, Edward L. *Southern Journey: The Migrations of the American South, 1790–2020*. Baton Rouge: Louisiana State Univeristy Press, 2020.

Baily, F., J. F. W. Herschel, and A. De Morgan. *Journal of a Tour in Unsettled Parts of North America in 1796 & 1797*. London: Baily Bros., 1856.

Baldwin, Leland D. *The Keelboat Age on Western Waters*. Pittsburgh: University of Pittsburgh Press, 1960.

Baptist, Edward E. *The Half Has Never Been Told: Slavery and the Making of American Capitalism*. New York: Basic Books, 2014.

Barnes, Celia. *Native American Power in the United States, 1783–1795.* Madison: Fairleigh Dickinson University Press, 2003.

Barnet, James E. Jr. *Mississippi's American Indians.* Jackson: University Press of Mississippi, 2012.

Barr, Daniel P. *A Colony Sprung from Hell: Pittsburgh and the Struggle for Authority on the Western Pennsylvania Frontier, 1744–1794.* Kent: Kent State University Press, 2014.

———. *Boundaries between Us: Natives and Newcomers along the Frontiers of the Old Northwest Territory, 1750–1850.* Kent: Kent State University Press, 2006.

Bartram, John, and William Bartram. *Catalogue of American Trees, Shrubs and Herbacious Plants.* Philadelphia, 1783.

Bartram, William. *Travels Through North and South Carolina: Georgia, East and West Florida, the Cherokee Country, the Extensive Territories of the Muscogulges or Creek Confederacy, and the Country of the Chactaws.* Philadelphia: James and Johnson, 1792.

Bates, Albert C., ed. *The Two Putnams, Israel and Rufus, in the Havanna Expedition 1762, and in the Mississippi River Exploration 1772–1773.* Hartford: Connecticut Historical Society, 1931.

Beckert, Sven. *Empire of Cotton: A Global History.* New York: Penguin Random House, 2014.

Bell, Richard. *We Shall Be No More: Suicide and Self-Government in the Newly United States.* Cambridge: Harvard University Press, 2012.

Benezet, Anthony. *Some Observations on the Situation, Disposition, and Character of the Indian Natives of this Continent.* Philadelphia: John Crukshank, 1784.

Berkin, Carol. *A Sovereign People: The Crises of the 1790s and the Birth of American Nationalism.* New York: Basic Books, 2017.

Berlin, Ira. *Generations of Captivity: A History of African-American Slaves.* Cambridge: Belknap Press, 2003.

Bernstein, R. B. *The Founding Fathers Reconsidered.* Oxford: Oxford University Press, 2009.

Berry, Daina Ramey. *The Price for Their Pound of Flesh: The Value of the Enslaved, from Womb to Grave, in the Building of a Nation.* Boston: Beacon Press, 2017.

Berry, Daina Ramey, and Leslie M. Harris, eds. *Sexuality and Slavery: Reclaiming Intimate Histories in the Americas*. Athens: University of Georgia Press, 2018.

Bilby, Joseph B., and Katherine B. Jenkins. *Monmouth Court House: The Battle That Made the American Army*. Yardley: Westholme, 2010.

Blanchard, Kendall. *The Mississippi Choctaws at Play: The Serious Side of Leisure*. Urbana: University of Illinois Press, 1981.

Blau, Joseph L., and Salo W. Baron, eds. *The Jews of the United States*. New York: Columbia University Press, 1963.

Bliss, Eugene F. *Dr. Saugrain's Relation of His Voyage Down the Ohio River from Pittsburgh to the Falls in 1788*. Worcester: Charles Hamilton, 1897.

———. *Dr. Saugrain's Note-Books, 1788: Stay Opposite Louisville, Observations upon Post Vincennes, Diary of a Journal from Louisville to Philadelphia*. Worcester: Davis Press, 1909.

Bolton, Herbert Eugene. *The Spanish Borderlands: A Chronicle of Old Florida and the Southwest*. New Haven: Yale University Press, 1921.

Booraem, Hendrik. *A Child of the Revolution: William Henry Harrison and His World, 1773–1798*. Kent: Kent State University Press, 2012.

Boucher, J. N., and J. W. Jordan. *History of Westmoreland County, Pennsylvania*. University City: Lewis Publishing Company, 1906.

Bowes, John P. *Land Too Good for Indians: Northern Indian Removal*. Norman: University of Oklahoma Press, 2016.

Brackenridge, Hugh Henry. *Incidents of the Insurrection in Western Pennsylvania in the Year 1794*. Philadelphia, 1795.

Brazy, Martha Jane. *An American Planter: Stephen Duncan of Antebellum Natchez and New York*. Baton Rouge: Louisiana State University, 2006.

Brissot de Warville, Jacques-Pierre. *New Travels in the United States of America*. London: J. S. Jordan, 1792.

Brooks, Joanna, and John Saillant, eds. *"Face Zion Forward"—First Writers of the Black Atlantic, 1785–1798*. Boston: Northeastern University Press, 2002.

Bruchey, Stuart Weems. *Cotton and the Growth of the American Economy, 1790–1860*. New York: Harcourt Brace, 1967.

Buchanan, Thomas C. *Black Life on the Mississippi*. Chapel Hill: University of North Carolina Press, 2004.

Burnard, Trevor. *Planters, Merchants, and Slaves: Plantation Societies in British America, 1650–1820*. Chicago: University of Chicago Press, 2015.

Burnet, Jacob. *Notes on the Early Settlement of the Northwestern Territory*. Cincinnati: Berby, Bradley & Co., 1847.

Bush, Robert D., ed. *Surveying the Early Republic*. Baton Rouge: Louisiana State University Press, 2016.

Butler, Pierce. *The Unhurried Years: Memories of the Old Natchez Region*. Baton Rouge: Louisiana State University Press, 1948.

Byars, William Vincent. *The First Scientist of the Mississippi Valley: A Memoir of the Life and Work of Doctor Antoine François Saugrain*. St. Louis: B. Von Phul, 1905.

Calloway, Colin G. *The American Revolution in Indian Country*. New York: Cambridge University Press, 1995.

———. *The Indian World of George Washington: The First President, the First Americans, and the Birth of the Nation*. New York: Oxford University Press, 2018.

———. *Pen and Ink Witchcraft*. New York: Oxford University Press, 2013.

———. *The Victory with No Name—The Native American Defeat of the First American Army*. New York: Oxford University Press, 2015.

———. *The World Turned Upside Down: Indian Voices from Early America*. 2nd ed. Boston: Bedford/St. Martin's, 2016.

Campbell, Gordon, ed. *King James Bible: 400th Anniversary Edition*. Oxford: Oxford University Press, 2010.

Cameron, Catherine M., Paul Kelton, and Alan C. Swedlund, eds. *Beyond Germs: Native Depopulation in North America*. Tucson: University of Arizona Press, 2015.

Carson, James Taylor. *Searching for the Bright Path: The Mississippi Choctaws from Prehistory to Removal*. Lincoln: University of Nebraska Press, 2003.

Carstens, Kenneth C., and Nancy Son Carstens, eds. *The Life of George Rogers Clark: Triumphs and Tragedies*. Westport: Praeger, 2004.

Carter, Clarence Edwin, ed. *The Territorial Papers of the United States. Volume 4, The Territory South of the River Ohio, 1790–1796*. 26 vols. Washington, DC: US Government Printing Office, 1934.

Carter, Harvey Lewis. *The Life and Times of Little Turtle*. Urbana: University of Illinois Press, 1987.

Catlin, George, and Peter Matthiessen, eds. *North American Indians*. New York: Penguin Books USA, 1989.

Caughey, John Walton. *Bernardo de Gálvez in Louisiana, 1776–1783*. Gretna: Pelican Firebird Press, 1998, original edition 1934.

———. *McGillivray of the Creeks*. Columbia: University of South Carolina Press, 2007, original edition 1938.

Cayton, Andrew R. L. *Frontier Indiana*. Bloomington: Indiana University Press, 1998.

———. *Contact Points: American Frontiers from the Mohawk Valley to the Mississippi, 1750–1830*. Chapel Hill: University of North Carolina Press, 1998.

Chávez, Thomas E. *Spain and the Independence of the United States: An Intrinsic Gift*. Albuquerque: University of New Mexico Press, 2002.

Chernow, Ron. *Washington: A Life*. New York: Penguin Press, 2010.

Claiborne, John F. H. *Mississippi as a Province, Territory, and State*. 2 vols. Jackson: Barksdale, 1880.

Clark, Daniel. *Proofs of the Corruption of Gen. James Wilkinson and of his Connexion with Aaron Burr. . . .* Philadelphia: W. Hall & G. W. Pierie, 1809.

Clark, George Rogers, Milo Milton Quaife, and Rand Burnette, eds. *The Conquest of the Illinois*. Carbondale: Southern Illinois University Press, 2001.

Clavin, Matthew J. *Aiming for Pensacola: Fugitive Slaves on the Atlantic and Southern Frontiers*. Cambridge: Harvard University Press, 2015.

Cobb, Charles L. *The Archaeology of Southeastern Native American Landscapes of the Colonial Era*. Gainesville: University Press of Florida, 2019.

Coleman, J. Winston. *Famous Kentucky Duels: The Story of the Code of Honor in the Bluegrass State*. Frankfort: Roberts Printing Co., 1953.

———. *John Bradford, Esq.—Pioneer Printer and Historian*. Lexington: Winburn Press, 1950.

Collot, Georges Henri Victor, and P. F. Tardieu. *A Journey in North America, Containing a Survey of the Countries Watered by the Mississippi, Ohio, Missouri, and Other Affluing Rivers*. Paris: Arthus Bertrand, 1796.

Cotterill, R. S. *The Southern Indians: The Story of the Civilized Tribes Before Removal*. Norman: University of Oklahoma Press, 1987.

Countryman, Edward. *Enjoy the Same Liberty: Black Americans and the Revolutionary Era*. Lanham: Rowman & Littlefield, 2012.

Cowger, Thomas W., and Mitchell Caver. *Piominko: Chickasaw Leader*. Ada, OK: Chickasaw Press, 2017.

Cramer, Zadok. *The Ohio and Mississippi Navigator*. 3rd ed. Pittsburgh: John Scull, 1802.

Craton, Michael, and Gail Saunders. *Islanders in the Stream: From Aboriginal Times to the End of Slavery*. 2 vols. Athens: University of Georgia Press, 1992.

Crèvecoeur, J. Hector St. John de, and Dennis D. Moore, ed. *Letters from an American Farmer and Other Essays*. Cambridge: Harvard University Press, 2013.

Crocker, Mary Wallace. *Historic Architecture of Mississippi*. Jackson: University Press of Mississippi, 1973.

Cronon, William, George Miles, and Jay Gitlin, eds. *Under an Open Sky: Rethinking America's Western Past*. New York: W. W. Norton & Co., 1992.

Crowder, Jack Darrell. *African Americans and American Indians in the Revolutionary War*. Jefferson: McFarland, 2019.

Culin, Stewart. *Games of the North American Indians*. New York: Dover Publications, 1907.

Cushman, Horatio Bardwell, and Angie Debo, eds. *History of the Choctaw, Chickasaw, and Natchez Indians*. Norman: University of Oklahoma Press, 1999, edited and annotated update to the 1899 edition.

Cutler, Julia. *The Founders of Ohio: Brief Sketches of the Forty-Eight Pioneers*. Cincinnati: Robert Clarke & Co., 1888.

Dandridge, Anne Spottswood. *The Forman Genealogy*. Cleveland: Forman Bassett Hatch Co., 1903.

Dant, Sara. *Losing Eden: An Environmental History of the American West*. Chichester: Wiley-Blackwell, 2016.

Davis, Ronald L. F. *Black Experience in Natchez: 1720–1880*. Denver: National Park Service, Department of the Interior, 1993.

Davis, William C. *Way Through the Wilderness: Natchez Trace and the Civilization of the Southern Frontier*. Baton Rouge: Louisiana State University Press, 1995.

Debo, Angie. *The Rise and Fall of the Choctaw Republic*. 2nd ed. Norman: University of Oklahoma Press, 1975.

Deetz, Kelley Fanto. *Bound to the Fire: How Virginia's Enslaved Cooks Helped Invent American Cuisine*. Lexington: University Press of Kentucky, 2017.

Delehanty, Randolph, Van Jones Martin, Ronald W. Miller, Mary Warren Miller, and Elizabeth Macneil Boggess. *Classic Natchez: History, Homes, and Gardens*. Athens: University of Georgia Press, 1996.

Denny, Ebenezer. *Military Journal of Major Ebenezer Denny with an Introductory Memoir*. Philadelphia: J. B. Lippincott & Co., 1859.

DeRosier Jr., Arthur H. *William Dunbar: Scientific Pioneer of the Old Southwest*. Lexington: University Press of Kentucky, 2007.

Diamond, Jared. *Guns, Germs, and Steel: The Fates of Human Societies*. New York: W. W. Norton, 1997.

Dowd, Gregory Evans. *A Spirited Resistance: The North American Indian Struggle for Unity, 1745–1815*. Baltimore: Johns Hopkins University Press, 1992.

Downes, Randolph C. *Council Fires on the Upper Ohio: A Narrative of Indian Affairs in the Upper Ohio Valley until 1795*. Pittsburgh: University of Pittsburgh Press, 1940, 1989 reprint.

Downey, Allan. *The Creator's Game: Lacrosse, Identity, and Indigenous Nationhood*. Vancouver: University of British Columbia Press, 2018.

Dunbar, Erica Armstrong. *Never Caught: The Washingtons' Relentless Pursuit of Their Runaway Slave, Ona Judge*. New York: Atria Books, 2017.

Dunbar-Ortiz, Roxanne. *An Indigenous Peoples' History of the United States*. Boston: Beacon Press, 2014.

Dupre, Daniel S. *Alabama's Frontiers and the Rise of the Old South*. Bloomington: Indiana University Press, 2018.

DuVal, Kathleen. *Independence Lost: Lives on the Edge of the American Revolution*. New York: Random House, 2016.

———. *The Native Ground: Indians and Colonists in the Heart of the Continent*. Philadelphia: University of Pennsylvania Press, 2006.

Earnest, Earnest. *John and William Bartram—Botanists and Explorers*. Philadelphia: University of Pennsylvania Press, 1940.

Egerton, Douglas R. *Death or Liberty: African Americans and Revolutionary America*. New York: Oxford University Press, 2009.

Ellicott, Andrew. *Message from the President of the United States . . . Relative to the Affairs of the United States on the Mississippi, the Intercourse with the Indian Nations, and the Inexecution of the Treaty between the United States and Spain*. Philadelphia: W. Ross, 1798.

———. *Journal of Andrew Ellicott*. Philadelphia: William Fry, 1803, 1814.

Ellis, Franklin, and Samuel Evans. *History of Lancaster County Pennsylvania with Biographical Sketches*. Philadelphia: Everts and Peck, 1883.

Enoch, Harry G. *Bound for New Orleans! John Halley's Journal of Flatboat Trips from Boonesborough in 1789 & 1791*. Privately published, 2015.

Equiano, Olaudah. *The Interesting Narrative of the Life of Olaudah Equiano*. Edited by Robert J. Allison. 3rd ed. Boston: Bedford/St. Martin's, 2016.

Erdoes, Richard, and Alfonso Ortiz, eds. *American Indian Myths and Legends*. New York: Random House, 1984.

Ethridge, Robin. *From Chicaza to Chickasaw: The European Invasion and the Transformation of the Mississippian World, 1540–1715*. Chapel Hill: University of North Carolina Press, 2010.

———. *Creek Country: The Creek Indians and Their World*. Chapel Hill: University of North Carolina Press, 2003.

Faber, Eberhard L. *Building the Land of Dreams: New Orleans and the Transformation of Early America*. Princeton: Princeton University Press, 2016.

Fairchild, Helen L., ed. *Travels in the Years 1791 and 1792 in Pennsylvania, New York and Vermont: Journals of John Lincklaen*. New York: G. P. Putnam's Sons, 1897.

———. *Three Revolutionary Soldiers: David Forman (1745–1797), Jonathan Forman (1755–1809), and Jonathan Marsh Forman (1758–1845)*. Cleveland: Forman-Bassett-Hatch Co., 1902.

Faragher, John, and Mack Faragher. *Daniel Boone: The Life and Legend of an American Pioneer*. New York: Henry Holt and Company, 1992.

Farman, Elbert Eli. *Foreman-Farman-Forman Genealogy*. New York: Tobias A. Wright, 1911.

Farrow, Anne, Joel Lang, and Jennifer Frank. *Complicity: How the North Promoted and Profited from Slavery*. New York: Ballantine Books, 2005.

Fenge, Terry, and Jim Aldridge, eds. *Keeping Promises: The Royal Proclamation of 1763, Aboriginal Rights, and Treaties in Canada*. Chicago: McGill-Queens University Press, 2015.

Ferling, John. *Almost a Miracle: The American Victory in the War of Independence*. New York: Oxford University Press, 2007.

Feros, Antonio. *Speaking of Spain—The Evolution of Race and Nation in the Hispanic World*. Cambridge: Harvard University Press, 2017.

Ferreiro, Larrie D. *Brothers at Arms: American Independence and the Men of France and Spain Who Saved It*. New York: Knopf, 2016.

Fischer, David Hackett. *Africa's Gifts*. New York: Oxford University Press, in preparation for 2022.

Fischer, David Hackett, and James C. Kelly. *Bound Away: Virginia and the Westward Movement*. Charlottesville and London: University of Virginia Press, 2000.

Fleming, Thomas. *The Strategy of Victory: How George Washington Won the American Revolution*. New York: Da Capo Press, 2017.

Follett, Richard, Sven Beckert, Peter Coclanis, and Barbara Hahn. *Plantation Kingdom: The American South and Its Global Commodities*. Baltimore: Johns Hopkins University Press, 2016.

Foner, Eric. *Give Me Liberty!: An American History*. 6th ed. New York: Norton & Co., 2020.

Ford, Emily, and Barry Stiefel. *The Jews of New Orleans and the Mississippi Delta*. Charleston: History Press, 2012.

Forman, Samuel S. *Annals of Cazenovia, 1793–1837*. Edited by Russell A. Grills. Cazenovia, New York: Friends of Lorenzo, Inc., Gleaner Press, 1982.

Forman, Samuel S., and Lyman C. Draper, eds. *Narrative of a Journey Down the Ohio and Mississippi in 1789–90*. Cincinnati: Robert Clarke & Co., 1888.

Forman, William P. *Records of the Descendants of John Foreman, Who Settled in Monmouth County, New Jersey about the Year A.D. 1685*. Cleveland: Short & Forman, 1885.

Forret, Jeff. *Slave Against Slave: Plantation Violence in the Old South*. Baton Rouge: Louisiana State University Press, 2015.

Fourtier, Alcée. *History of Louisiana*. 2nd ed. 4 vols. Baton Rouge: Claitor's Book Store, 1966 facsimile of 1904 edition.

Fowler, William M. *American Crisis: George Washington and the Dangerous Two Years after Yorktown, 1781–1783*. New York: Walker & Co., 2011.

Fradera, Josep Maria. *Imperial Nation: Ruling Citizens and Subjects in the British, French, Spanish, and American Empires*. Princeton: Princeton University Press, 2018.

Frank, Andrew K., and A. Glenn Crothers. *Borderland Narratives: Negotiation and Accommodation in North American Contested Spaces, 1500–1850*. Gainesville: University Press of Florida, 2017.

———. *Creeks and Southerners: Biculturalism on the Early American Frontier*. Lincoln: University of Nebraska Press, 2005.

Franklin, Benjamin. *Information to Those Who Would Remove to America*. Passy, France, 1784.

Franklin, Wayne, Philip F. Gura, and Arnold Krupat, eds. *The Norton Anthology of American Literature*. New York: Norton & Company, 2007.

Friend, Craig Thompson, and Lorri Glover, eds. *Reinterpreting Southern Histories: Essays in Historiography*. Baton Rouge: Louisiana State University Press, 2020.

Freneau, Philip, and Harry Hayden Clark, eds. *Poems of Freneau*. New York: Harcourt, Brace and Co., 1929.

Gallay, Alan. *The Indian Slave Trade*. New Haven: Yale University Press, 2002.

Galloway, Patricia. *Choctaw Genesis*. Lincoln: University of Nebraska Press, 1995.

Garraty, John A., and Mark C. Carnes, eds. *American National Biography*. 24 vols. New York: Oxford University Press, 1999.

Gates, Henry Louis Jr., and Valerie Smith, eds. *The Norton Anthology of African American Literature*. 3rd ed. Vol. 1. New York: W. W. Norton & Co., 2014.

Gayarre, Charles. *History of Louisiana*. 4 vols. New Orleans: Armand Hawkins Publisher, 1885.

———. *History of Louisiana—The Spanish Domination*. New York: Redfield, 1854.

Geggus, David, ed. *The Haitian Revolution: A Documentary History*. Indianapolis: Hacket Publishing, 2014.

Gigantino, James J. II, ed. *The American Revolution in New Jersey*. New Brunswick: Rutgers University Press, 2014.

———. *The Ragged Road to Abolition: Slavery and Freedom in New Jersey, 1775–1865*. Philadelphia: University of Pennsylvania Press, 2015.

Gilbert, Alan. *Black Patriots and Loyalists: Fighting for Emancipation in the War for Independence*. Chicago: University of Chicago Press, 2012.

Gillis, Norman G. *Early Inhabitants of the Natchez District*. Greenville: Southern Historical Press, Inc., 1999, reprint of a 1963 edition.

Girard, Philippe. *Toussaint L'Ouverture: A Revolutionary Life*. New York: Basic Books, 2016.

Gontar, Cybèle T., and Beatriz E. Caro, eds. *Salazar: Portraits of Influence in Spanish New Orleans, 1785–1802*. New Orleans: Ogden Museum of Southern Art/University of New Orleans Press, 2018.

Gordon-Reed, Annette, and Peter S. Onuf. *Most Blessed of the Patriarchs: Thomas Jefferson and the Empire of the Imagination*. New York: Norton & Co., 2016.

Gordon, Thomas F. *The History of New Jersey: From Its Discovery by Europeans to the Adoption of the Federal Constitution*. Trenton: D. Fenton, 1834.

Grandin, Greg. *The Empire of Necessity*. New York: Picador, Henry Holt and Company, 2014.

Green, Richard. *Chickasaw Lives*. Ada: Chickasaw Press, 2007–2012.

Greer, Allan. *Property and Dispossession: Natives, Empires and Land in Early Modern North America*. New York: Cambridge University Press, 2018.

Grenier, John. *The First Way of War: American War Making on the Frontier, 1607–1814*. Cambridge: Cambridge University Press, 2005.

Griffin, Patrick. *American Leviathan: Empire, Nation, and the Revolutionary Frontier*. New York: Hill and Wang, 2007.

Griffin, Patrick, ed. *Experiencing Empire: Power, People, and Revolution in Early America*. Charlottesville: University of Virginia Press, 2017.

Grundset, Eric G., Brianna L. Diaz, Hollis L. Gentry, and Jean D. Strahan, eds. *Forgotten Patriots: African American and American Indian Patriots of the Revolutionary War*. Washington, DC: Daughters of the American Revolution, 2008 and 2012 supplement.

Gustafson, Sandra M. *Eloquence Is Power: Oratory and Performance in Early America*. Chapel Hill: University of North Carolina Press, 2000.

Guthman, William H. *March to Massacre: A History of the First Seven Years of the United States Army 1784–1791*. New York: McGraw-Hill Book Company, 1975.

Hall, Gwendolyn Midlo. *Africans in Colonial Louisiana: The Development of Afro-Creole Culture in the Eighteenth Century*. Baton Rouge: Louisiana State University Press, 1992.

———. *Slavery and African Ethnicities in the Americas: Restoring the Links*. Chapel Hill: University of North Carolina Press, 2005.

Hamnett, Brian R. *The End of Iberian Rule on the American Continent, 1770–1830*. Cambridge: Cambridge University Press, 2017.

Harless, Richard. *George Washington and Native Americans: "Learn Our Arts and Ways of Life."* Fairfax: George Mason University Press, 2018.

Harper, Rob. *Unsettling the West: Violence and State Building in the Ohio Valley*. Philadelphia: University of Pennsylvania Press, 2018.

Harris, Alex. *Biographical History of Lancaster County*. Lancaster: Elias Barr & Co., 1872.

Harrison, Richard A. *Princetonians, 1769–1775: A Biographical Dictionary*. Princeton: Princeton University Press, 1980.

Hartog, Hendrik. *The Trouble with Minna: A Case of Slavery and Emancipation in the Antebellum North*. Chapel Hill: University of Carolina Press, 2018.

Hay, Thomas Robson, and M. R. Werner. *The Admirable Trumpeter*. Garden City: Doubleday, Doran & Co., 1941.

Haynes, Robert V. *The Natchez District and the American Revolution*. Jackson: University Press of Mississippi, 1976.

Heath, William. *William Wells and the Struggle for the Old Northwest*. Norman: University of Oklahoma Press, 2015.

Heckewelder, Gottlieb E., and William C. Reichel. *History, Manners, and Customs of the Indian Nations Who Once Inhabited Pennsylvania and Neighboring States*. Philadelphia: Lippincott Press, 1876.

Heckewelder, John C., Don Heinrich Tolzman, and H. A. Ratterman, eds. *The First Description of Cincinnati and Other Ohio Settlements: The Travel Report of Johann Heckewelder (1792)*. Lanham: University Press of America, 1988.

Heckewelder, John G. *A Narrative of the Mission of the United Brethren among the Delaware and Mohegan Indians*. Philadelphia: McCarty & Davis, 1820.

Hildreth, Samuel P. *Pioneer History: Being an Account of the First Examinations of the Ohio Valley, and the Early Settlement of the Northwest Territory*. Cincinnati: H. W. Derby & Company, 1848.

Hinderaker, Eric. *Elusive Empires: Constructing Colonialism in the Ohio Valley, 1673–1800*. New York: Cambridge University Press, 1997.

Hixson, Walter L. *American Settler Colonialism: A History*. New York: Palgrave Macmillan, 2013.

Hodges, Graham Russell. *Slavery and Freedom in the Rural North: African Americans in Monmouth County, New Jersey, 1665–1865*. Madison: Madison House, 1997.

Hodges, Graham Russell, and Alan Edward Brown, eds. *"Pretends to Be Free": Runaway Slave Advertisements from Colonial and Revolutionary New York and New Jersey.* New York: Garland Publishing Inc., 1994.

Hodges, Graham Russell, Susan Hawkes Cook, and Alan Edward Brown, eds. *The Black Loyalist Directory: African Americans in Exile after the American Revolution.* New York: Garland Publishers, 1996.

Hodson, Christopher. *The Acadian Diaspora: An Eighteenth-Century History.* Oxford: Oxford University Press, 2012.

Hoffman, Elizabeth Cobbs. *American Umpire.* Cambridge: Harvard University Press, 2013.

Hogeland, William. *Autumn of the Black Snake: The Creation of the U.S. Army and the Invasion That Opened the West.* New York: Farrar, Straus & Giroux, 2017.

———. *The Whiskey Rebellion: George Washington, Alexander Hamilton, and the Frontier Rebels Who Challenged America's Newfound Sovereignty.* New York: Scribner, 2006.

Holmes, Jack D. L. *Documentos Indetiyos para las Historia de la Luisiana, 1792–1810.* Madrid: Ediciones Jose Porrua Turanzas, 1963.

———. *Gayoso: The Life of a Spanish Governor in the Mississippi Valley, 1789–1799.* Baton Rouge: Louisiana State University Press, 1985.

Holmes, Oliver Wendell. *The Poems of Oliver Wendell Holmes.* Boston: Ticknor and Fields, 1864.

Holton, Woody. *Black Americans in the Revolutionary Era: A Brief History with Documents.* New York: Bedford/St. Martin's, 2009.

Horton, James Oliver, and Lois E. Horton. *In Hope of Liberty: Culture, Community and Protest among Northern Free Blacks, 1700–1860.* New York: Oxford University Press, 1997.

Hotchkin, J. H. *A History of the Purchase and Settlement of Western New York, and of the Rise, Progress, and Present State of the Presbyterian Church in That Section.* New York: M. W. Dodd, 1848.

Howard, Clinton N. *The British Development of West Florida, 1763–1769.* Berkeley: University of California Press, 1947.

Hoxie, Frederick E., ed. *Encyclopedia of North American Indians.* Boston: Houghton Mifflin Company, 1996.

————, ed. *Indians in American History: An Introduction.* Arlington Heights: Harlan Davidson, 1988.

Hoxie, Frederick E., and Harvey Markowitz. *Native Americans: An Annotated Bibliography.* Pasadena: Salem Press, 1991.

Hrastar, John. *Breaking the Appalachian Barrier: Maryland as the Gateway to Ohio and the West, 1750–1850.* Jefferson: McFarland & Co., 2017.

Hubley, Bernard Jr. *History of the American Revolution.* Northumberland: Andrew Kennedy printer, privately published, 1805.

Hulbert, Archer Butler. *The Records of the Original Proceedings of the Ohio Company.* Volume I. Marietta: Marietta Historical Commission, 1917.

Hurley, Daniel, and Paul A. Tenkotte. C*incinnati: The Queen City, 225th Anniversary Edition.* San Antonio: HPN Books, 2014.

Hurt, R. Douglas. *The Indian Frontier 1763–1846.* Albuquerque: University of New Mexico Press, 2002.

————. *The Ohio Frontier: Crucible of the Old Northwest, 1720–1830.* Bloomington: Indiana University Press, 1996.

Hutchins, Thomas. *An Historical Narrative and Topographical Description of Louisiana, and West-Florida.* Philadelphia: Robert Aitken, 1784.

Imlay, Gilbert, and John Filson. *A Topographical Description of the Western Territory of North America. . . .* 3rd ed. London: J. Debrett, 1797.

Isenberg, Nancy. *Fallen Founder: The Life of Aaron Burr.* New York: Viking, 2007.

Jackson, Donald, and Dorothy Twohig, eds. *The Diaries of George Washington.* 6 vols. Charlottesville: University of Virginia Press, 1976–1979.

Jackson, Maurice. *Let This Voice Be Heard: Anthony Benezet, Father of Atlantic Abolitionism.* Philadelphia: University of Pennsylvania Press, 2009.

Jacobs, James Ripley. *Tarnished Warrior: Major-General James Wilkinson.* New York: Macmillan, 1938.

James, D. Clayton. *Antebellum Natchez.* Baton Rouge: Louisiana State University Press, 1993.

James, James Alton. *The Life of George Rogers Clark.* Chicago: University of Illinois Press, 1928.

———. *Oliver Pollock—The Life and Times of an Unknown Patriot*. New York: Appeton-Century Company, 1937.

Jennings, Francis. *The Invasion of America: Indians, Colonialism, and the Cant of Conquest*. Chapel Hill: University of North Carolina Press, 1975.

John, Elizabeth A. H. *Storms Brewed in Other Men's Worlds: The Confrontations of Indians, Spanish, and French in the Southwest, 1540–1795*. College Station: Texas A&M University Press, 1975.

Johnson, Cecil. *British West Florida, 1763–1783*. New Haven: Yale University Press, 1943.

Johnson, Walter. *River of Dark Dreams: Slavery and Empire in the Cotton Kingdom*. Cambridge: Harvard University Press, 2013.

Jones-Rogers, Stephanie E. *They Were Her Property: White Women as Slave Owners*. New Haven: Yale University Press, 2019.

Kane, Hanett T. *Natchez on the Mississippi*. New York: William Morrow & Co., 1947.

Kappler, Charles J., ed. *The Indian Treaties 1778–1883*. New York: Interland Publishing Co., 1972.

Kastor, Peter J., ed. T*he Louisiana Purchase: Emergence of an American Nation*. Washington, DC: CQ Press, 2002.

Kendi, Ibram X. *Stamped from the Beginnings: The Definitive History of Racist Ideas in America*. New York: Nation Books, 2016.

Kendi, Ibram X., and Keisha N. Blain. *Four Hundred Souls: A Community History of African America, 1619–2019*. New York: One World, 2021.

King, Thomas. *The Inconvenient Indian: A Curious Account of Native People in North America*. Minneapolis: University of Minnesota Press, 2013.

Klaus, Ian. *Forging Capitalism: Rogues, Swindlers, Frauds and the Rise of Modern Finance*. New Haven: Yale University Press, 2014.

Kleber, John E. *The Encyclopedia of Louisville*. Lexington: University Press of Kentucky, 2001.

Kolchin, Peter. *American Slavery, 1619–1877*. First revised ed. New York: Hill and Wang, 2003.

Kovarsky, Joel S. *The True Geography of Our Country: Jefferson's Cartographic Vision*. Charlottesville: University of Virginia Press, 2014.

Kraft, Herbert C. *The Lenape-Delaware Indian Heritage: 10,000 B.C.–A.D. 2000.* New Jersey: Lenape Books, 2001.

Lakwete, Angela. *Inventing the Cotton Gin: Machine and Myth in Antebellum America.* Baltimore: Johns Hopkins University Press, 2005.

Langley, Lester P. *The Long American Revolution and Its Legacy.* Athens: University of Georgia Press, 2019.

Leal, Guillermo Calleja, and Gregorio Calleja Leal. *Gálvez and Spain in the American Revolution.* Valencia: Albatros Ediciones, 2017.

Lee, Jacob F. *Masters of the Middle Waters: Indian Nations and Colonial Ambitions along the Mississippi.* Cambridge: Harvard University Press, 2019.

Lewis, Kay Wright. *A Curse upon the Nation: Race, Freedom, and Extermination in America and the Atlantic World.* Athens: University of Georgia Press, 2017.

Libby, David J. *Slavery and Frontier Mississippi, 1720–1835.* Jackson: University Press of Mississippi, 2004.

Lincklaen, John. *Journals of John Linklaen, Agent of the Holland Land Company: Travels in the Years 1791, and 1792.* New York: Putnam and Sons, 1897.

Linklater, Andro. *An Artist in Treason: The Extraordinary Double Life of General James Wilkinson.* New York: Walker Publishing Company, 2009.

Longfellow, Henry Wadsworth. *The Belfry of Bruges and Other Poems.* Cambridge: Metcalf and Company, 1846.

Lorant, Stefan. *Pittsburgh: The Story of an American City.* New York: Doubleday & Co., 1980.

Lowrie, Walter. *Early Settlers of Mississippi as Taken from Land Grants in the Mississippi Territory.* Easley: Southern Historical Press, 1986.

Mancall, Peter C. *Deadly Medicine: Indians and Alcohol in Early America.* Ithaca: Cornell University Press, 1995.

Marshall, Theodora Britton, and Gladys Crail Evans. *They Found It in Natchez.* New Orleans: Pelican Publishing Company, 1939.

Martin, Michael T. *Mississippi—A Guide to the Magnolia State: Writers' Program of the Works Progress Administration in the State of Mississippi.* New York: Viking Press, 1938.

Mathews, Catherine Van Cortlandt. *Andrew Ellicott: His Life and Letters.* New York: Grafton Press, 1908.

McBee, M. W. *The Natchez Court Records, 1767–1805: Abstracts of Early Records.* Greenwood, Mississippi, n.p., 1953.

McCaleb, Walter Flavius. *The Aaron Burr Conspiracy and a New Light on Aaron Burr.* New York: Argosy Antiquarian, 1966.

McCullough, David. *The Pioneers: The Heroic Story of the Settlers Who Brought the American Ideal West.* New York: Simon & Schuster, 2019.

McLemore, Richard Aubrey. *A History of Mississippi.* Hattiesburg: University and College Press of Mississippi, 1973.

McManus, Edward. *Black Bondage in the North.* Syracuse: Syracuse University Press, 1973.

McMichael, F. Andrew. *Atlantic Loyalties: Americans in Spanish West Florida, 1785–1810.* Athens: University of Georgia Press, 2008.

Middlekauff, Robert. *The Glorious Cause—The American Revolution, 1763–1789.* New York: Oxford University Press, 2005.

Miles, Tiya. *The House on Diamond Hill: A Cherokee Plantation Story.* Chapel Hill: University of North Carolina Press, 2010.

———. *Ties That Bind: The Story of an Afro-Cherokee Family in Slavery and Freedom.* University of California Press, 2015.

Mombert, J. I. *An Authentic History of Lancaster County in the State of Pennsylvania.* Lancaster: J. E. Barr & Co., 1869.

Moore, John Hebron. *The Emergence of the Cotton Kingdom in the Old Southwest: Mississippi, 1770–1860.* Baton Rouge: Louisiana State University Press, 1988.

Morris, Christopher. *Becoming Southern: The Evolution of a Way of Life, Warren County and Vicksburg, Mississippi, 1770–1860.* New York: Oxford University Press, 1995.

Narrett, David. *Adventurism and Empire: The Struggle for Mastery in the Louisiana-Florida Borderlands, 1762–1803.* Chapel Hill: University of North Carolina Press, 2015.

Nash, Gary B., and Jean R. Soderland. *Freedom by Degrees: Emancipation in Pennsylvania and Its Aftermath.* New York: Oxford University Press, 1991.

Nasatir, Abraham P. *Borderland in Retreat—From Spanish Louisiana to the Far Southwest*. Albuquerque: University of New Mexico Press, 1976.

Nash, Gary B. *Red, White, and Black: The Peoples of Early North America*. 7th ed. New York: Prentice-Hall, 2014.

Nelson, Larry L. *A Man of Distinction among Them: Alexander McKee and the Ohio Country Frontier, 1754–1799*. Kent: Kent State University Press, 1999.

Nelson, Paul David. *Anthony Wayne: Soldier of the Early Republic*. Bloomington: Indiana University Press, 1985.

———. *General Horatio Gates: A Biography*. Baton Rouge: Louisiana State University, 1976.

Nester, William R. *George Rogers Clark: I Glory in War*. Norman: University of Oklahoma Press, 2012.

Nichols, David Andrew. *Engines of Diplomacy: Indian Trading Factories and the Negotiation of American Empire*. Chapel Hill: University of North Carolina Press, 2016.

O'Brien, Greg. *Choctaws in a Revolutionary Age, 1750–1830*. Lincoln: University of Nebraska Press, 2002.

O'Brien, Greg, ed. *Pre-Removal Choctaw History*. Norman: University of Oklahoma Press, 2008.

Ogg, Frederic Austin. *The Opening of the Mississippi*. New York: Macmillan Company, 1904.

O'Malley, George E. *Final Passages: The Intercolonial Slave Trade of British America, 1619–1807*. Williamsburg: University of North Carolina, 2014.

Ortiz, Paul. *An African American and Latinx History of the United States*. Boston: Beacon Press, 2018.

Ostler, Jeffrey. *Surviving Genocide: Native Nations and the United States from the American Revolution to Bleeding Kansas*. New Haven: Yale University Press, 2019.

Page, Jack. *In the Hands of the Great Spirit: The 20,000 Year History of American Indians*. New York: Free Press, 2003.

Parkhurst, Jacob. *Sketches of the Life and Adventures of Jacob Parkhurst. . . .* Henry County, Indiana, 1842.

Parkinson, Robert G. *Creating Race and Nation in the American Revolution*. Chapel Hill: University of North Carolina, 2016.

Peirce, Charles. *A Meteorological Account of the Weather in Philadelphia: From January 1, 1790, to January 1, 1847*. Philadelphia: Lindsay & Blakiston, 1847.

Perkins, Elizabeth A. *Border Life: Experience and Memory in the Revolutionary Ohio Valley*. Chapel Hill: University of North Carolina Press, 1998.

Persac, A. *Plantations on the Mississippi River from Natchez to New Orleans*. New Orleans: Pelican Publishing Company, 1967.

Peterson, Dawn. *Indians in the Family: Adoption and the Politics of Antebellum Expansion*. Cambridge: Harvard University Press, 2017.

Phillips, Charles, and Charles Alexrod, eds. *Encyclopedia of the American West*. 4 vols. New York: Simon & Schuster, 1996.

Pickett, Albert James, and James P. Pate, eds. *The Annotated Pickett's History of Alabama and Incidentally of Georgia and Mississippi*. Montgomery: NewSouth Books, 2018.

Piecuch, Jim. *Three Peoples, One King: Loyalists, Indians, and Slaves in the Revolutionary South*. University of South Carolina Press, 2008.

Pinnen, Christian, and Charles A. *Colonial Mississippi: A Borrowed Land*. Jackson: University Press of Mississippi, 2021.

Powell, J. H. *Bring Out Your Dead: The Great Plague of Yellow Fever in Philadelphia in 1793*. Philadelphia: University of Pennsylvania Press, 1993.

Quarles, Benjamin. *The Negro in the American Revolution*. New York: Norton & Co., 1973.

Quintero Saravia, Gonzalo M. *Bernardo de Gálvez: Spanish Hero of the American Revolution*. Chapel Hill: University of North Carolina Press, 2018.

Raum, John O. *The History of New Jersey: From Its Earliest Settlement to the Present Time*. Philadelphia: J. E. Potter and Co., 1877.

Reilly, F. Kent III, and James F. Garber, eds. *Ancient Objects and Sacred Realms: Interpretations of Mississippian Iconography*. Austin: University of Texas Press, 2009.

Richter, Daniel K. *Before the Revolution—America's Ancient Pasts*. Cambridge: Harvard University Press, 2011.

———. *Facing East from Indian Country: A Native History of Early America*. Cambridge: Harvard University Press, 2003.

———. *Trade, Land, Power: The Struggle for Eastern North America*. Philadelphia: University of Pennsylvania Press, 2013.

Roberts, Robert B. *Encyclopedia of Historic Forts: Military, Pioneer, and Trading Posts of the United States*. New York: Macmillan Publishing Company, 1988.

Rodney, Thomas. *A Journey Through the West: Journey from Delaware to the Mississippi Territory*. Edited by Dwight L. Smith and Ray Swick. Louisville: The Filson Historical Society, 1997.

Rood, Daniel B. *The Reinvention of Atlantic Slavery: Technology, Labor, Race, and Capitalism in the Greater Caribbean*. Oxford: Oxford University Press, 2017.

Roosevelt, Theodore. *The Winning of the West*. 4 vols. Vol. 3, The Founding of the Trans-Alleghany Commonwealths, 1784–1790; Vol. 4, Louisiana and the Northwest, 1791–1807. New York: G. P. Putnam's Sons, 1903.

Rothman, Adam. *Slave Country: American Expansion and the Origins of the Deep South*. Cambridge: Harvard University Press, 2005.

Rowland, Dunbar. *History of Mississippi: The Heart of the South*. Vol. 2. Chicago: S. J. Clarke Publishing Company, 1925.

Rowland, Eron. *Life, Letters and Papers of William Dunbar*. New York: J. J. Little and Ives Co., 1930.

[Sargent, Winthrop]. Papers in Relation to the Official Conduct of Governor Sargent. Boston, 1801.

[———]. *Political Intolerance, or the Violence of Party Spirit. . . .* Boston: Benjamin Russel, 1801.

Saugrain de Vigny, Antoine François. *L'odyssée américaine d'une famille française*. Baltimore: Johns Hopkins University, 1936.

Saunt, Claudio. *The New Order of Things: Property, Power, and the Transformation of the Creek Indians, 1733–1816*. New York: Cambridge University Press, 1999.

———. *West of the Revolution: An Uncommon History of 1776*. New York: Norton and Company, 2014.

Savage, Henry Jr., and Elizabeth J. Savage. *André and François André Michaux*. Charlottesville: University Press of Virginia, 1986.

Savelle, Max. *George Morgan: Colony Builder*. New York: Columbia University Press, 1932.

Savoy, Lauret Edith. *Trace: Memory, History, Race, and the American Landscape*. Berkeley: Counterpoint Press, 2015.

Schermerhorn, Calvin. *Unrequited Toil: A History of United States Slavery*. Cambridge: Cambridge University Press, 2018.

Schloesser, Pauline. *The Fair Sex: White Women and Racial Patriarchy in the Early American Republic*. New York: New York University Press, 2002.

Schutt, A. *Peoples of the River Valleys: The Odyssey of the Delaware Indians*. Philadelphia: University of Pennsylvania Press, 2007.

Schwartz, Marie Jenkins. *Ties That Bound: Founding First Ladies and Slaves*. Chicago: University of Chicago Press, 2017.

Shields, Joseph Dunbar. *Natchez—Its Early History*. Louisville: John P. Morton and Co., 1930.

Silver, Peter. *Our Savage Neighbors: How Indian War Transformed Early America*. New York: W. W. Norton and Company, 2008.

Silverman, David J. *Thundersticks: Firearms and the Violent Transformation of Native America*. Cambridge: Harvard University Press, 2016.

Sinha, Manisha. *The Slaves' Cause: A History of Abolition*. New Haven: Yale University Press. 2016.

Skaggs, David Curtis, and Larry L. Nelson, eds. *The Sixty Years War for the Great Lakes, 1754–1814*. East Lansing: University of Michigan Press, 2001.

Skemp, Sheila M. *Judith Sargent Murray: A Brief Biography with Documents*. New York: Bedford/St. Martin's, 1998.

Slaughter, Thomas P. *The Whiskey Rebellion: Frontier Epilogue to the American Revolution*. New York: Oxford University Press, 1986.

Sleeper-Smith, Susan. *Indigenous Prosperity and American Conquest: Indian Women and the Ohio River Valley, 1690–1792*. Chapel Hill: University of North Carolina Press, 2018.

Smith, Billy G., and Richard Wojtowicz. *Blacks Who Stole Themselves: Advertisements for Runaways in the Pennsylvania Gazette, 1728–1790.* Philadelphia: University of Pennsylvania, 1989.

Smith, David G. *On the Edge of Freedom: The Fugitive Slave Issue in South Central Pennsylvania, 1820–1870.* New York: Fordham University Press, 2012.

Smith, Edward Y., Earl G. Gieser, George J. Goss, Frank Z. Kovach, R. Stanford Lanterman, eds. *The History of Freemasonry in New Jersey, 1787-1987,* [Grand Lodge of New Jersey], u.d. [1988].

Smith, Gene Allen, and Sylvia L. Hilton, eds. *Nexus of Empire: Negotiating Loyalty and Identity in the Revolutionary Borderlands, 1760s–1820s.* Gainesville: University Press of Florida, 2010.

Smithers, Gregory D. *Slave Breeding: Sex, Violence, and Memory in African American History.* Gainesville: University Press of Florida, 2013.

Snyder, Christina. *Slavery in Indian Country: The Changing Face of Captivity in Early America.* Cambridge: Harvard University Press, 2010.

Spero, Patrick. *Frontier Country: The Politics of War in Early Pennsylvania.* Philadelphia: University of Pennsylvania Press, 2016.

Spencer, Oliver M. *Indian Captivity: A True Narrative of the Capture of the Rev. O. M. Spencer by the Indians.* New York: B. Waugh and T. Mason, 1835.

St. Clair, Arthur. *A Narrative of the Manner in Which the Campaign against the Indians, in the Year One Thousand Seven Hundred and Ninety-One, Was Conducted.* Philadelphia: n.p., 1812.

Stagg, J. C. A. *Borderlines in Borderlands: James Madison and the Spanish-American Frontier 1776–1821.* New Haven: Yale University Press, 2009.

Starr, J. Barton. *Tories, Dons, and Rebels: The American Revolution in British West Florida.* Gainesville: University Presses of Florida, 1976.

Stewart, Kelly Lloyd. *An Illustrated History of the Society of the Cincinnati in the State of New Jersey.* Society of the Cincinnati in the State of New Jersey, 2016.

Stiggins, George, Virginia Pounds Brown, and William Stokes Wyman, eds. *Creek Indian History.* 2nd ed. Tuscaloosa: University Alabama Press, 2003.

Stockwell, Mary. *Unlikely General: Mad Anthony Wayne and the Battle for America*. New Haven: Yale University Press, 2018.

Stoddard, Amos. *Sketches, Historical and Descriptive, of Louisiana*. Philadelphia: Mathew Carey, 1812.

Strang, Cameron B. *Frontiers of Science: Imperialism and Natural Knowledge in the Gulf South Borderlands, 1500–1850*. Chapel Hill: University of North Carolina Press, 2018.

Strauss, Jill, and Dionne Ford, eds. *Slavery's Descendants: Shared Legacies of Race and Reconciliation*. New Brunswick: Rutgers University Press, 2019.

Stubbs, Tristan. *Masters of Violence: The Plantation Overseers of Eighteenth-Century Virginia, South Carolina, and Georgia*. Columbia: University of South Carolina Press, 2019.

Sugden, John. *Blue Jacket, Warrior of the Shawnees*. Lincoln: University of Nebraska Press, 2000.

Swanton, John. *Social and Religious Beliefs of the Chickasaw Indian*. Washington, DC: US Government Printing Office, 1928.

———. *Source Material for the Social and Ceremonial Life of the Choctaw Indians*. University of Alabama Press: University of Alabama Press, 2001.

Sword, Wiley. *President Washington's Indian War: The Struggle for the Old Northwest, 1790–1795*. Norman: University of Oklahoma Press, 1985.

Symmes, John Cleves, Beverly Waugh Bond, and Anna Tuthill Symmes, eds. *The Intimate Letters of John Cleves Symmes and His Family Including Those of His Daughter Mrs. William Henry Harrison*. Cincinnati: Historical and Philosophical Society of Ohio, 1956.

Symmes, Frank R. *History of the Old Tennent Church*. Cranberry: George W. Burroughs, 1904.

Tewell, Jeremy J. *A Self-Evident Lie: Southern Slavery and the Threat to American Freedom*. Kent: Kent State University Press, 2013.

Thompson, Robert J. *Colonel James Neilson: A Business Man of the Early Machine Age in New Jersey, 1784–1862*. New Brunswick: Rutgers University Press, 1940.

Thwaites, Reuben Gold. *Early Western Travels, 1748–1846: A Series of Annotated Reprints of Some of the Best and Rarest Contemporary Volumes of Travel, Descriptive of the Aborigines and Social and Economic Conditions in the Middle and Far West.* Cleveland: A. H. Clark Co., 1904.

Torget, Andrew J. *Seeds of Empire: Cotton, Slavery, and the Transformation of the Texas Borderlands, 1800–1850.* Chapel Hill: University of North Carolina Press, 2015.

Treuer, Anton, Karenne Wood, William W. Fitzhugh, George P. Horse Capture, Theresa Lynn Frazier, Miles R. Miller, Miranda Belarde-Lewis, and Jill Norwood. *Indian Nations of North America.* Washington, DC: National Geographic, 2013.

Trogdon, Jo Ann. *The Unknown Travels and Dubious Pursuits of William Clark.* Columbia: University of Missouri Press, 2015.

Trumbull, John. *Autobiography, Reminiscences and Letters of John Trumbull from 1756 to 1841.* New Haven: B. L. Hamlin 1841.

Trotter, Joe William Jr., and Eric Ledell Smih, eds. *African Americans in Pennsylvania—Shifting Historical Perspectives.* University Park: Pennsylvania Historical and Museum Commission, Pennsylvania State University Press, 1997.

Twain, Mark. *Life on the Mississippi.* Edited by J. C. Levenson. Minneapolis: Dillon Press, 1967.

Unser, Daniel H. Jr. *American Indians in the Lower Mississippi Valley: Social and Economic Histories.* Lincoln: University of Nebraska Press, 1998.

Van Buskirk, Judith L. *Standing in Their Own Light: African American Patriots in the American Revolution.* Norman: University of Oklahoma Press, 2017.

Van Engen, Abram C. *City on a Hill: A History of American Exceptionalism.* New Haven: Yale University Press, 2020.

Vanderwerth, W. C., ed. *Indian Oratory—Famous Speeches by Noted Indian Chieftains.* Norman: University of Oklahoma, 1971.

Vaughan, Alden T. *The Roots of American Racism: Essays on the Colonial Experience.* New York: Oxford University Press, 1995.

Vennum, Thomas Jr. *American Indian Lacrosse: Little Brother of War.* Washington, DC: Smithsonian Institution Press, 1994.

Voelz, Peter M. *Slave and Soldier: The Military Impact of Blacks in the Colonial Americas.* New York: Garland Publishing, 1993.

Wagner, Henry R. *The Spanish Southwest 1542–1794.* Albuquerque: The Quivera Society, 1937.

Wagner, Mark J. *The Wreck of the America in Southern Illinois: A Flatboat on the Ohio River.* Carbondale: Southern Illinois University, 2015.

Walker, James B. *Experiences of Pioneer Life in the Early Settlements and Cities of the West.* Chicago: Sumner & Co., 1881.

Wallach, Jennifer Jensen, ed. *Dethroning the Deceitful Pork Chop: Rethinking African American Foodways from Slavery to Obama.* Fayetteville, AR: University of Arkansas Press, 2015.

Walter, Dierk. *Colonial Violence: European Empires and the Use of Force.* Oxford: Oxford University Press, 2017.

Warren, Stephen. *The Worlds the Shawnees Made: Migration and Violence in Early America.* Chapel Hill: University of North Carolina Press, 2014.

Waselkov, Gregory A., Peter H. Wood, and M. Thomas Hatley, eds. *Powhattan's Mantle: Indians in the Colonial Southeast.* Lincoln: University of Nebraska, 2006.

Watkins, T. H. *Mark Twain's Mississippi: A Pictorial History of America's Greatest River, Also Selected Excerpts from Mark Twain's Life on the Mississippi.* Palo Alto: American West Publishing Co., 1974.

Weeks, Charles A. *Paths to a Middle Ground: The Diplomacy of Natchez, Boukfouka, Nogales, and San Fernando de las Barrancas, 1791–1795.* Tuscaloosa: University of Alabama Press, 2005.

Weem, John Edwards. *Men Without Countries—Three Adventurers of the Early Southwest.* Boston: Houghton Mifflin, 1969.

Weslager, Clinton Alfred. *The Delaware Indians—A History.* New Brunswick: Rutgers University Press, 1989.

———. *The Delaware Indian Westward Migration: With the Texts of Two Manuscripts, 1821–22, Responding to General Lewis Cass's Inquiries about Lenape Culture and Language.* Wallingford: Middle Atlantic Press, 1978.

Whitaker, Arthur Preston. *Spanish-American Frontier, 1783–1795*. Lincoln: University of Nebraska Press, 1927.

———. *The Mississippi Question 1795–1803: A Study in Trade, Politics, and Diplomacy*. New York: D. Appleton Century Company, 1934.

White, Richard. The *Middle Ground: Indians, Empires, and Republics in the Great Lakes Region, 1650–1815*. New York: Cambridge University Press, 1991.

White, Shane. *Stories of Freedom in Black New York*. Cambridge: Harvard University Press, 2002.

White, Sophie. *Voices of the Enslaved: Love, Labor, and Longing in French Louisiana*. Chapel Hill: University of North Carolina Press, 2019.

Whitten, David O., ed. *Eli Whitney's Cotton Gin, 1793–1993*. Washington, DC: Agricultural History Society, 1994.

Wickman, Patricia Riles. *In the Tree That Bends: Discourse, Power, and the Survival of the Maskókí People*. Tuscaloosa: University of Alabama Press, 1999.

Wiggin, Bethany. *Babel of the Atlantic*. University Park: Pennsylvania State University Press, 2019.

Wilkerson, Isabel. *Caste: The Origins of Our Discontents*. New York: Random House, 2020.

Wilkinson, James. *Memoirs of My Own Times*. Philadelphia: Abraham Small. 1816.

Williams, Eric. *Capitalism and Slavery*. Chapel Hill: University of North Carolina Press, 1994, original edition 1944.

Williams, Patrick C., Charles S. Bolton, and Jeannie M. Whayne, eds. *A Whole Country in Commotion—The Louisiana Purchase and the American Southwest*. Fayetteville: The University of Arkansas Press, 2005.

Williamson, C. W. *History of Western Ohio and Auglaize County with Illustrations and Biographical Sketches of Pioneers*. Columbus: W. M. Linn & Sons, 1905.

Wilson, Maurine T., and Jack Jackson. *Philip Nolan and Texas: Expeditions to the Unknown Land, 1791–1801*. Waco: Texian Press, 1987.

Winkler, John F. *Fallen Timbers*. New York, Oxford: Osprey Publishing, 2012.

———. *Wabash 1791: St. Clair's Defeat.* Long Island City: Osprey Publishing, 2011.

Wood, Gordon S. *Empire of Liberty: A History of the Early Republic.* New York: Oxford University Press, 2009.

Wood, Jerome H. Jr. "The Negro in Early Pennsylvania: The Lancaster Experience." In *Plantation, Town, and County: Essays on the Local History of American Slave Society,* edited by Elinor Miller and Eugene D. Genovese. Urbana: University of Illinois Press, 1974.

Woodward, Ruth L., and Wesley Frank Craven. *Princetonians, 1784–1790: A Biographical Dictionary.* Princeton: Princeton University Press, 2014.

Worman, B. *Father Tammany's Almanac, for the Year of Our Lord, 1791 . . . The Astronomical Calculations by B. Workman.* Philadelphia: William Young, 1790.

Worthington, Chauncey Ford, ed. *List of the Benjamin Franklin Papers.* Manuscript Division of the Library of Congress. Washington, DC: US Government Printing Office, 1905.

Yater, George H. *Two Hundred Years at the Fall of the Ohio: A History of Louisville and Jefferson County.* 2nd ed. Louisville: Filson Club, 1987.

Young, Calvin M. *Little Turtle: The Great Chief of the Miami Indian Nation: Being a Sketch of His Life Together with That of Wm. Wells.* Greenville: Calvin M. Young, 1917.

Zilversmit, Arthur. *The First Emancipation: The Abolition of Slavery in the North.* Chicago: University of Chicago Press, 1965.

Index